DA 125 .A1 H37 2013

Heath, A. F. (Anthony
Francis), author, Author.

The political integration of
ethnic minorities in Britain

The Political Integration of Ethnic Minorities in Britain

The Political Integration of Ethnic Minorities in Britain

WILLOW INTERNATIONAL LIBRARY

Anthony F. Heath
Stephen D. Fisher
Gemma Rosenblatt
David Sanders
Maria Sobolewska

UNIVERSITY PRESS

OXFORD
UNIVERSITY PRESS

Great Clarendon Street, Oxford, OX2 6DP,
United Kingdom

Oxford University Press is a department of the University of Oxford.
It furthers the University's objective of excellence in research, scholarship,
and education by publishing worldwide. Oxford is a registered trade mark of
Oxford University Press in the UK and in certain other countries

© Anthony F. Heath, Stephen D. Fisher, Gemma Rosenblatt, David Sanders,
and Maria Sobolewska 2013

The moral rights of the authors have been asserted

First Edition published in 2013

Impression: 1

All rights reserved. No part of this publication may be reproduced, stored in
a retrieval system, or transmitted, in any form or by any means, without the
prior permission in writing of Oxford University Press, or as expressly permitted
by law, by licence or under terms agreed with the appropriate reprographics
rights organization. Enquiries concerning reproduction outside the scope of the
above should be sent to the Rights Department, Oxford University Press, at the
address above

You must not circulate this work in any other form
and you must impose this same condition on any acquirer

Published in the United States of America by Oxford University Press
198 Madison Avenue, New York, NY 10016, United States of America

British Library Cataloguing in Publication Data

Data available

ISBN 978–0–19–965663–9

Printed in Great Britain by
CPI Group (UK) Ltd, Croydon, CR0 4YY

Acknowledgements

This study could not have taken place without the generous funding and support from the Economic and Social Research Council (ESRC), to whom we are once again deeply indebted. We would like to thank our case officer at the ESRC, Ian Farnden, and the anonymous referees and assessors for whose advice we are very grateful. The ESRC also funded the main British Election Survey (BES), to which our Ethnic Minority Study is in effect a companion. We are thus doubly indebted to the ESRC. We have made very extensive use of the BES dataset, and we are most grateful to the BES team of Harold Clarke, David Sanders, Marianne Stewart, and Paul Whiteley for including many of our questions from the Ethnic Minority British Election Survey (EMBES) in the main post-election questionnaire so that we could make comparisons between ethnic minorities and other British citizens.

The Electoral Commission has throughout been a partner in the research on voting and registration and has given us extensive support and backup. We are particularly grateful to Sam Younger, the founding chairman of the Electoral Commission, who gave us his full and enthusiastic backing.

We have also drawn on the research carried out as part of the Managing Cultural Diversity study at the Department of Psychology, University of Oxford, under the direction of Miles Hewstone. We are very grateful to the Leverhulme Trust, who funded the study, and to our colleagues on the project, Miles Hewstone, Katarina Schmid, Ananthi Al-Ramiah, Neli Demireva, Ceri Peach, Sarah Spencer, and Steve Vertovec.

The fieldwork for the EMBES survey was carried out by TNS-BMRB, who did an outstanding job for us. They have contributed greatly to our research, not only through their collection of the data but through their intellectual contributions, practical support, and encouragement. We are particularly grateful to Nick Howat, Oliver Nordern, Emily Pickering, and Joel Williams. It has been a great pleasure working with them, and we have learned a great deal.

We have also had great support and encouragement from many colleagues. In particular, we wish to thank the members of our Advisory Board, Irene Bloemraad, Chris Bryant, John Curtice, Harry Goulbourne, Maajid Nawaz, Lucinda Platt, Peter Riddell, Shamit Saggar, Will Somerville, and David Voas.

Acknowledgements

We are also very grateful to Mohammed Ali, Sundas Ali, Jennifer Birchall, Neli Demireva, Ed Fieldhouse, Maria Grasso, Jane Greig, Omar Khan, Yaojun Li, Jane Pearce, Iqbal Wahhab, Simon Woolley, and the many participants at workshops and conferences where we have presented our draft papers and who have given us invaluable feedback.

Any academic study always owes a debt to the previous scholars whose work has shaped the field. The citations at the end of this book give some indication of the wide range of scholars, most unknown to us personally, from whom we have learned a great deal. We would like to thank especially David Butler, whose remarkable book (with Donald Stokes) *Political Change in Britain* pervades all subsequent British work on electoral behaviour. Readers of the present book will also realize the immense intellectual debt that we owe to Garry Runciman, whose landmark study *Relative Deprivation and Social Justice* is one of the great classics of British social science. Both of these scholars have also been great supporters of our endeavours to continue work in the intellectual tradition that they themselves helped to create.

Our greatest debt is to our EMBES respondents and to the BES respondents. We hope that we have faithfully recorded their views, and that our study will in its small way allow their voices to be heard.

AFH, SDF, GR, DS, MS

Contents

List of Figures   ix
List of Tables   xi
List of Abbreviations   xv

1. Exclusion or Integration?   1
2. Diversity and Integration of British Ethnic Minorities   15
3. Political Orientations: Home or Away?   40
4. The Ethnic Minority Agenda(s)   60
5. Representation of Ethnic Minority Concerns   81
6. Partisanship   105
7. Eligibility, Registration and Turnout   132
8. Voting, Abstention, and Defection   154
9. Varieties of Political Engagement: Activists and Dissidents   174
10. Satisfaction or Disaffection from British Democracy?   190

Appendices
   1. *The Ethnic Minority British Election Survey (EMBES)*   207
   2. *Coding of the variables*   210
References   213
Index   227

List of Figures

5.1	Summary of manifesto commitments on immigration and redress for racial discrimination	84
5.2	Discrimination and immigration legislation 1951–2010	87
5.A1	Manifesto statements on immigration and redress for racial discrimination	99
6.1	Ethno-religious group consensus on Labour policies and Labour partisanship	120

List of Tables

2.1	Black Caribbean adult migrants	20
2.2	Indian adult migrants	22
2.3	Pakistani adult migrants	24
2.4	Bangladeshi adult migrants	25
2.5	Black African adult migrants	26
2.6	English fluency, national identity, cultural practices, and ethnic identification	29
2.7	Bonding social capital	31
2.8	Structural integration	33
2.9	Generational differences in social, cultural, and structural integration	34
3.1	Interest in home country and British politics among first-generation (adult) migrants	43
3.2	Duty to vote among first-generation (adult) migrants	49
3.3	Generational differences in political orientations and knowledge	52
4.1	Most important issue facing Britain today	63
4.2	Attitudes to spending/tax cuts, civil liberties, immigration, and Afghan war by ethnic group	65
4.3	Attitudes to minority opportunities and affirmative action by ethnic group	69
4.4	Attitudes to introduction of culturally specific institutions and practices	71
4.5	Socio-economic differences within the majority and minority ethnic groups on key issues	73
5.1	Numbers of ethnic minority candidates and MPs 1979–2010	89
5.2a	Perceptions of party positions: ethnic minorities	91
5.2b	Perceptions of party positions: white British	92
5.3a	Perceptions that the parties look after group interests very or fairly well: ethnic minorities	93
5.3b	Perceptions that the parties look after group interests very or fairly well: white British	93
5.4	Minority feelings about their representation	95

List of Tables

6.1	Partisanship by ethnic group, 2010	111
6.2	Socio-economic differences in Labour partisanship within the main ethnic minorities and majority group	113
6.3	Attitudinal differences in Labour partisanship within the main ethnic minorities and majority group	114
6.4	Ethnic group feelings of fraternal relative deprivation	115
6.5	Support for Labour in 2010 by year of arrival (first generation) and year of entry to the electorate (one point five and second generations)	117
6.6	Multilevel logit models of Labour partisanship among majority and minority groups	121
6.7	Multilevel logit models of Labour partisanship among minority groups	123
7.1	Validated voting and non-voting	136
7.2	Citizenship by ethnic group, adult migrants only	137
7.3	Registration among those eligible (British and Commonwealth citizens)	140
7.4	Self-reported and validated turnout	143
8.1	Patterns of voting in 2010	156
8.2	Labour voting and partisanship by ethnic group, 1997 and 2010	156
8.3	Voting patterns in 2010 among Labour partisans	157
8.4	Net evaluations of Labour record and party leaders	160
8.5	Net perceptions of how ethnic and religious groups had fared over the last few years: Labour partisans	162
8.6	Explaining departures from Labour support (Labour partisans only)	164
8.7	Canvassing (all respondents)	166
9.1	Participation in voluntary organizations	178
9.2	Participation in protest, petition, or boycott	179
9.3	Generational differences in political participation	180
9.4	Predictors of non-electoral participation	182
10.1	Satisfaction with democracy and trust in institutions	194
10.2	Religious differences in satisfaction and trust	194
10.3	Generational differences in political trust and satisfaction	195
10.4	Satisfaction and trust: second-generation minorities compared with their white British peers	196
10.5	Generational differences in feelings of exclusion and in bonding social capital	198
10.6	Predictors of ethnic minority satisfaction and trust in British politics	200

List of Tables

Chapter appendices: Supplementary Tables

3.A1	Significant associations with interest, knowledge, and duty: first generation (adult migrants)	54
3.A2	Test of differences between generations: OLS regressions	55
3.A3	Test of differences between parental and filial generations: OLS regressions	56
4.A1	Multiple regression of attitudes to selected issues: BES respondents only	76
4.A2	Percentages adopting left-wing views on left/right questions	76
4.A3	Percentages adopting libertarian views on civil liberties	77
4.A4	Percentages adopting progressive views on immigration	77
4.A5	Percentages adopting progressive views on Afghanistan	78
5.A1	Regression analyses of representation (ordered logit for separate party, logistic for no party)	98
6.A1	Logistic regression of no party identity (none versus any)	125
6.A2	Logistic regression of Labour identity—socio-economic characteristics	126
6.A3	Logistic regression of Labour identity—issues	127
7.A1	Logistic regressions of citizenship: first-generation ethnic minorities	146
7.A2	Logistic regressions of registration: ethnic minorities and white British (among those eligible)	147
7.A3	Logistic regressions of registration	148
7.A4	Logistic regressions of validated turnout: ethnic minorities and white British (registered electors only)	149
7.A5	Logistic regressions of turnout among registered electors: all and first-generation ethnic minorities	150
8.A1	Partisanship and vote in 2010 (all minorities)	169
8.A2	Multinomial logistic regression of departures from Labour identity	169
8.A3	Vote and vote change among 2005 Labour voters	170
8.A4	Distributions of different ethnic groups' opinions on key performance measures: Labour partisans only	170
8.A5	Expanded model for explaining deviations from Labour support among ethnic minority Labour identifiers: multinomial logistic regression	171
9.A1	Associations between different forms of non-electoral participation (ethnic minorities only)	186
9.A2	Cluster analysis of the different forms of non-electoral participation	187
10.A1	Generational differences in duty, interest, identification, and participation	205
A1.1	The achieved sample sizes in BES, EMBES, and ONS mid-year estimates for 2007	209

List of Abbreviations

AME	Average Marginal Effect
BES	British Election Survey
BME	Black and Minority Ethnic
CAPI	Computer assisted personal interviewing
EHRC	Equality and Human Rights Commission
EMBES	Ethnic Minority British Election Survey
ESRC	Economic and Social Research Council
IDEA	Institute for Democracy and Electoral Assistance
IMD	Index of Multiple Deprivation
ISCED	International Standard Classification of Education
LGBT	Lesbian, Gay, Bisexual and Transgender
LPBS	Labour Party Black Sections
LSOA	Lower level Super Output Area
MCDS	Managing Cultural Diversity Survey
MIPEX	Migrant Integration Policy Index
MP	Member of Parliament
NHS	National Health Service
ONS	Office for National Statistics
PSI	Policy Studies Institute
PSU	Primary sampling unit
UKIP	UK Independence Party

1

Exclusion or Integration?

One of the most remarkable changes that Britain has seen over the last fifty years has been its transformation into a diverse multi-ethnic society, with growing numbers of citizens whose roots are to be found in the Caribbean, Africa, or South Asia. We estimate that around 8 per cent of the electorate is now from these origins, and in some areas of the country, especially London, the proportion is much higher. This is set to increase substantially given the youthful age profile of the minority population.

This transformation has presented many different opportunities and challenges to Britain. Not least, it challenges Britain to turn its liberal principles of equality of opportunity and fair play into reality. The first post-war migrants were actively recruited from new (a euphemism for non-white) Commonwealth countries by British employers and government in order to help fill vacancies in Britain's recovering economy and its new welfare state. But the welcome was not always a warm one, and Britain's record of prejudice, harassment, and discrimination is not one to be proud of. A great deal of evidence has shown that, even today, the children and grandchildren of these post-war migrants suffer varying degrees of exclusion and disadvantage in the British labour market. Ethnic minority unemployment rates have consistently been much higher than those of the white British majority group, and a long series of field experiments has demonstrated discrimination by employers.[1]

In this book we set out to explore the extent and nature of the political rather than the economic exclusion and integration of Britain's growing ethnic minority population. Political exclusion can take the form of exclusion of ethnic minority members from becoming MPs or local councillors, or it can take the form of exclusion of ethnic minority interests and concerns from mainstream party politics. We will focus primarily on the latter form of exclusion, although we will also consider whether economic exclusion has political repercussions. Exclusion does not need to be a result of deliberate or conscious acts of discrimination by political elites. The law holds that indirect discrimination, when standard practices and procedures unwittingly but disproportionately disadvantage certain groups, is illegal. Exactly the same would hold in politics. Practices for selecting candidates for Parliament or policies for inclusion in a manifesto may have evolved and become entrenched before Britain became a multi-ethnic society. But they may nonetheless disproportionately disadvantage Britain's ethnic minorities in comparison with the established ethnic majority.

Political integration can take many forms, and it is not our intention to set up any single ethical ideal of what should count as integration. However, it may be useful as a starting point to distinguish integration from its absence. In particular, we would argue that a situation analogous to the Troubles in Northern Ireland, where a significant proportion of the Catholic minority were hostile to or in active conflict with the British state, would count as lack of integration. A second potential case of lack of integration might be one where members of a particular minority disproportionately withdraw from any form of political engagement either in conventional politics (such as putting forward candidates for local councils or Parliament, or turning out to vote) or in protest politics.

In between these two contrasting cases of non-integration there may be various different forms of positive integration. One version would be engagement in conventional mainstream politics as individual citizens, similar to the white British majority group, turning out to vote in general elections and engaging in the standard repertoire of legal political action. Another version would be collective action by the minority, either in the form of pressure-group activity or the formation of separate (minority) parties aiming to advance minority interests. In this case, the minority might engage in British politics but in ways that are different from those practised by the majority group. Moreover, different minorities might well follow different models of political integration. It is not our purpose to establish a single one as the 'gold standard'.[2]

Our questions

Why might we think that there is any risk of either form of non-integration—withdrawal or conflict—occurring? One fear is that the same kinds of exclusion may occur in politics as have happened, and continue to happen, in the labour market. Scarcely any ethnic minority MPs were elected until 1979, and even after the 2010 general election, which saw a larger number of minority MPs (twenty-seven) elected than ever before, it was still the case that they made up only 4 per cent of the House of Commons, half the percentage of ethnic minorities in the electorate. Perhaps more importantly, as Donley

Studlar and Zig Layton-Henry have argued, ethnic minority political interests and concerns may be sidelined by the main political parties in Britain, and in effect may be excluded from the mainstream political agenda.[3]

Exclusion, whether from the labour market or politics, is inconsistent with the official rhetoric of Britain's leaders, who, like the great majority of British citizens, espouse liberal principles of equality of opportunity. Political exclusion also has worrying implications for the health and legitimacy of democracy, since it means that the voices and viewpoints of certain electors will not be heard in the political process. At its worst it has led to the 'tyranny of the majority', where a majority systematically excludes a minority from political influence but justifies their exclusion by majoritarian principles. Historically, Northern Ireland might well be regarded as an example, where it took three decades of Troubles to lead to the establishment of power-sharing arrangements.

There are, to be sure, many differences between the historical situation in Northern Ireland (or in other divided states that have been torn apart by ethnic conflict) and that facing post-war migrants and their descendants. In the case of migrants, the more usual current concern is with their low political participation. In many countries, migrants (and perhaps their children) appear to exhibit particularly low levels of turnout in elections and low levels of engagement with the mainstream parties; and in Britain too there has been some evidence in the past that black electors have low levels of turnout.[4] The eminent US political scientist Sidney Verba and his colleagues have argued that low participation by minorities matters, since distinctive concerns of minorities will be heard less in the political arena than will others' concerns, and that this constitutes 'a violation of the principle of equal protection of interests' (1993, p. 455). They go on to argue that any such violation rests upon two fundamental criteria, namely whether minority interests and preferences differ from those of the majority, and whether abstention is the product of free and voluntary choice. To be sure, some commentators have suggested that minorities do not actually have any distinct interests and policy preferences but simply share the same political agenda as the wider British public. If this really does hold true, then the issue of exclusion of their political interests (if not of their candidates) does not arise. We clearly need to examine this.

Some key questions for us are:

Do minorities have distinct political concerns and interests that are different from those of the majority?

If so, are minorities excluded from British politics in the sense that these distinctive political interests and concerns are ignored or sidelined by the mainstream political parties?

In turn, does any such exclusion lead to withdrawal and lack of engagement or participation on the one hand, or to alienation, discontent, and protest on the other?

While our starting point is a fear that lack of political integration might be a consequence of the same kind of exclusion that has already been demonstrated in the labour market, we have to recognize that exclusion is not the only process that might be at work in generating withdrawal or alienation. As Sidney Verba's argument implies, minorities might freely choose not to participate. While the notion of a free choice is a rather slippery one, we can readily imagine a number of reasons why recent migrants might quite reasonably choose not to participate in British politics. They might, for example, see themselves as temporary sojourners who plan to return to their origin countries, and therefore do not care to take out British citizenship. Even if they plan to settle in Britain, they might have family and friends remaining abroad, perhaps in politically unstable situations, and they might choose to concentrate their energies on the politics of their origin country rather than on less pressing British political controversies.

While orientations towards the home country might lead to lack of interest in British politics and voluntary withdrawal from active participation, some public figures have raised less benign worries. There have, for example, been some suggestions in the recent debates about social cohesion and multiculturalism in Britain that minorities might choose to remain within separate ethnic communities, and that this might in turn have adverse implications for political integration. Social segregation was a major theme in the Cantle report of 2001 on the disturbances in Oldham, Burnley, and Bradford, and the issue of the extent to which minorities lead separate lives from the white British majority has been a recurring theme in the debates over multiculturalism.[5] The Cantle report in particular focused on the extent of social segregation in these cities, and the implications for conflict and disorder.

In this kind of account, disorder and support for extremism is seen to grow out of social and cultural segregation, with minorities choosing or being encouraged to live separate lives and to maintain values, attitudes, and identities that are at odds with those of the British mainstream. As the eminent political theorist Brian Barry argued, 'a situation where groups live in parallel universes is not one well calculated to advance mutual understanding or encourage the cultivation of habits of co-operation or sentiments of trust' (Barry 2001, p. 88). This kind of account focuses particularly on Muslim groups, tending to ignore the various black groups who have long been known to have high levels of intermarriage with white British partners and high levels of social and residential integration.

To be fair, the Cantle report emphasized repeatedly that the formation of separate communities might not be a simple matter of choice but might also reflect exclusionary practices in the housing market and constraints imposed by the wider society. The report also emphasized the importance of grievances over economic deprivation and disadvantage as a powerful ingredient in the sense of alienation among some ethnic communities. Cantle's segregation thesis should not be seen as in any way inconsistent with the exclusion thesis. Nevertheless, the main thrust of the Cantle report and its recommendations is that bridges need to be constructed between the parallel communities in order to promote understanding and cohesion.

A quite different formulation, however, might see segregation as an (indirect) source of political integration rather than an obstacle. Rahsaan Maxwell, for example, has claimed that social concentration may facilitate positive economic and political outcomes, since the strong social ties within separate communities can provide an effective basis for group organization in pursuit of common ethnic interests. This in turn can provide incentives for the established party elites to respond to minority concerns, and thus ensure that they are incorporated into the mainstream political agenda.[6] A related stream of work has suggested that voter numbers are higher in socially and residentially concentrated ethnic communities. Cohesive ethnic communities might therefore foster rather than hinder political integration by encouraging members to participate in mainstream politics, and ensuring that their voices are heard.[7]

Key questions arising from these perspectives are thus:

> *To what extent do minorities have positive orientations towards and interest in mainstream British politics?*
>
> *Can lack of engagement with British politics be explained by minorities' focus on politics in their countries of origin?*
>
> *Do minorities lead separate social lives, apart from the mainstream?*
>
> *If so, do separate lives, perhaps when accompanied by grievances over deprivation, lead to alienation and disaffection?*
>
> *Or do cohesive ethnic communities provide collective resources fostering participation and engagement with mainstream politics?*

These alternative perspectives all implicitly assume that, in one way or another, the ethnic minority experience of life in Britain has distinctive features, whether in terms of discrimination and exclusion, orientations to the home country, or separate social lives, which set them apart from other sections of British society. An alternative perspective emphasizes the commonalities. Minorities will surely have many of the same political concerns as fellow citizens from the majority group—for example, over the parlous state of the economy, high levels of unemployment, or cuts in public spending. Many, whether brought up in Commonwealth countries or, in the case of second-generation children of migrants, brought up and educated in British schools, may share the same commitment to democratic values and norms of political engagement as other Britons—or, indeed, they may share the same cynicism and distrust of politicians that has become a widespread feature of young people in modern Western democracies.

Minorities might also be internally divided, for example by socio-economic position, in just the same way as the majority group is divided. Some of the sources of political participation and engagement, and some of the dividing lines in party preferences, might thus be very similar among minorities and the majority. Low minority rates of participation, or high levels of support for the Labour Party, might be explained by the same kinds of socio-economic interests and resources that explain participation and partisanship among the white British. Or might ethnicity trump class?

On this account we might expect to find similarities in minority- and majority-group patterns of engagement, particularly among those in similar socio-economic positions. This might be even more marked in later generations. Interest in the politics of the homeland, for example, might be stronger among recent arrivals from overseas and much weaker among later generations educated or born in Britain. Similarly, the most recent arrivals may not be so fluent in the English language, and may have little choice but to remain within the ethnic enclave. But the second generation will have acquired greater fluency, will be more likely to hold British citizenship, will have had greater opportunities for mixing with white British counterparts, and might hence exhibit more typically British patterns of engagement.

British studies, both official government and academic studies, have largely ignored issues of generational change. This may perhaps reflect the fact that immigration is a relatively recent phenomenon in Britain compared with the classic countries of immigration such as Australia, Canada, and the USA, where studies of generational change are standard. It may also reflect British antipathy towards US theories of generational assimilation, and the assumption in some older US accounts that minorities *ought* to assimilate (although many US scholars would dispute the claim that their theories imply any particular normative stances).[8]

We do not ourselves believe that assimilation is in any sense an ideal, just as we do not accept that there is any single ideal model of political integration. But it must at the very least be an important empirical question as to whether there are generational changes in patterns of political integration, and whether the first generation or recent arrivals from overseas have distinctive patterns of political orientations, identity, and behaviour, while the second and later generations look more like their white British peers.

Moreover, generational change might in principle move in very different directions, depending on the focus of our attention. For example, drawing on experience from other countries, we might expect to find that participation and engagement in British politics was particularly low among recent arrivals, for reasons we have already sketched, while in the second generation we might see convergence with British levels of engagement. In contrast, the second generation might actually feel more strongly about discrimination and unfair treatment, and thus become more alienated or more radical than migrants. For example, the first (migrant) generation may tend to compare themselves with their compatriots who did not migrate rather than with the British, with whom they may have little contact or of whom they may have little knowledge. In contrast, the second generation, born and educated in Britain, may compare themselves with their white British peers, and may well expect to be treated in the same way and have the same opportunities in life. The frame of reference, and the comparisons made, may thus change between generations, and the new frame of reference may actually lead the second generation to feel more discontented, as they will be more aware of the exclusion and inequality of opportunity that they face.

We therefore have further questions to address:

> *In what respects do minorities and the majority share common political concerns that cut across ethnic divisions?*
>
> *To what extent are minorities, like the majority, internally divided by socio-economic interests; or does ethnicity 'trump' class?*
>
> *Do the second and later generations converge with British patterns of political engagement and participation?*
>
> *Or do later generations of ethnic minorities come to feel more alienated and/or disengaged as they become more aware of the exclusion that they experience?*

The Ethnic Minority British Election survey

To answer our questions, we draw on a major new survey (funded by the ESRC) conducted immediately after the 2010 general election.[9] The aim of the survey was to provide a comprehensive resource covering the social and political attitudes, the electoral behaviour, and political integration, broadly defined, of the major established ethnic minorities in Britain—namely people of Indian, Pakistani, Bangladeshi, black Caribbean, and black African background. We reluctantly decided to exclude people of Chinese background, as this is a rather small and geographically scattered group that we would not have been able to sample in a cost-effective manner. We also excluded the larger numbers of recently arrived white minorities from the European Union. Few of these would have been eligible to vote in a general election, and they also have much higher rates of return migration to their origin countries than do the established minorities on whom we focus.[10]

Our survey was both large-scale (at least by the standards of academic studies) and rigorous, conducted to the highest standards of representative sampling and fieldwork. It thus gives us an authoritative basis for describing and understanding ethnic minority integration. It is the first study of this kind since 1997, when we conducted a smaller-scale exercise under Shamit Saggar's leadership. As with the 1997 exercise, our survey was closely integrated with the main British Election Survey, and we are thus able for many questions, although unfortunately not all, to compare the responses of our ethnic minority respondents with those of the white British.

The survey inevitably has its limitations. While it is national in coverage, it does not allow us to explore local politics, which is a major arena for minority engagement. And while it is relatively large, with 2,787 respondents (1,339 men and 1,448 women), it is not nearly large enough to investigate rare phenomena such as engagement in forms of extremist political behaviour. In any event, we very much doubt whether a survey of this kind is a sensible vehicle for investigating extremism, since extremists will almost certainly refuse to take part or to answer questions honestly. So while we are interested in questions about minority disaffection and protest, we must emphasize that this is quite different from extremism.

Our main findings

In Chapter 2, we begin by introducing our main ethnic groups. We provide the historical background to the migration of the five groups, and give some essential statistics about the socio-economic profile of each group. An important point that emerges from this chapter is the diversity both between and within each of the main ethnic groups, especially the Indian and most of all the black African groups (both in terms of ethno-religious differences and socio-economic situation). It would be quite wrong to think of the five main ethnic groups on which the book focuses as monolithic. The chapter also shows some major ways in which the groups differ across generations, with the second generation typically showing higher levels of British identity and higher levels of social integration than the first. The chapter also casts considerable doubt on the claim that, even in the first generation, minorities lead separate or parallel lives.

Chapter 3 starts by focusing on the orientations of the first generation who migrated to Britain as adults. It confirms that adult migrants do show quite high levels of interest in the politics of their homeland, while their interest in and knowledge of British politics is rather lower than that of the British majority group. But interest in homeland and British politics are not either/or alternatives. Instead, we find that they often go together, and that membership of ethnic organizations often goes with increased interest in politics generally. Moreover, there is a major decline across generations in levels of interest in homeland politics, and a convergence towards British patterns. There is no sign that particular minorities, for example Muslim groups, are more resistant to change than others.

We also find that the first generation is highly committed to the duty to vote, even more so than the typical British citizen, although again we find some convergence with British norms across generations, albeit from the opposite direction. This is a very positive start to our story.

Chapter 4 asks whether there is a distinct ethnic agenda (or distinctive agendas), while Chapter 5 looks at the extent to which any such agenda is incorporated into mainstream politics. First, and unsurprisingly, we find that minorities share many of the concerns of white British voters, especially on issues like the state of the economy. Secondly, however, even on the mainstream agenda, minorities on average differ from the majority in the priority that they assign to various issues. For example, minorities assign a greater priority to unemployment, but are less concerned to maintain government spending; are somewhat more concerned to protect the rights of the accused and to help asylum-seekers; and are on average more supportive of the war in Afghanistan. These majority/minority differences on the mainstream issues should not, however, be taken to represent a fundamentally distinct ethnic agenda. There are very substantial differences between minorities on some of the issues, especially on asylum (on which the black African groups tend to be most supportive) and Afghanistan (where Muslim groups tend to be most opposed). These differences between minorities are sometimes much larger than those between the majority and the minority overall, with some minorities being more 'progressive' and some much less 'progressive' than the majority.

However, there is a distinct and dramatic majority/minority difference on the issue of securing equal opportunities for ethnic minorities and redress for racial discrimination. This is an issue that unites all the different minorities, but on which their views are not shared by their white British fellow-citizens, raising the crucial question of whether this central minority concern is excluded from the mainstream political agenda.

Chapter 5 sets out to determine how far this concern is represented by the major political parties, and also asks about minorities' perceptions of the main parties' commitment to their concerns. The key finding is that, despite the increasing number of ethnic minority candidates, neither the Labour nor Conservative manifestos for the 2010 general election made any explicit new commitments for redressing ethnic inequalities or addressing racial discrimination. There seems to be something of a mismatch between the increasing number of ethnic minority MPs and a declining attention to the redress of racial discrimination. Nevertheless, minorities still perceive Labour as being much more supportive of their concerns than the Conservatives, quite possibly because of the legacy of previous Labour legislation. Curiously, even though the Liberal Democrats were the one party in 2010 to bring forward an explicit new policy to address ethnic inequality, minorities did not seem to be aware of this.

Chapter 6 takes a first look at political engagement, and asks whether minorities engage with British politics in the sense of identifying with a particular party. Here we find, in striking contrast to results from some other countries such as the USA, that Britain's ethnic minorities are just as likely as their white British fellow-citizens to identify with a political party— overwhelmingly the Labour Party. Minorities continue to show much higher levels of allegiance to Labour than does the rest of the electorate, while black groups show even higher levels of Labour allegiance than do South Asian groups. These differences cannot be explained by differences in socio-economic status or ideology: minorities' allegiance to Labour is much higher than that of other disadvantaged groups, while ethnicity trumps class in the sense that middle-class blacks show the same high levels of support for Labour as do working-class blacks. We go on to show that this remarkable level of Labour allegiance can best be explained by enduring collective norms, and sentiments that 'Labour is the party of ethnic minorities', akin to the older but now largely vanished sentiment that 'Labour is the party of the working class'.

Chapter 7, the first of three chapters focusing on political behaviour rather than on orientations, preferences, and identities, asks about minorities' participation in the electoral process. We find that the great majority of our five ethnic minorities, even in the first generation, are eligible to vote (either as British or as Commonwealth citizens). Unlike many other countries, citizenship is not a major barrier in Britain to political incorporation. Registration, however, does prove to be a barrier, with registration rates ten points lower than among the white British. Even in the second generation, rates of registration among those eligible are markedly lower than among the white British. We attribute this to the socio-economic marginalization of some members of minority communities, just as among the white British the highest rates of registration are among those who are most established (such as middle-class home-owners). However, among those who are registered, minority rates of turnout (measured by the official registers) were very similar to white British ones, and we find no evidence for the common assumption that black people of Caribbean background are less likely to go to the polls than are other minorities. Indeed, among those who are registered, Caribbean turnout is effectively the same as the white British rate.

Chapter 8 looks at voting at the 2010 general election, and in particular at patterns of abstention and defection from the predominant Labour partisanship. Did minorities abandon their Labour allegiance as a result of Labour's failure in office in the same way that the majority group did? Or was there evidence of greater loyalty to Labour among their ethnic minority supporters?

What we find is a move away from Labour in 2010 among minorities, just as among the white British, and reflecting similar concerns about government performance. But ethnic minorities showed greater loyalty to Labour than did the white British, in the sense that minorities were much less likely to switch from Labour to another party, opting instead for abstention. Black groups showed the highest loyalty to Labour, just as they showed the highest levels of Labour allegiance in Chapter 6; and the same collective norms and sentiments that we introduced in Chapter 6 to explain minority allegiance to Labour also explain in part their loyalty in 2010. However, another major factor in 2010 (and probably in previous elections too) was that other parties made little active effort through canvassing and the like to win over minority voters. To some extent, Labour did well by default, and the electoral success of the Respect Party in 2005, and in a few seats in 2010, indicates the vulnerability of Labour to active campaigns to win minority voters. While Labour is the beneficiary of community norms arising from past Labour commitments, these norms could well be eroded, just as working-class norms of support for Labour have historically been eroded. Labour should not take minority support for granted. If other parties seriously wished to win over minority voters, active campaigning on issues that minorities care about would be a good way to start.

Chapter 9 turns to non-electoral forms of participation, looking at organizational activity, petitions, protests and demonstrations, donations to political causes, and participation in boycotts. A particular focus of this chapter is on the processes that might be expected to lead to discontent and protest, such as grievances over exclusion, or the separate lives that some have speculated might lead to conflict.

In practice, however, the profile of minority non-electoral participation looks very similar to that of other British citizens. As with the white British, the most prevalent option is non-participation, but among those who do take part minority and majority profiles are, as far as we can detect, very similar, just as they were in patterns of political interest, political engagement, and electoral turnout. We find a consistent pattern running throughout the chapters: levels and forms of minority engagement and participation are scarcely aberrant, and, especially in the second generation, closely resemble white British ones. Moreover, we find little evidence that minority social and residential segregation fosters withdrawal or retreat, or conversely that it leads to protest and conflict.

Finally, in Chapter 10, we review how minorities feel about British democracy, and how much they trust British political institutions. Once again, just as in Chapter 3, the central finding is of convergence across the generations towards the white British profile, the first generation showing markedly greater satisfaction with democracy and trust in parliamentary institutions than does the second generation. To be sure, this is not a wholly comforting picture, since British citizens generally are less satisfied and less trusting than they used to be, and there is certainly work to be done by the British political elite to reconnect with the public, both with minority and majority groups alike. The democratic deficit is not something restricted to European institutions, or to ethnic minorities whose voices are not heard.

But there is one very important exception to this pattern of convergence, and there is one important group whose voices are even less heard or recognized than usual by elites. Our evidence shows clearly that young second-generation people of black Caribbean or mixed heritage are notably more disaffected from British democracy and institutions than are other minorities or other British citizens, and this disaffection is clearly linked to feelings of exclusion and unfairness in the allocation of rewards. Just as the second-generation black groups are the ones who suffer the largest ethnic penalties in the labour market, so they are the ones who feel most alienated from the political process.

Our key messages

Our central message is that ethnic minority migrants came to Britain with highly positive orientations towards British democracy and with a positive attitude towards political integration, while also retaining substantial interest in the politics of their home countries. We find evidence of cohesive ethnic communities, although here we could find no evidence of especially negative consequences; rather, we incline to the view that ethnic communities typically play positive roles in fostering engagement in the political process.

Across the generations, we then find convergence with prevalent British patterns of political engagement, electoral and non-electoral participation, albeit second-generation minorities becoming more critical in their view of British democracy, just like their white peers. In these respects, we find no widespread departures from political integration either in the form of withdrawal and disengagement or of protest and dissent. To be sure, we find evidence of political exclusion, especially the current neglect of minority concerns about inequality of opportunity and redress for discrimination, and this we believe may have serious and neglected implications for social cohesion and disaffection. We also find that socio-economic exclusion, and the feelings of relative deprivation to which it gives rise, plays a major role in shaping a wide range of political attitudes, and in particular feelings of distrust and disaffection.

Some of these processes of convergence we would naturally attribute to wider social trends that have little to do with politics. These social trends include increasing fluency in the English language, greater social contact with other British citizens, and greater exposure and participation in British institutions at school and work. But we also suspect that politics has played a part, and could continue to do so. Most notably, the Labour Party's early espousal of ethnic minority concerns over inequality of opportunity, and the succession of Acts passed by Labour governments to outlaw racial discrimination (with Acts in 1965, 1968, 1976, and 2000, as well as the Racial and Religious Hatred Act of 2006) established Labour as 'the' party of minorities just as Labour used to be 'the' party of the working class. On the one hand, we suspect that this commitment to minorities was a key historical source for the development of pro-Labour norms and sentiments among minority communities, and these norms and collective identities in turn encouraged engagement and participation in the political process. On the other hand, Labour has been rewarded with remarkably many and loyal supporters from the ethnic minorities. The growing size of the ethnic minority population which the 2011 census has shown is likely to make their support even more crucial in future general elections.

We should not paint too positive or fanciful a portrait of Labour virtue. Undoubtedly, Labour's record on immigration has not always been its strongest source of appeal to minorities, with a series of acts to restrict immigration from the new Commonwealth. Labour's adventures in Iraq and Afghanistan have also alienated many Muslim voters, and eroded Labour support among British citizens of Pakistani background. The interventions of the Respect Party in 2005 demonstrated that minority support for Labour is not unconditional and cannot be taken for granted. Collective norms and sentiments, just like individual allegiance to a party, provide a legacy from the past that can be drawn upon by current incumbents. But the current incumbents can preserve or waste their political legacies just as individuals can develop or waste financial ones. In particular, despite Labour's past history of legislation, major inequalities of opportunity persist, together with widespread feelings of fraternal relative deprivation. Perhaps the most important theme of this book is the role of these feelings of relative deprivation in explaining political attitudes and behaviour, and the need for mainstream political parties to address them.

Notes

1. In these field experiments, written applications are sent to actual employers who have advertised vacancies. These applications are matched in all respects except the name of the applicant, one application having a recognizably minority name and the matched one a name typical of the majority group. Firms' responses to these application letters are then monitored. Examples of work in this tradition include Daniel (1968) (which used actors rather than written applications), Jowell and Prescott-Clarke (1970), Brown and Gay (1985), Wood et al. (2009).
2. Our concept of integration is thus very close to that of Laura Morales, who writes: 'Our notion of political integration leaves room for migrants to define patterns of engagement with politics in ways that diverge in important ways from that of the natives or the mainstream, as long as this divergence does not entail their political exclusion' (Morales 2011, p. 41).
3. On ethnic MPs see Sobolewska (2013), and on exclusion from the mainstream political agenda see Bulpitt (1986) and Studlar and Layton-Henry (1990). This research is discussed in detail in Chapter 5.
4. See for example Hajnal and Lee (2011) Table 5.1 on Latino and Asian-American turnout in the USA; González-Ferrer (2011) Table 4.2 for turnout in a range of European cities; Bird et al. (2011). On Britain see Studlar (1986), Anwar (2001), and Purdam et al. (2002).
5. Perhaps the most notable contribution was that of David Cameron with his speech in 2011 to the Munich Security conference (Cameron 2011).
6. See Maxwell (2012), pp. 22–3.
7. For two important studies that show the relationship between residential ethnic density and rates of registration and turnout see Fieldhouse and Cutts (2008a and 2008b).
8. Alba and Nee (1999) have provided a highly influential reworking of the concept of assimilation without implying normative assumptions. As they point out, W. Lloyd Warner and Leo Srole (1945) did indeed betray various normative assumptions in their early account of ethnic assimilation in New Haven, but Alba and Nee argue that, shorn of these assumptions, the concept of assimilation remains a valuable tool for social scientists.
9. For technical details see Appendix 1 and Howat et al. (2011).
10. For details of rates of return migration see Dustmann and Weiss (2007). Moreover, because this new migration wave from Europe is so recent, there was no detailed and reliable evidence from the 2001 census on their geographical distribution that would have allowed us to undertake effective sampling.

2

Diversity and Integration of British Ethnic Minorities

Before we get down to business, we need to introduce our five main ethnic groups. There are a lot of half-truths in circulation about British ethnic minorities, and it is not a bad idea to try and dispel some of them; especially as our survey is one of the most up-to-date and comprehensive surveys of minorities available, with a much richer array of data than the 2011 census. To be sure, any survey or census is only a snapshot of a dynamic reality, and we should not pretend that this chapter gives the last word; but we hope it will be a useful introduction.

We begin with a brief discussion of the concept and measurement of ethnicity. We then introduce the migration history of our five main groups and the extent of diversity within each of them. When and why did the minorities, or their pioneering predecessors, migrate to Britain? We then explore the cultural, social, and structural integration of the five minority groups, focusing on those aspects which are most relevant for understanding political integration. How fluent are they in English? To what extent do they feel British or conform to British practices, such as wearing a poppy on Remembrance Day? To what extent do they live parallel lives and exhibit ethnic solidarity? How disadvantaged are they economically, and are they internally stratified by social class? We conclude by summarizing patterns of generational change.

The concept and measurement of ethnicity

A good starting place for understanding the sociological approach to ethnicity is Max Weber's definition. Weber stated that 'we shall call "ethnic groups" those human groups that entertain a subjective belief in their common descent because of similarities of physical type or of customs or both, or because of memories of colonization and migration' (Weber [1922] 1978, p. 389). The key component of this definition, as in most sociological approaches to ethnicity, is the central role accorded to subjective beliefs: whether a particular group of people can be counted as an ethnic group is a matter for the members of that group to decide, not for outside observers to stipulate. In this respect, ethnic groups are rather like nations—they are 'imagined communities' (to use the expression coined by Benedict Anderson). Ethnicity is essentially a self-defined social identity, akin to national identity or class identity.

Social identities are by no means fixed or immutable: they can change over time or across generations. For example, many of the first migrants from the Caribbean thought of themselves as Jamaican or Antiguan depending on their national country of origin, but by the second generation many had come to think of themselves as black British with a shared black identity, irrespective of their parents' original homeland. There is also some evidence suggesting that 'pan-ethnic' identities might be emerging, with black Caribbean and black African groups, for example, developing a wider and shared black identity.[1]

The salience of social identities can also vary between individuals and groups. In the USA, where the study of ethnicity has a much longer history, sociologists have demonstrated how many of the European groups, such as Italians or Irish, who migrated there in large numbers at the beginning of the twentieth century, were originally stigmatized and disadvantaged, yet have now been accepted into the US mainstream. There has been a gradual blurring of boundaries between these groups and the previously dominant Anglo groups; hyphenated identities as Irish-American or Italian-American have replaced separate Irish or Italian identities, and these ethnicities are no longer major bases of social organization. Richard Alba, for example, has described what he calls 'the twilight of European ethnicity' in late twentieth-century USA.[2] In Britain, Robin Cohen has written about the 'fuzziness' of concepts of British and English identity, and the same idea might well be applied to some ethnic identities too.[3] In particular, the distinctions between black and mixed white and black and white have become rather fuzzy ones in the British context, unlike the US context where the 'one drop' rule is much clearer.[4]

In practice in our research, we have had to use an overly static framework, based on the official British classification of ethnic groups. But we need always to be aware, when interpreting the findings of our research, of the fluidity and fuzziness of the categories that are being measured.

The question that we used was:

> Now I'd like to ask you some questions about your ethnic background and national identity.
>
> Firstly, please could you look at this card and tell me which of these best describes your ethnic group?

WHITE
  1. *White—British*
  2. *White—Irish*
  3. *White—Gypsy or Irish Traveller*
  4. *Any other White background*

MIXED
  5. *Mixed White and Black Caribbean*
  6. *Mixed White and Black African*
  7. *Mixed White and Asian*
  8. *Any other mixed background*

ASIAN
  9. *Asian or Asian British—Indian*
  10. *Asian or Asian British—Pakistani*
  11. *Asian or Asian British—Bangladeshi*
  12. *Any other Asian/Asian British background*

BLACK
  13. *Black or Black British—Caribbean*
  14. *Black or Black British—African*
  15. *Any other Black/Black British background*
  16. *Chinese*
  17. *Any other ethnic group*

Although the Canadian concept of 'visible' minorities is not officially used in Britain, it is applicable to the British way of measuring ethnicity, and for much the same reason. That is to say, the five main headings listed above—White, Mixed, Asian, Black and Chinese—are partly defined by their colour and visibility. The latter four also tend to cover the groups that suffer discrimination on the grounds of race or colour, and who consequently experience major ethnic penalties in British society, whereas the various white groups (apart from Gypsies and Travellers) appear to suffer much less in the way of disadvantage.[5] This almost certainly reflects the racism still prevalent in wider British society.

While the official categories had extensive testing and consultation with ethnic groups before being adopted for the purposes of government classifications, they are nonetheless somewhat contentious, particularly because of their use of the 'racial' terminology of white and black.[6] Furthermore, they do not necessarily map onto the Weberian concept of ethnicity in any very consistent way: it is not at all clear that ethnic minorities actually think of themselves in terms of the official classifications—although the power of official concepts may well lead to people eventually adopting the official classification. Some people may choose to define themselves in terms of religion—for example, as Muslim—and may see themselves as part of a worldwide *ummah* of the faithful rather than as a member of a specific ethnic group.

Others may define themselves as members of more specific ethnic groups—as Punjabi or Azad Kashmiri rather than Pakistani, for example. The official classification tends to take a national approach (Indian, Pakistani, or Bangladeshi) or supra-national (African or Caribbean), but nations are not the same as ethnic groups, and there may be important ethnic differences within nations.[7] A prime example is that of Punjabi Sikhs, who would normally be classed as Indian in the official classification but who think of themselves as a separate ethno-religious group, and have indeed been accepted under British law as an ethnic group following the legal case of Mandla versus Dowell-Lee [1983] 2 AC 548.[8]

In practice, we shall generally have to follow the official classification, since our sample size is not really sufficient to enable us to make finer distinctions. We shall for simplicity refer to our five main groups as ethnic minorities, and we will often contrast them with the white British, who constitute the ethnic majority. We need to remember that this white British majority group is also internally divided into different ethnic or national minorities (Irish, Scottish, Welsh, and so on) as well as being stratified by social class and region. We need to be continually aware, therefore, of the diversity within all our groups.

History and diversity

In this section of the chapter we will briefly describe the patterns of migration of each of our five main groups, and will use the information supplied by the *adult migrants* (that is, people who migrated to Britain as adults, aged sixteen or over) in our sample to illustrate the diversity of these five groups in terms of national origins, religious affiliation, reasons for migration, and home language. We recognize, of course, that the characteristics of our sample cannot tell us about the characteristics of the first pioneering migrants, except for the most recently arrived group of black Africans. Moreover, some characteristics—notably citizenship status—will have changed since the migrant arrived in Britain. But evidence on the pioneers is simply not available, and the data in our survey is useful as an indicator of the diversity within our sample. (Another reason for focusing on adult migrants is that some interesting information, for example on reasons for migration, can only sensibly be answered by adult migrants.)

Black or Black British—Caribbean

Our main groups arrived over somewhat different periods, with different legal statuses, with different reasons for migration, under different immigration rules, and meeting varying conditions in the labour market and British society more generally. The first of our five main groups to arrive in substantial numbers were the black Caribbeans, who were actively recruited after the war to work on the London Underground and as nurses in the NHS. There is an ironic poster showing Enoch Powell, then Minister for Health but later the most virulent opponent of immigration, asking black Caribbean nurses to come to Britain.

The black Caribbean migrants who came to Britain largely came from British colonies. The largest number came from Jamaica, but there were other sizeable inflows from other Caribbean countries. The first migrants came at a time when Britain gave Citizenship of the United Kingdom and Colonies to all citizens of the colonies (as Jamaica and the other sending countries in the Caribbean still were). This status gave them free right of entry to the UK, and immediate citizenship and voting rights on arrival. The 1962 Commonwealth Immigrants Act took away this right of entry in an attempt to limit immigration from the new Commonwealth, and work vouchers became necessary for further immigration. We can thus think of the initial migrants from the Caribbean as being colonial or (after independence) postcolonial migrants.

In some ways, the black Caribbean men were the equivalent of the so-called guest-workers who came from Turkey and South Europe after the war to fill labour shortages and undertake less-skilled and poorly paid work in north European industries in Austria, Belgium, Germany, and the Netherlands, although they tended to be more highly skilled than the continental guest-workers. Moreover, black Caribbean women who came as nurses were particularly well qualified and highly skilled. Also unlike the so-called guest-workers, the black Caribbean migrants spoke English (albeit with a distinct accent and sometimes dialect). They were typically Christian, and had also been socialized under British rule and been exposed to British institutions and values. Many had served, or their families had traditions of serving, in the British armed forces or merchant navy during the Second World War, supplying an additional link with, and impetus to migrate to, Britain. They thus had much stronger affiliations and affinities with Britain than did continental guest-workers in their respective destination countries.

In addition, again unlike the guest-workers, the migrants from the Caribbean were primarily voluntary migrants, responding individually to advertisements rather than coming as part of government-to-government deals (although there were some direct sponsorship arrangements too). As a result they were what economists have tended to describe as 'positively' rather than 'negatively selected'.[9] In other words, the Caribbean migrants were not drawn from the lowest levels of Caribbean societies but were actually above average, when compared with non-migrants in their countries of origin, in terms of their skills and qualifications.[10] This is not surprising, since individual voluntary migration was a big step to take (especially in the 1950s), and involved considerable expense and effort. This implies that many of the migrants would have been particularly dynamic people, and probably more adventurous and optimistic than those who did not migrate. This in turn may have implications for their orientations towards, and participation in, British politics. Britain was fortunate with its migrants from the Caribbean. Compared with continental guest-workers, they were more selective, more attuned to British society, and more similar in culture and traditions.

Migration from the Caribbean continued throughout the 1950s and 1960s, although the net rate of inflow declined after the 1962 Act.[11] By the early twenty-first century there were about 615,000 people of black Caribbean background in England and Wales, roughly 1.1 per cent of the population.[12] Because of their relatively early immigration to Britain, a high proportion in our sample (55 per cent) were British-born (including a substantial number with British-born parents too), while even among the migrants from the Caribbean many have been here for considerable periods of time. This can be seen from Table 2.1, which summarizes the picture for the adult migrants in our 2010 sample.

We must not extrapolate backwards in time from a 2010 survey to draw conclusions about the first migrants to Britain from the Caribbean. The adult migrants in our survey will be somewhat different from the pioneers, while some of the attributes in the tables such as language spoken at home may have changed since arrival. Nevertheless, earlier sources do indicate that many of the features displayed in Table 2.1 are quite long-standing.[13]

Table 2.1 shows the dominance of Jamaica as the main origin country in the Caribbean, the emphasis on moving for a 'better life' in Britain, the relatively

Table 2.1. Black Caribbean adult migrants

Main countries of origin	Jamaica 59%	Barbados 6%	Trinidad 4%	Antigua 4%	Dominica 4%
Reasons for migration	Better life 40%	Join family 26%	Earn money 22%	Live in Britain 12%	To be a student 10%
Average time since arrival	23 years				
Citizenship	British 89%	Commonwealth 7%	Other 4%		
Main language spoken at home	English 98%	French 1%	Spanish 1%		
Religion	Other Christian 31%	Pentecostal 22%	None 18%	Catholic 15%	Anglican 12%
Secondary or higher foreign qualifications	16%				

Notes: Percentages do not sum to 100 as only major categories are reported. Reasons for migration are multicoded. British citizenship includes dual citizenship. The base for foreign qualifications excludes those who reported having any British qualifications.

Source: EMBES 2010, weighted data. N = 165

early dates of arrival (as shown by the average length of time the migrants have now spent in Britain), their British citizenship, use of the English language, and membership of the Christian religion, with relatively large numbers of Pentecostals.

People of black Caribbean background have also been especially notable for their very high rates of intermarriage (or interethnic partnership) with the white British.[14] There is now a substantial and rapidly growing number of people—about 450,000 in England and Wales—of mixed white and black Caribbean heritage.[15] We should not really think of people of mixed background as representing a distinct ethnic group. Perhaps instead they should be thought of as straddling the blurred boundary between the majority group and the black minority group, and people with similar ancestries may well choose to define themselves in different ways.

We have a number of people who described themselves as having mixed background in our sample. Our interviewers, when on the doorstep, asked if anyone from one of the five target groups was resident at the address. However, on securing an interview, quite a number of interviewees then described themselves as coming from a mixed black Caribbean and white background. We decided to continue with the interviews anyway, although we must emphasize that our interviewees are not a representative sample of people of mixed background. Our interviewers' experience does, however, bring out the fuzzy nature of the official categories. When we report results for people of mixed black/white background throughout this book, we also include a small number who reported mixed white and black African background.

Asian or Asian British—Indian

The next main group(s) to arrive in Britain were the Indians. These were an even more disparate group than the migrants from the Caribbean—both socially and ethnically. Migration from India began in the 1950s, with some highly educated Indians coming from Gujerat to work as doctors in the NHS. There were also considerable inflows of Sikhs from the Punjab. Many Sikhs had already been dislocated from their original homes in the west of the Punjab following the partition of India in 1947, and had been allocated poorer land in what remained of the Indian Punjab. Linked to this was a history of protest and discontent in the Punjab.[16] Dislocation and displacement have of course been major sources of migration throughout South Asia and Sub-Saharan Africa. Another factor, as with black Caribbeans, was a history of military service in the British armed forces, which recruited particularly from the Punjab.[17]

There had also been an earlier Indian diaspora to other British colonies, particularly East Africa, where many Indians had been recruited by the British for government service as clerks and lower-level officials, while others had become entrepreneurs and businessmen. They have been described as 'the filling in the colonial sandwich', holding positions below that of the dominant British colonists but above that of the subordinate African population.[18] When these East African countries finally secured independence from Britain in the 1960s, a number followed policies of Africanization. Some Indians were forcibly expelled, most notoriously from Uganda by Idi Amin who gave the Indians ninety days to leave the country in 1972, but also from Kenya a few years earlier. The British government, which had already restricted entry rights for New Commonwealth citizens in 1962 and again in 1968, attempted to bar the East African Indians from entering Britain but eventually allowed many to enter, although others took their skills elsewhere to the USA and Canada, where they have been notably successful.[19]

As with the migrants from the Caribbean, and unlike many migrants to the continental countries, Indians were positively selected, quite probably even more so than the Caribbeans. They are now the largest (1.4 million) but also one of the most disparate of Britain's visible ethnic minorities, making up 2.5 per cent of the population of England and Wales. Since they are more recent arrivals than the Caribbeans, the overseas-born currently make up around 67 per cent of the group in our sample.

Table 2.2 shows the diverse origins of the Indian group, although our 2010 data probably undercounts the proportion of Indians who originally came from East Africa. In addition, we can see that there is very considerable diversity in the languages and religions of the Indian migrants to Britain, with Catholics outnumbering Muslims in our sample. (Western Christian missionaries to India converted considerable numbers of *adivasis*—tribal groups believed to be the aboriginal population of India—who were outside the

Table 2.2. Indian adult migrants

Main countries of origin	India 86%	Kenya 4%	Uganda 2%	Mauritius 2%	Sri Lanka 1%
Reasons for migration	Join family 40%	Better life 24%	Earn money 24%	To be a student 19%	Live in Britain 6%
Average time since arrival	17 years				
Citizenship	British 51%	Commonwealth 48%			
Main language spoken at home	English 35%	Punjabi 18%	Gujerati 15%	Hindi 11%	Tamil 7%
Religion	Hindu 48%	Sikh 21%	Catholic 10%	Sunni Muslim 7%	None 5%
Secondary or higher foreign qualifications	76%				

Notes: As for Table 2.1.
Source: EMBES 2010, weighted data. N = 317

dominant Indian religious traditions.) We also see that family reunion was a more important motivation than among the Caribbean migrants, reflecting the fact that Indian men rather than women tended to be the primary migrants. And we also suspect that caste is a further element of stratification and diversity within the Indian communities in Britain, though it was not something on which we felt able to collect data as British Indians might find it offensive.

It is also noticeable that the figures for British citizenship are much lower than for most of the other groups that we cover in this study. This is almost certainly because India, unlike Britain, has not in the past allowed dual citizenship, and has regarded Indians who take out citizenship of another country as terminating their Indian citizenship (although some changes are now underway).

Asian or Asian British—Pakistani

There are several similarities between the Pakistani migration to Britain and the Indian migration. Some Muslims from what is now Pakistan had settled in East Africa in the same roles as the Indian middlemen, and were expelled or pressured to leave during the processes of Africanization. (We should remember that to talk of Indians and Pakistanis in the case of people who migrated from British India to East Africa before partition is anachronistic.) Many Muslim Punjabis were also displaced by partition in the same way that Sikh Punjabis were, and many British Pakistanis have come from the northern Punjab. Many too had served in the British armed forces, as with the Indians.

Another major group of migrants were those who came from Azad Kashmir (disputed territory between India and Pakistan), and particularly from the Mirpur district.[20] Emigration from Mirpur was accelerated by the Pakistani government's construction of the huge Mangla dam in 1961–7, which submerged over 250 villages and displaced 100,000 people.

The period of migration was also fairly similar to that from India, and as with Indian migration a great deal of more recent migration has taken the form of family reunion. Men tended to be the primary migrants during the early phases, and subsequently brought over their wives and families. However, Pakistani traditions of marriage to close kin from one's *birādarī*[21] (and desires for social advancement or to circumvent Britain's restrictive immigration laws) have also led to many British Pakistani women acquiring husbands from their families' villages in Mirpur or the Punjab. Family reunion (see Table 2.3) does not therefore apply only to women. In fact, 36 per cent of the men in our sample gave family reasons for their migration, compared with 21 per cent of men overall (but 88 per cent of Pakistani women).

Most commentators have concluded that the Pakistani migration to Britain, especially from Mirpur, was more of a rural phenomenon than the Indian

Table 2.3. Pakistani adult migrants

Main countries of origin	Pakistan 95%	India 2%	Kenya 1%		
Reasons for migration	Join family 61%	Better life 22%	To be a student 13%	Earn money 8%	Live in Britain 2%
Average time since arrival	17 years				
Citizenship	British 74%	Commonwealth 25%			
Main language spoken at home	Urdu 36%	Punjabi 25%	English 24%	Mirpuri 10%	Pashtu 3%
Religion	Sunni Muslim 85%	Other Muslim 13%			
Secondary or higher foreign qualifications	46%				

Notes: As for Table 2.1.
Source: EMBES 2010, weighted data. N = 312

migration. But overall, Pakistani migrants were also positively selected, though somewhat less so than in the Indian case. They (together with their descendants) now constitute the second largest of Britain's visible ethnic minorities, over a million in number, making up 2.0 per cent of the population of England and Wales. Similarly to the Indians, the overseas-born currently make up around 64 per cent of the group in our sample, reflecting their similar period of arrival.

Most British commentators tend to think of people of Pakistani background as constituting a rather homogeneous ethnic group, but as we can see from the diversity of languages spoken among our adult migrants to Britain, this is not really the case. There is a stereotype that most Pakistani migrants to Britain were poorly educated and low-skilled migrants from rural areas like Mirpur. We must once again emphasize that our sample of adult migrants to Britain is by no means representative of the pioneers, but our data warn us to beware of this kind of 'stylized fact'. Certainly, it is clear that our sample has a high proportion with foreign secondary or degree-level qualifications. They cannot all have been rural agriculturalists.

Asian or Asian British—Bangladeshi

Bangladeshis were the last of the main South Asian groups to arrive in Britain. Many came from Sylhet, a relatively poor and rural area in Northern Bangladesh, which had been dislocated by the war of independence against Pakistan in 1971. Some Sylhetis had already been displaced by the partition of eastern India after independence, while there was also a tradition of working in the British merchant navy, establishing links with Britain comparable to those of Sikhs in the British armed forces.[22]

Diversity and Integration of British Ethnic Minorities

Table 2.4. Bangladeshi adult migrants

Main countries of origin	Bangladesh 99%	India 1%			
Reasons for migration	Join family 51%	Better life 27%	To be a student 20%	Earn money 10%	Freedom 6%
Average time since arrival	16 years				
Citizenship	British 75%	Commonwealth 23%			
Main language spoken at home	Bengali 82%	English 15%	Sylheti 2%		
Religion	Sunni Muslim 88%	Other Muslim 9%	Hindu 3%		
Secondary or higher foreign qualifications	37%				

Notes: As for Table 2.1.
Source: EMBES 2010, weighted data. N = 102

As with migration from Pakistan, there has been continuing entry to Britain despite the progressively stricter immigration laws, many coming to join family or to marry co-ethnics in Britain. Reflecting their more recent arrival, around 73 per cent of people of Bangladeshi background in our sample were born in Bangladesh.

They are also perhaps the most homogeneous of the five main ethnic groups. They are not ethnically or religiously divided, and the distinction in Table 2.4 between Bengali and Sylheti speakers is almost certainly artificial: Sylheti is in effect a dialect of Bengali, and many British Bangladeshis are likely to say that they speak Bengali as they will assume that British interviewers will not know about or recognize Sylheti.

While the anthropologists who have studied migrants from Sylhet to Britain have emphasized their rural and less-educated background, it should be noted that 36 per cent of our sample actually had qualifications at secondary level or above—a considerably higher proportion than among the migrants from the Caribbean. To be sure, few of the migrants in our sample will have been among the first arrivals, and Bangladesh like many other developing countries has seen substantial improvements in education in recent years. But it is important not to fall into the trap of stereotyping the migrants from Bangladesh as being uniformly ill-educated.

Black or Black British-African

The most recent large-scale arrivals have been migrants from Sub-Saharan Africa. This has been by far the most diverse group of migrants in any of our five main groups. It includes some post-colonial migrants from countries such as Nigeria and Ghana, although a considerable proportion of these were not labour migrants, like those from the Caribbean or South Asia, but highly educated young people from fairly affluent backgrounds who came to study at British universities. As Patricia Daley has described them, many were 'students who stayed'.[23]

However, alongside the postcolonial migrants from former colonies, the black Africans have included a considerable number of refugees, fleeing civil war and persecution, coming from non-Commonwealth countries such as Somalia and the Congo. These are the first largish group of 'visible' minorities who do not have a strong colonial or postcolonial tie with Britain (though part of what is now Somalia had actually been a British protectorate from 1888, although briefly occupied by Italy during the Second World War).

In recent years black Africans have been the fastest growing of the five main groups of visible minorities. There are now around one million, making up around 1.8 per cent of the population of England and Wales, and 88 per cent in our sample were overseas-born. In the case of some of the black African groups, for example the most recent arrivals from Somalia, the data in Table 2.5 do tell us about the initial arrivals.

As we can see from Table 2.5, the black Africans in our sample are highly diverse, and indeed they have come from thirty-two different African countries. Broadly speaking, however, we need to remember that the largest number come from Commonwealth countries (58 per cent of the adult migrants), with high proportions speaking English and belonging to various Christian denominations. Alongside these are more recent arrivals, many fleeing war or persecution in their countries of origin and a considerable number being Muslims. However, it is also important to recognize the complexities. While many of the refugees are Muslims coming from the Horn of Africa, others are Christians fleeing conflicts in the Congo or Zimbabwe.[24]

Table 2.5. Black African adult migrants

Main countries of origin	Nigeria 27%	Ghana 14%	Somalia 13%	Zimbabwe 8%	Congo 6%
Reasons for migration	Better life 28%	To be a student 23%	Join family 22%	War 12%	Persecution 8%
Average time since arrival	13 years				
Citizenship	British 58%	Commonwealth 29%	Other 14%		
Main language spoken at home	English 64%	Somali 9%	French 5%	Yoruba 3%	Akan/Twi 4%
Religion	Pentecostal 31%	Catholic 17%	Other Christian 15%	Sunni 14%	Other Muslim 12%
Secondary or higher foreign qualifications	82%				

Notes: As for Table 2.1.
Source: EMBES 2010, weighted data. N = 342

Diversity and complexity are therefore key themes that emerge from all our five main groups. A second key theme is that these groups are all, to varying degrees, positively selected.[25] They were not people coming from the lowest social levels of their societies but were typically exceptional (relative to their non-migrant peers in their countries of origin) in their educational levels, and were probably exceptional in other ways too, such as their drive and determination. It is also important to recognize that these groups were generally voluntary migrants (apart from some of the refugees). In this way they are quite unlike, say, African-Americans, who were involuntary migrants. John Ogbu in particular has emphasized how the involuntary character of the African-American situation in the USA may have a crucial role in explaining their reactions to life in US society, and we should therefore be very careful in extrapolating from US research on African-Americans to the very different situation of the black British.[26]

Minorities today: cultural, social, and structural integration

In this section we turn from adult migrants to look more generally at all members of the five minority groups in our sample, focusing on their cultural, social, and economic integration. Our key objective here is to introduce the main intellectual characters who will be taking various parts, some heroes, a few villains, and several walk-on parts, in our drama. Many authors have cast cultural and social insularity as potential villains that might explain lack of political integration. In contrast, in our own previous writings, we have tended to cast discrimination and barriers to labour market success as the potential villains. We shall have to see what happens as the drama unfolds over the next eight chapters, but first to the introductions.

Cultural integration

Classic studies of ethnicity, such as Milton Gordon's work, emphasized acculturation as the first stage of immigrant adaptation.[27] By acculturation he had in mind the idea that newcomers will typically adopt the language, dress, and daily customs of the host society. Gordon saw this as one step in the direction of assimilation, a concept that has been heavily criticized, and which we do not accept either as a necessary normative ideal or as a likely empirical reality for most groups in the foreseeable future.

While the moral and political assumptions underlying the concept of assimilation are questioned by many British commentators, it is empirically the case that some aspects of acculturation such as fluency in English are important for some of the migrants' own objectives, especially those in the economic sphere. They are also likely to be very important from the point of view of political participation. Lack of English is certainly a major barrier to occupational advancement, and possibly to political participation as well. Fluency in the host-country language—in our case English—should not, however, be equated with loss of the minority language. Bilingualism potentially has many advantages over monolingualism, and the experience of bilingual Welsh and English speakers in Britain is an important precedent.

Other aspects of culture that may be important for political integration include the extent to which minorities feel themselves to be British and to be part of a British political community. Conversely, ethnic or race consciousness has been emphasized by US scholars as a source of desires to split away from mainstream parties and support a specifically black-oriented party.[28] British debates have focused more on British identity than on race consciousness, with politicians in particular being concerned over the need to develop loyalty to Britain. Most notorious was Norman Tebbit's 'cricket test'. Tebbit (a member of the cabinet in Margaret Thatcher's Conservative administrations), in a 1990 interview with the *Los Angeles Times*, said: 'A large proportion of Britain's Asian population fail to pass the cricket test. Which side do they cheer for? It's an interesting test. Are you still harking back to where you came from or where you are?'[29]

As we shall see in the final section of this chapter, there is a great deal of generational change in language use, ethnic identity, and British identity. For now, though, we summarize the patterns for our five groups. Given the fuzziness of the distinction between the black Caribbean and mixed black/white terms, we also include in these tables the figures for this mixed group (who incidentally are largely born in Britain, as might be expected). As we can see, in many respects they closely resemble our respondents of black Caribbean background.

In Table 2.6 we report ethnic group differences in the fluent use of English, adoption of British practices such as wearing a poppy on Remembrance Day, British and black/Asian identities, and an overall measure of ethnic identity. One result that runs strongly counter to stereotypes about minorities in Britain is our finding that the overwhelming majority are fluent in English: 63 per cent reported that English was their main language at home, while a further 18 per cent said that they spoke English fluently. We also see high numbers reporting that they followed the quintessentially British practice of wearing a poppy on Remembrance Day. (Unfortunately, this question was not asked in the main BES, but one suspects that the white British proportion would not be much higher.)

Turning next to identity, we asked respondents whether they felt black (or Asian) *not* British, *more* black (or Asian) than British, *equally* black (or Asian) and British, and so on. As we can see, the modal response for all groups is to

Table 2.6. English fluency, national identity, cultural practices, and ethnic identification
Cell percentages

Ethnic background	Fluent in English	Wears poppy	More black or Asian than British	Equally British and black or Asian	More British than black or Asian	Bothered if relative marries white person	Ethnic identification scale (mean score)	N
Indian	80	69	29	48	19	29	4.6	586
Pakistani	70	53	21	51	26	36	4.6	667
Bangladeshi	63	46	29	45	22	28	4.5	269
Black Caribbean	100	74	36	51	11	13	4.4	596
Black African	85	55	46	44	6	18	4.7	523
Mixed white/black	91	70	–	–	–	14	4.2	93
All minorities	81	62	31	48	17	24	4.6	2782

Notes: Identity questions were not asked of people of mixed background. Ns are for the item on wearing a poppy.
Source: EMBES 2010, weighted data

report dual identities with 48 per cent overall saying that they felt equally British and black or Asian. The balance among the other responses was towards the ethnic rather than the British pole, with 32 per cent feeling more black or Asian, compared with 17 per cent feeling more British. (The remaining 3 per cent gave other answers.) Interestingly, these figures are very close to the ones we found in our 1997 survey. These are long-standing patterns.[30] So ethnicity is clearly an important social identity, and for some it is their most salient identity. For a greater number, however, the ethnic and British identities have more or less equal salience. As Alan Manning and Sanchari Roy conclude from their detailed examination of the evidence, fears of a culture clash between Britons and Muslims are grossly exaggerated.[31]

There are also unsurprising differences between ethnic groups in Table 2.6. The biggest differences are with respect to language and practices such as wearing a poppy on Remembrance Day, with people of Caribbean and mixed background showing the highest levels of acculturation. There are also some important differences in levels of concern about intermarriage with a white person, which almost certainly reflect religious as much as ethnic differences. In the final column of the table, we report scores on an overall measure of ethnic identification.[32] As we can see, average differences between our five main groups are quite small, with the most recently arrived black Africans not surprisingly showing the highest level of ethnic identification.

Social integration

As we remarked in Chapter 1, lack of social integration is often thought of as a potential villain, undermining other forms of integration. Some dissenters, though, think it might be an important resource, potentially promoting integration. Clearly, we need to take it seriously.

Sociologists and political scientists have tended to distinguish between 'bridging' and 'bonding' social capital.[33] In essence, bonding social capital arises where groups have strong relationships binding them to other members of their ethnic community. These can be either informal social relationships through family, friends, and neighbours, or they can be more formal ones based on membership of ethnic associations. In contrast, bridging social capital involves relationships which bridge ethnic boundaries and link the members of one group with members of other groups (with a natural tendency to focus on links with the majority group). Bridging social capital typically involves weaker ties than the strong ties of family that underpin bonding social capital, but weak ties can also be effective. They have been shown to be important as channels for communication, especially about job opportunities, and there is a large psychological literature on the role of social contact in reducing prejudice and hostility between groups.[34] Bridging ties might therefore be important for political integration through providing access to knowledge about mainstream politics and entry into mainstream pressure groups.

Just as ethnic and British identities should not be seen as necessarily in conflict with one another, bridging and bonding social capital should not be seen as inherently in opposition to one another. They are not either/or phenomena: individuals and groups can in principle have high levels of both. As Bob Putnam has argued, the most disadvantaged individuals may be the ones who have neither bridging nor bonding ties.[35]

Table 2.7 shows some measures of bonding social capital. We focus on three indicators of informal social ties—co-ethnic partnerships, co-ethnic friendship networks, and co-ethnic residential neighbourhoods—and two indicators of associational bonding capital. (We shall later see that the informal and associational forms of bonding capital work in rather different ways.) We also include an overall measure of bonding social capital.[36]

Broadly speaking, Table 2.7 shows that the stronger the tie the more likely there is to be in-group choice. Thus we see the highest level of in-group choice in the case of partnership, with most ethnic groups apart from people of Caribbean or mixed background overwhelmingly choosing partners of their own ethnicity. In-group choice is still high for friends, but is considerably lower for neighbours. Church membership also shows a high level of bonding, while membership in an ethnic or cultural association is rather lower.

The contrast between the very high percentages who report having a co-ethnic partner and the much lower percentages in the previous table who indicated that they were bothered about marriage with a white person deserves some discussion. We need to remember that many partnerships will have been formed abroad before people migrated to Britain, and even

Table 2.7. Bonding social capital
Cell percentages

Ethnic background	Co-ethnic partner	Friends mainly co-ethnic	Neighbours mainly co-ethnic	Belongs to predominantly co-ethnic church	Belongs to ethnic or cultural association	Bonding social capital scale (mean score)	N
Indian	94	50	17	72	44	3.2	585
Pakistani	96	58	38	73	22	3.1	667
Bangladeshi	98	57	26	52	27	2.6	269
Black Caribbean	67	44	7	32	29	1.6	595
Black African	90	49	8	37	33	2.0	523
Mixed white/black	44	27	5	19	10	0.9	93
All minorities	90	51	19	58	33	2.6	2780

Notes: 'Mainly co-ethnic' covers respondents who said that all or most of their friends were from the same ethnic background, and likewise for the other items. The base for partnership excludes those who are not partnered. For the mixed respondents, co-ethnic partner is defined as either of black or mixed white/black background. The Ns are for the item on friends.
Source: EMBES 2010, weighted data

after arrival in Britain rates of inter-ethnic partnership will depend on the size and nature of the pool of eligibles with whom one comes into contact.[37]

The overall differences between groups in rates of intermarriage, and levels of bonding social capital more generally, follow closely the patterns that might be expected. The key point is that the three South Asian groups have the highest levels of bonding social capital. This will be driven partly by religion, non-religious people having the lowest levels of bonding social capital, and Sikhs, Hindus, Pentecostals, and Muslims all having high levels of bonding. But we must not exaggerate the importance of religion: other attributes such as age, education, social class, and generation are also significantly associated with bridging and bonding.

Structural integration

By structural integration we mean integration into the educational and employment spheres of British life. This is potentially important in a number of ways for political integration—a standard theory advanced by political scientists is that educational and financial resources facilitate political participation.[38] A standard theory advanced by sociologists is that middle-class occupations will be associated with support for right-wing economic values and with voting for the Conservative Party, while higher education will promote more liberal or progressive values.

It is well known that minorities have not all been equally successful in Britain, with Indians tending to be more successful than the other main groups. Nevertheless, all the five groups have now developed substantial middle classes and are now quite strongly stratified internally by social class. It would be quite wrong to typify minorities nowadays, as they were once (rightly) typified when the first arrivals came to Britain, as filling the lowest levels of the class structure. There is now a substantial black and Asian middle class.

However, while it would be wrong to stereotype minorities as occupying the lowest rungs of the occupational ladder, it is still true that minorities experience substantial 'ethnic penalties'. Anthony Heath and Dorren McMahon coined the term to cover 'all the sources of disadvantage that might lead an ethnic group to fare less well in the labour market than do similarly qualified whites'.[39] The key idea here is that minorities statistically have higher unemployment rates than do comparable white people of the same age and educational level. Furthermore, this holds true at all levels of education—it is not a phenomenon restricted to the less qualified, and so even relatively successful groups like Indians still suffer ethnic penalties, and may find it more difficult than their similarly qualified white peers to obtain employment commensurate with their educational qualifications. Discrimination is one fairly obvious explanation for the existence of ethnic penalties, but it is by no means the only explanation: lack of bridging social capital and the social connections which help people find and secure jobs might also play a role, as might lack of language skills.

In Table 2.8 we show a range of indicators of structural integration, together with estimates of the size of the ethnic penalties experienced by each group, and self-reported levels of discrimination on grounds of race, language, or religion.

A detailed interpretation of Table 2.8 would require one to take account of the minorities' age and generational profiles. There are also some important gender differences, which vary across the different ethnic groups. However, there are a number of important points that hold true even after taking age, gender, and generation into account. First, we can see that men and women of an Indian background are the most successful, and experience the smallest ethnic penalties. There is a somewhat more varied picture for the other groups, with patterns also varying between men and women. But it is noticeable that all three black groups (those of black Caribbean, black African, and mixed black/white background) report large ethnic penalties and the highest levels of discrimination. These patterns replicate those found in previous research using large government surveys and the census, and we can have considerable confidence that they provide an accurate picture.[40]

There are also some substantial variations within the five main groups. Among men of Indian background, Hindus and the twice-migrants from East Africa

Table 2.8. Structural integration
Cell percentages

Ethnic background	Home owner	Middle class	Routine class or unwaged	Graduate	Un-qualified	Reports discrimination	Ethnic penalty (men)	N
White British	72	52	35	16	30	–	0	2754
Indian	69	56	32	41	18	28	0.5	577
Pakistani	73	33	48	24	28	25	0.6	658
Bangladeshi	40	29	54	18	28	27	1.1	265
Black Caribbean	49	42	41	15	20	44	1.2	583
Black African	20	39	47	33	17	35	1.0	509
Mixed white/black	28	26	64	11	31	41	0.9	93
All minorities	55	43	42	27	22	33	–	2732

Notes: Middle class includes those in professional and managerial, clerical and small employer categories; routine/unwaged includes those in routine occupations plus those dependent on unemployment or other benefits; discrimination includes discrimination on grounds of race, language, or religion; ethnic penalties are with respect to unemployment. They are measured on the logit scale. The Ns are for the item on home ownership. Ns for social class are substantially lower because of missing data.
Sources: BES 2010, EMBES 2010; estimates of the ethnic penalties are taken from Heath and Martin 2012

are rather more successful economically than the Sikhs or Indian Muslims. Among the black African group, the situation of men of Somali or Congolese background is disturbingly disadvantageous. As we noted earlier, many of these will have come as asylum-seekers, and their disadvantageous situation in the labour market may well reflect the government's refusal to allow asylum-seekers to undertake paid work while their applications are being considered, with knock-on consequences for future participation in the labour market.

Generational change

Sociological studies of ethnicity have emphasized the importance of changes across generations. In particular, we anticipate that recent arrivals will tend to be more strongly embedded within their ethnic communities, partly because ethnic community networks can provide important sources of social support and know-how about coping with a new environment, and partly because lack of fluency in English will make it difficult to engage outside the ethnic community. The second generation, who have been born in Britain and educated in British schools and colleges, can be expected to be much less dependent on their ethnic community.

In this study we distinguish between the first, the 'one point five', and the second generation (in which we include the small numbers in the third or later generations). More formally, we define these groups as follows:

- First generation—born abroad and arrived as adults, that is at age sixteen and above.
- One point five generation—born abroad and arrived before adulthood, that is before age sixteen. They will thus have arrived either before or during the period of compulsory schooling in Britain, and will have had some experience of British education.
- Second plus generation—born in Britain (the second generation having parents who were born outside Britain, and the third generation having British-born parents).

Table 2.9 gives some summary statistics, clubbing together the different minorities to save space, although we need to remember that the groups are not evenly distributed across generations. It is also important to recognize that this is cross-sectional rather than longitudinal data. That is to say, some members of our first generation will be relatively recent arrivals, and may indeed be quite young, and so they cannot be treated as the parents of our second generation. To get a better handle on processes of intergenerational change, we have also constructed a 'quasi-parental' generation who broadly correspond to the parents of the second generation.[41]

Table 2.9 highlights once again the dangers of oversimplification and stylized facts. We do indeed see some major generational change, especially with respect to acculturation, where there are huge increases in the use of English at home and substantial decreases in ethnic (rather than British) identity. There is also a big decline in informal bonding social ties, but this contrasts with an absence of any significant change in membership of an ethnic or cultural

Table 2.9. Generational differences in social, cultural, and structural integration
Cell percentages

	1st generation	Quasi-parents	1.5 generation	2nd + generation
English main language at home	44	55	60	**83**
More black/Asian than British	**41**	24	27	19
Friends mainly co-ethnic	53	**57**	51	42
Belongs to ethnic or cultural association	31	40	37	34
Middle class	40	36	38	**50**
No qualifications	31	**46**	19	8
Reports discrimination	26	19	32	**39**
N	1308	332	448	993

Notes: Quasi-parents defined as respondents born abroad who were aged fifty-five or over in 2010 and had been resident in Britain for twenty-five years or more. Ns are for the item on co-ethnic friends. Figures in bold are significantly higher than expectation. Comparing first, 1.5 and second-plus generations chi^2 (English) = 401.6, $p < 0.001$; (ethnic identity) = 75.4, $p < 0.001$; (friends) = 70.1, $p < 0.001$; (ethnic association) = 2.3, $p > 0.05$; (class) = 18.7, $p < 0.001$; (qualifications) = 208.4, $p < 0.001$; (discrimination) = 74.3, $p < 0.001$ (all with 2 degrees of freedom).
Source: EMBES 2010, weighted data

association. Similarly, we see a big increase in educational qualifications but a much more modest (albeit still significant) change in class position. And in the case of discrimination we see, in line with our theory of changing frames of reference which we outlined in Chapter 1, that members of the second generation are the ones most likely to report experiencing discrimination.

We need to be careful in drawing any strong conclusions from these summary statistics, since they do not take account of possible confounding factors, such as the differing ethnic composition of each generation (with black Africans being a large component of the recent arrivals, and the black Caribbeans predominating in the second generation). Our estimates for the 'quasi parents' probably provide the best guide to the actual generational change, since their ethnic profile is very close to that of the second generation.

More detailed studies using a wider range of data sources have also found that rates of generational change vary across different outcomes, and that ethnic penalties in the labour market have been particularly resistant to change.[42] It makes intuitive sense that processes of acculturation might show the most rapid changes, with use of English being a necessity for getting by in British schools or workplaces. Conversely, social support from co-ethnics might continue to be important in the face of a somewhat hostile reception from the majority group.

Emerging themes

There are three central themes that arise from this brief overview. The first theme is that we must beware of stylized facts and oversimplification. There is very considerable diversity between ethnic groups, but there is also diversity within ethnic groups—more so within some groups than others. There are also ongoing processes of change, and these too are diverse, with some changes being more rapid than others. We must be very careful to avoid 'essentializing' ethnic minorities, and assuming that they are somehow fixed, monolithic, and unchanging.

The second theme is that, despite all the diversity, there do appear to be some pan-ethnic patterns, with the black groups being clearly rather different from the South Asian groups on a number of criteria. This is most evident with bridging and bonding social capital, all three black groups having lower bonding scores than any of the South Asian groups. The black groups also all report higher levels of discrimination—and remember that our measure includes religious- and language-based discrimination as well as racial discrimination—and they tend to experience greater ethnic penalties. This may at first sight appear a paradoxical collection of differences, but it may well be that they are in fact intimately related: it may be precisely because the black British have greater contacts with the white British majority and are more likely to use English that they are more aware of the ethnic penalties and discrimination that they suffer. As we shall see in later chapters, this theme resonates throughout the book.

The third key theme is that all our main groups were in economists' jargon 'positively selected'. That is, they were on average more educated than the non-migrants who remained in their countries of origin, and most probably were also more dynamic and more highly motivated. They were also typically voluntary migrants who came to Britain in pursuit of a better life, rather than involuntary migrants or contracted guest-workers who expected to return home in due course. In most cases the pioneer migrants to Britain also had strong prior ties with Britain, as members of former colonies, and often with prior links through service in Britain's armed forces during the Second World War. They would also have had some experience of British institutions, or institutions inherited from British colonial times. To be sure, this was not equally true of all groups, and the most recent arrivals from the Congo do not fit this bill. But many of the earlier migrants from the Caribbean and South Asia would fit this account, and in our sample will be many of their children who have grown up in British institutions.

This leads in turn to the inference that British minorities do not fit the typical pattern of either African-Americans in the USA, on whom a great deal of theorizing has been based, or of so-called guest-workers in Austria, Belgium, and Germany. True, there are large post-colonial minorities in France and the Netherlands who share many of the same characteristics as British minorities, so we should not make a claim for British exceptionalism. But equally we should not expect either US or continental theorizing to apply straightforwardly to the political integration of minorities in Britain, and we should not be surprised if our results challenge established theories and findings imported from other countries.

Notes

1. Lopez and Espiritu (1990) provide an important account of the concept of panethnicity. Muttarak (forthcoming) gives relevant evidence for Britain.
2. Alba (1981, 1985, and 1990) provides authoritative accounts of changes in European identities in the USA.
3. See Cohen (1995) for a detailed account of the notion of fuzziness.
4. According to the one-drop rule, an American with any known black ancestry, even if it is only one grandparent or great grandparent, is counted as black rather than as having mixed heritage. However, this may be changing with recent changes in the US census' classification of racial and ethnic groups. For a detailed account and comparison with other countries see Patterson (2005).

5. For example Cheung and Heath (2007) show that second-generation people of Irish or West European background do not suffer significant ethnic penalties in the British labour market. It is of course too soon to say whether the children of the most recent waves of migrants from Europe will be equally fortunate.
6. For a cogent critique of the official measure see Ballard (1996).
7. See Mateos et al. (2009) on the problems of aggregation in the census classification.
8. A Sikh boy was refused entry to Park Grove School, Birmingham by the headmaster, because his father refused to make him stop wearing a turban and cut his hair. Mandla and his father (who were supported by the Commission for Racial Equality) lost the case, and also lost in the Court of Appeal, where Lord Denning held that Sikhs were not a racial or ethnic group. However, on appeal to the House of Lords, Lord Fraser (employing arguments basically the same as Max Weber's) agreed that Sikhs did count as a racial group for the purpose of the 1976 Race Relations Act.
9. Two classic but differing accounts of selection by economists are those of Borjas (1987) and Chiswick (1999). Feliciano (2005) provides an important empirical investigation of the degree to which migrants to America were actually positively or negatively selected.
10. For discussions of the history of Caribbean migration to Britain see Peach (1968) and Foner (1977).
11. For further details see Peach (1996).
12. ONS (2011) provides detailed estimates for mid-2009, which can be updated in due course from the 2011 census.
13. The major previous surveys are the series conducted on behalf of the PSI—Daniel (1968), Smith (1977), Brown (1984) and Modood et al. (1997). Studlar (1986) also shows the reasons for migration given by blacks and Asians in a 1978 survey, which are quite close to the ones we report from the 2010 survey.
14. Berrington (1996) and Muttarak and Heath (2010) provide detailed accounts of ethnic intermarriage and partnership.
15. ONS (2011) estimates for 2009 suggested that there were 315,000 people from mixed white and black Caribbean backgrounds, but latest estimates from the 2011 census indicate 448,000. There can be little doubt that the proportion is growing rapidly, and some commentators have suggested that the proportion who self-report mixed backgrounds may be considerably lower than the proportion whose parents reported having different backgrounds.
16. Guha (2007) provides a masterly account of Sikh demands for the formation of a separate Sikh state of Khalistan.
17. See Shaw (2000), pp. 22–3.
18. See Ballard (2008).
19. For further details of East African migration to Britain see Bhachu (1985), and on Indian migration generally see Ballard (1994).
20. Shaw (2000) provides the most authoritative recent account of the Pakistani community in Britain and their history.
21. Shaw (2000) describes the *birādarī* as 'the kinship group I belong to', with the sense of kinship widening or narrowing its focus depending on context (Shaw 2000, pp. 140–3).

22. Gardner and Shukur (1994) have given us a detailed account of Sylheti migration, especially the prior history of migration and work in the merchant navy, and the disruption caused by the reallocation of Sylhet from Assam to East Pakistan on the partition of British India.
23. Daley (1996) provides a detailed account of black Africans in Britain, drawing on the 1991 census.
24. Mitton and Aspinall (2010) give us a much fuller account of black African diversity.
25. The classic empirical study of positive selection of migrants is Feliciano (2005). Evidence for Britain shows that all five of the main ethnic groups were positively selected, the least positively selected being the migrants from Bangladesh (next least those from Pakistan). See van de Werfhorst et al. (2012).
26. John Ogbu (1978 and many later publications) has provided a highly influential account of the oppositional culture developed by involuntary migrants in the USA. This has developed a considerable secondary literature.
27. See Gordon (1964).
28. There has been an extensive US literature on this, although it is not clear how far the concept can be transposed from the African-American to the British context. Classic treatments are those of Miller et al. (1981) and Dawson (1994).
29. Cited by Manning and Roy (2010).
30. In our 1997 survey, 6 per cent of Indian respondents, 8 per cent of Pakistani, 6 per cent of black Caribbeans and 22 per cent of black Africans gave the ethnic not British response, while 91 per cent, 80 per cent, 86 per cent, and 68 per cent respectively volunteered dual ethnic and British identities.
31. See Manning and Roy (2010). Also Platt, Maxwell, etc.
32. We use the items on ethnic and British identity, how much in common respondents feel they have with other British people and with co-ethnics, and their concerns about intermarriage to construct the index of ethnic identification.
33. The classic treatment of bridging and bonding social capital is that of Putnam (2000), pp. 22–3 although Putnam gives credit for coining these labels to Ross Gittell and Avis Vidal (1998).
34. On the economic value of bridging ties see Petersen et al. (2000), Lancee (2010). On the role of contact in mitigating prejudice and distrust see Dovidio et al. (2003) and Hewstone (2009).
35. Putnam develops the notion of 'hunkering down' to describe those individuals who, particularly in diverse communities, may limit their social contacts both with in-group and out-group members. See Putnam (2007).
36. Our measures of informal social capital are essentially ones that are simultaneously measures of bonding and of bridging social capital, since they ask respondents to report whether all, most, about half, a few, or none of their friends have the same ethnic background. It is not useful, therefore, to construct separate measures of informal bridging and bonding social capital. We can, however, distinguish between associational bridging and bonding.
37. For a detailed discussion of intermarriage rates and their explanation see Muttarak and Heath (2010).

38. The classic statement of the resource theory is presented in Brady et al. (1995), while Verba et al. (1993) give an application to ethnic minorities.
39. See Heath and McMahon (1997), p. 91 for a detailed definition of the concept of ethnic penalty and empirical measures.
40. See Heath and McMahon (1997), Berthoud (2000), Carmichael and Woods (2000), and Cheung and Heath (2007) for discussions and estimates of ethnic penalties.
41. We construct our measure of quasi-parents by selecting individuals from the first or one point five generations who arrived in Britain more than twenty-five years ago and who were aged fifty-five or over in 2010. These are not the actual parents of the second generation, but they are broadly a sample from the cohort which will have included the actual parents.
42. See the articles in the special issue of *Ethnic and Racial Studies* (forthcoming) on generational change.

3

Political Orientations: Home or Away?

In a number of countries, migrants appear to exhibit political apathy rather than engagement. In a classic study in Germany, Claudia Diehl and Michael Blohm showed that migrants expressed very low levels of interest in German politics, and low levels of political engagement in other respects too.[1] As we argued in Chapter 1, disengagement is important for several reasons: it is likely to mean that the views of the non-participants are not properly represented, and hence our democracy runs the risk of violating the principle of equal protection of interests. And if the disengagement is the result of exclusion, then, as appears possible from the German research, minorities may turn away from the mainstream parties to more militant separatist ones.

One natural explanation for why minorities, especially the first generation who migrated as adults, might choose not to engage with destination-country politics is that they may primarily be oriented to life in the country from which they came. British politics might appear to be rather irrelevant to their main life-concerns. For example, there is evidence that some migrants, at least initially, see themselves as sojourners for whom working abroad is intended only to be a temporary stage of life, with the eventual goal of earning enough money in order to return home and buy land or set up a business.[2] Research from Germany has also suggested that migrants whose primary motive for migration was economic rather than political tend to have lower levels of political engagement with German politics than those who came for broader or more political reasons.[3] To be sure, German migration at least in the early years was dominated by guest-workers, who were expected to be temporary migrants and who were not readily granted citizenship; so this kind of argument might apply more forcibly in Germany than in Britain, where postcolonial migrants might well have had greater commitments to making a new life in Britain, as well as easier access to citizenship.

Moreover, even among migrants who have longer-term intentions to settle, it would not be very surprising if they were initially more familiar with and more interested in the politics of their homeland than in the politics of

Britain. Many will still have families in their country of origin and strong ties with them: remittances back home from migrants to family members are a major source of income to many developing countries. Many migrants regularly return to their home country, watch television channels from their origin country, and read origin-language newspapers and media. Moreover, family and kin remaining behind in the homeland often face rather troubled political circumstances, as in Pakistan today or in India in the 1980s, when agitation for a separate Sikh state of Khalistan was at its height. This might very understandably lead migrants to focus more on the politics of their origin country than on the comparatively peaceful political scene in Britain. This focus on the home country might perhaps be fostered by living in a cohesive ethnic community with high levels of bonding social capital. Previous academic research has suggested that bonding social capital strengthens migrants' interest and engagement in the political affairs of their origin country, and hinders engagement with the politics of their new country of residence.[4] Do separate social lives therefore lead minorities to focus on their origins and to turn away from mainstream British politics?

It would therefore be eminently reasonable for many migrants to opt out of British politics and to take more interest in what is going on in their country of origin. We might, however, expect to see some change over time as migrants become more established in Britain, and even more so across the generations, as their children come to see their long-term future as lying in Britain. (We might also expect there to be some selective return migration, so that individuals with sojourner orientations would be the ones most likely to return home relatively soon after arriving, and thus to disappear from our sample.)

Additionally, there might be barriers to getting involved in British politics, notably linguistic barriers. People who lack fluency in English are inevitably going to be restricted in their access to information about British politics. Lack of citizenship has also been found to be a major barrier in other countries.[5] But our evidence suggests that these barriers weaken the longer people spend in Britain, and even more so across generations. An orientation towards the home country and lack of interest in Britain or British politics might therefore be rather transitory phenomena rather than permanent features of minority life in Britain.

A second set of issues, again highlighted both by politicians and academic commentators, is whether minorities share British democratic norms and values. Our particular focus in this chapter is on the duty to vote, a key principle of British democracy and one that might go some considerable way to overcoming lack of interest. Certainly, among the British electorate as a whole, a feeling of duty to vote is one of the strongest predictors of whether people actually will go to the polling booth and cast their vote.[6] However, we might expect to find differences between migrants from different countries. Some migrants come from well-established democracies such as India, Mauritius, and Jamaica, where democratic norms are as secure as those in Britain, and rates of turnout are similar to British ones.[7] In contrast, migrants from some non-democratic countries may well not have been imbued with democratic norms. For example, migrants from countries such as Somalia or the Congo, which lack democratic traditions, or from countries such as Bangladesh and Pakistan, which have had long periods of military rule, might not have been exposed to or socialized into democratic values or modes of participation.

The primary aim of this chapter, then, is to explore whether there are differences of this sort in minorities' commitment to and interest in British electoral politics, and whether these vary among different national groups or generations. Our starting point is the first generation, who arrived as adults, and the orientations that they brought with them—in a sense the starting point of their political integration in Britain. How interested are they in politics in Britain, or are they more focused on their origin countries? Do we find that migrants who are more embedded in their ethnic communities, and who may lead the kind of separate lives castigated by British politicians, fail to engage with British politics? To what extent is interest in the home country, and lack of interest in British politics, a transitory phenomenon that changes the longer people spend in Britain? Do the children of migrants, educated in British schools, fluent in English, and exposed to the British mass media, converge with British patterns of political engagement?

Interest in origin-country and in British politics

We begin by charting the minorities' interest in British and in origin-country politics, focusing initially on the adult migrants. (We will look at intergenerational change at the end of the chapter.) We asked two general questions about interest in British and in homeland politics:

Let's talk for a few minutes about politics in general. How much interest do you generally have in what is going on in British politics?

And how much interest do you generally have in what is going on in politics in your country of birth?[8]

Political interest tends to be associated strongly with political knowledge, which might in turn be relevant for understanding how individuals engage with the democratic process. Political knowledge is also a fairly objective measure, which gives us some hard evidence with which to back up respondents' own reports. In our questionnaire we included a short quiz designed to measure knowledge about British political arrangements. It consisted of just four items:

> Please tell me if you think that the following statements are true or false. If you don't know, just say so and we will skip to the next one. Remember—true, false, or don't know.
> 1. Polling stations close at 10.00p.m. on election day.
> 2. The minimum voting age is 16.
> 3. The Chancellor of the Exchequer is responsible for setting interest rates in the UK.
> 4. Any registered voter can obtain a postal vote if they want one—by contacting their local council and asking for a postal vote.

All four questions were also included in the main British Election Survey, and so we can make direct comparisons with the knowledge of the white British majority group. Incidentally, in case you were wondering, the first and fourth statements are true, and the second and third are false.

Table 3.1 shows that, for most of our first-generation groups, interest in British politics and in home-country politics is more or less balanced—overall, just over one third of the first generation has a great deal or quite a lot of interest in each type of politics. Interest in British politics is slightly lower than among the white British majority group, although only by four percentage points overall, as is knowledge of British politics.[9] On this criterion the adult migrants to Britain cannot be characterized as disengaged. To put our figures in perspective, Claudia Diehl and Michael Blohm found that in Germany, migrants' level of interest was only half that of the German majority group (with 15 per cent of migrants having 'much' or 'very much' interest in German politics compared with 30 per cent of the majority group).[10] Only the Bangladeshi migrants in Britain approach this low level of interest.

Table 3.1. Interest in home country and British politics among first-generation (adult) migrants
Cell percentages/means

Ethnic background	Interest in home country politics	Interest in British politics	Average score on quiz	N
White British (all generations)	–	41	2.9	2761
Indian	33	41	2.6	317
Pakistani	27	24	2.4	312
Bangladeshi	22	16	2.1	118
Black Caribbean	36	39	2.6	165
Black African	45	50	2.5	358
All adult migrants	35	37	2.5	1270

Notes: 'Don't know' responses are included in the base, but refusals are excluded. For the two political interest items, the percentages are those saying 'a great deal' or 'quite a lot' of interest. Figures significantly higher than expectation are in bold. The mixed group is excluded as there were so few adult migrants from this group. Chi^2 (interest in origin politics) = 38.4 (5 df), p < 0.001; (interest in British politics) = 59.5 (5 df), p < 0.001.
Sources: BES 2010, EMBES 2010, weighted data

The most striking finding from Table 3.1, however, is that interest in home-country politics and in British politics are not either/or phenomena. There are some minor differences in emphasis, with the migrants of Pakistani and Bangladeshi background giving slightly greater prominence to home-country politics than to British politics, while the reverse is true for the other three groups. But the big story is that these two groups are less interested in politics generally than are the other minorities. This is reinforced by the finding that they have lower levels of knowledge about British politics as well. This is clearly not a case where these migrants are interested in the politics of their homeland instead of British politics, but rather a case of lower political interest generally among migrants from Pakistan and Bangladesh. So we cannot blame low interest in British politics on separate lives or strong orientations towards their countries of origin.

More generally, there seems to be a tendency for some groups to be more politically engaged than others, with some of the black African migrants having especially high levels of interest in both origin-country and British political arenas. More detailed analysis confirms that individuals who have a high level of interest in one area of politics also tend to have high interest in the other. In other words, interest in British and in homeland politics are not mutually exclusive.[11]

This finding suggests that some of the natural explanations for lack of interest in British politics that we touched on in the introduction—short-term or narrowly economic reasons for migrating to Britain, ties with the homeland, lack of bridging social capital, or barriers owing to lack of fluency in English—are unlikely to be particularly powerful, since they would not in themselves seem to be plausible explanations for lack of interest in the politics of the origin country. We need to be looking for explanations that can account for lack of interest in politics in both origin and destination countries alike.

One possibility is that lack of engagement with politics may be a legacy of authoritarian rule in the country of origin: an authoritarian regime which discourages participation and gives no opportunities for practising civic skills, and which cracks down on political dissent, might turn people away from democratic politics generally. This has been suggested by a number of authors as an explanation for migrants' lack of commitment to democratic norms, and it might in principle apply to lack of engagement with politics more generally.[12] Since both Pakistan and Bangladesh have had periods of authoritarian military rule (especially at the times when our migrants would have been living there) this is not an implausible explanation. An alternative explanation is that they may reflect differences in individual characteristics rather than differences in the political regimes of the origin countries. In particular, studies of the British population as a whole have found that levels of education are strongly associated with political interest,[13] and as we saw in Chapter 2 some groups such as black African migrants to Britain are much more highly educated than other groups of migrants, whereas migrants from Bangladesh and Pakistan tend to fit more into the model of migrant workers with lower levels of education. Gender could also be an important factor, especially for people coming from more traditional societies where there are strong patriarchal norms, with politics being seen as part of the man's world.

We therefore carried out a number of analyses of the main predictors of interest in homeland and in British politics, exploring a range of individual and country characteristics (for details see Table 3.A1).[14] What we find is that our potential predictors fall into three main groups. First, there is a set of attributes that is associated with increased interest in homeland politics but largely unrelated to interest in British politics; second, there is a set that is associated with increased interest in both arenas. And third, there is a somewhat more ambiguous set which is associated with reduced interest in both arenas. (There are also several attributes that prove not to be significant in either analysis.)

First, the attributes associated with interest in *origin-country* politics but having lesser or no relationship with interest in British politics, are:

- Recent arrival in Britain
- Lack of British citizenship
- Family in origin country
- Ethnic identification
- Coming to Britain to flee persecution

Second, there are several attributes that are associated with *greater* interest in *both* arenas:

- Educational qualifications
- Reads daily newspaper
- Engaging in British practices, such as wearing a poppy on Remembrance Day
- Fluency in the English language
- Coming to Britain in order to study
- Associational bonding social capital, specifically membership of an ethnic or cultural association[15]
- Associational bridging social capital, specifically membership of a voluntary association where co-ethnics are not in the majority[16]
- Exposure to ethnic media

Third, there are a number of attributes associated with *lesser* interest in *both* arenas:

- Gender—women less interested in both political arenas
- Coming to Britain for family reunion
- Main language at home is not English
- High levels of informal bonding social capital[17]
- Living in a neighbourhood with a higher proportion of ethnic minority residents

We need to be cautious in our interpretation of these findings, since the causal direction is not always uncontroversial. For example, does newspaper readership stimulate political interest, or does it work the other way round, with political aficionados being more likely to read newspapers? Given the added risk of false positives, it is probably wise not to focus too closely on individual associations but to attempt to discern the broader patterns.[18]

Fortunately, our results exhibit some straightforward and interpretable patterns which offer clear pointers to the kinds of process that may be operating. First of all, it is clear that there is a coherent grouping of factors—ethnic identification, transnational links with the home country, non-British citizenship, and political persecution—linked with a focus on the politics of the origin country. What is interesting about this group of attributes is that they tend to be transitory or impermanent ones: ethnic identification tends to be strongest among recent arrivals, and then declines the longer migrants have spent in Britain. Visits to the home country also tend to decline over time, while migrants are more likely to acquire British citizenship the longer they remain in Britain. So, overall, we have good grounds for supposing that a primary focus on origin-country politics is most common among recent arrivals and declines the longer that people remain in Britain. This process of disengagement with the origin country and integration into the new country is unsurprising, and has been reported from other research too.[19]

The majority of our predictors, however, are not so much transitory as stable attributes of the individuals concerned. Thus we find a number of education-related influences that serve to promote interest in both origin and destination-country politics alike. The role of education in increasing political interest is a standard finding in research on Western countries, and it is hardly surprising that it is associated with greater interest in both origin and destination countries among migrants too. Nor is it surprising that migrants who came to Britain in order to study share this interest in politics. Fluency in English is more intriguing, since this serves to increase interest in origin-country as well as in British politics. Lack of fluency in the English language per se probably should not be regarded as a barrier to political engagement, therefore, since it would not be a barrier to following home-country politics. Rather, we suspect that our measure of fluency in English taps the cognitive skills that political scientists argue are associated with political engagement.

More surprising is the role of associational bonding capital and attention to ethnic media (such as ethnic newspapers or television channels). Membership of ethnic or cultural associations goes with increased political interest generally, and does not, as one might naively have supposed, lead members to engage with their homeland and to turn their backs on British political life. This finding has also been shown by previous research: Laura Morales and Katia Pilati report that involvement in ethnic associations works in exactly the same way in several European cities.[20] We must confess that we cannot be sure about the precise causal mechanisms involved. One possibility (following the standard political science literature on the 'civic voluntarism model' developed by Sydney Verba and his colleagues) is that associational membership fosters the cognitive skills associated with political engagement.[21] But it might not be a causal effect at all: maybe political interest leads people to join organizations rather than the other way round. Still, even if this were the case, it would seem that ethnic associations cannot to any great extent be channelling such interests away from Britain and back towards the home country. At the very least, we can conclude that ethnic associations are not playing any harmful role with regard to engagement with British politics.

Finally, there are a number of gender-related influences. Women show lower levels of political interest in both origin and destination politics than do men, and people who have migrated for family reunion also evince less political interest. White British women also report less interest in politics than men do, so this finding is not specific to women coming from traditional backgrounds. However, we see that this set of measures also includes speaking a language other than English at home, having high levels of informal bonding capital, and living in an ethnically dense area. The precise mechanisms involved are far from clear, but the key point is that they reduce interest in both origin and destination politics alike: they do not lead to a focus on the home country at the expense of integration into Britain.

These results provide, therefore, some support for a thin version of the separate lives thesis. While separate social lives do not lead to an emphasis on homeland politics at the expense of British politics, they nevertheless seem to be associated with lack of political engagement. Our interpretation is that informal ethnic social relations, among our migrants at least, tend to be relatively apolitical. To be interested in politics is the exception, not the rule, and they are not the main topic of conversation between friends and neighbours, even in the majority population. Informal relationships, therefore, and cohesive ethnic communities may have other more important things to focus on, such as coping with the day-to-day strains of adapting to a new society, rather than engaging in political debate.[22] Furthermore, this could well explain why it is that migrant communities from Bangladesh and Pakistan have the lowest levels of political interest: these are the two communities (as we saw in Chapter 2, Table 2.7) which have the highest levels of informal bonding social capital and the lowest levels of associational capital.

Commitment to the duty to vote

Politicians have frequently raised doubts about whether minorities share British values, and while we did not have the space in our questionnaire to cover the full range of British values we did ask about one of the fundamental principles of democracy, the duty to turn out and vote.[23] Voting is, of course, one of the cornerstones of a democracy, and indeed in many democracies, although not Britain, the duty to vote is enshrined in law, and voting in general elections is compulsory. Rules for compulsory voting make sense, since the institutions of representative democracy are usually thought to provide little in the way of rational incentive for anyone to vote unless they are compelled to: one's own vote is extremely unlikely to make any difference to the outcome in one's constituency (and one's constituency result is extremely unlikely to make any difference to the overall outcome), so the rational selfish voter, standard theory holds, will not bother to go to the polling booth. Rational individualists will prefer to be 'free-riders'. In practice, a majority of eligible citizens do turn out and vote, at least in general elections, and, alongside political interest, a feeling of duty to vote is one of the strongest predictors of whether people actually will go to the polling booth.[24] In short, moral and psychological incentives are needed to overcome the absence of any material incentives to participate in a general election. (There is a more general discussion of the free-rider problem in Chapter 7, where we discuss actual rates of turnout.)

In our survey, respondents were asked whether they agreed that

It is every citizen's duty to vote in an election

Respondents were also asked a number of other questions about voting which enable us to cross-check the responses to the 'duty to vote' question. One question in particular is relevant here in any discussion of norms. We asked whether the respondent agreed that

Most of my family and friends think that voting is a waste of time

Disagreement with this statement can give us some indication of whether there is a norm of voting among the respondent's social network. (Basically, a community of free-riders will agree with the statement that voting is a waste of

Table 3.2. Duty to vote among first-generation (adult) migrants
Cell percentages

Ethnic background	Agree every citizen's duty to vote	Disagree family and friends think voting a waste of time	N
White British (all generations)	78	70	2761
Indian	96	80	311
Pakistani	92	74	313
Bangladeshi	93	80	108
Black Caribbean	84	72	183
Black African	89	73	375
All minorities	91	75	1290

Notes: 'Don't know' responses included in the base, but refusals are excluded. Figures in bold are significantly higher at the 5% level than expectation. Chi^2 (duty) = 118.1 (5 df), $p < 0.001$; (waste of time) = 26.9 (5 df), $p < 0.001$.
Sources: BES 2010, EMBES 2010, weighted data

time.) Table 3.2 shows how our first-generation migrants who had arrived as adults (that is, at age sixteen or above) answered these two questions.

Overall, we see rather high levels of commitment to this fundamental aspect of British democracy on the part of our migrants. Indeed, the levels of commitment shown by the migrants are distinctly higher than those among the majority group of white British, with 91 per cent of first-generation minorities strongly agreeing with the duty to vote (48 per cent strongly agreeing) compared with 78 per cent of white British (only 39 per cent strongly agreeing). The same holds true for the second question on perceptions of free-riding among friends and family. So whereas levels of political interest were slightly lower on average among migrants, this is more than counterbalanced by greater normative commitments.

There is a second contrast with Table 3.1 on political interest. In Table 3.2 we see no sign of lower commitment among the migrants from Pakistan or Bangladesh. Indeed, if anything the normative commitment is slightly lower among the two groups of black migrants from the Caribbean and Africa (though they are still higher than among the majority group). These differences between the results for political interest and political duty suggest that the predictors may be rather different too. We therefore carried out the same analyses as we had done for political interest in order to check which attributes are associated with the duty to vote (see Table 3.A2).

The results are quite striking. Very few of our predictors proved to have statistically strong and significant relationships with the duty to vote, but they are ones of considerable theoretical relevance. They are:

- Educational qualifications
- Church attendance
- Associational bonding social capital
- Participation in British practices
- Coming from a more democratic origin country[25]

The roles of education and church attendance are not especially surprising, as there is a considerable literature showing an association between education, church-going, and civic attitudes generally. But it is also striking that, just as with political interest, ethnic organizations seem to promote a sense of civic duty, or at the very least do not inhibit it. They are not the villains that critics of multiculturalism seem to suggest.

It is also intriguing that democratic origins appear to promote the duty to vote, whereas there was no sign that they promoted political interest (indeed, if anything the reverse). The most likely interpretation is that migrants from democratic origins have already been exposed, perhaps through their schooling in democratic countries of origin such as India and Jamaica, to democratic norms.

It follows from this that many other predictors are non-significant. Most notably, there was no sign that any of the following played a substantial role:

- Ethnic identification
- Transnational links
- Informal bonding social capital
- Recent arrival in Britain
- British citizenship
- Reasons for coming to Britain
- Fluency in the English language
- Exposure to ethnic media
- Percentage non-white in the neighbourhood

There is absolutely no sign, therefore, that recent arrival, or the other transitory phenomena that were linked to interest in origin-country politics, or the separate lives within an enclave that politicians like to criticize, deflect from commitment to one's democratic duty to vote.

Our failure to find many significant predictors in turn implies another important conclusion: in essence, there is a broad consensus among migrants of all sorts and backgrounds on the civic obligation to vote. This sense of obligation does not vary according to how recently people arrived in Britain or to other transitory phenomena, such as lack of English. Nor is it significantly structured by enduring attributes such as gender. In this respect, our findings are very different from the ones we find among the white British, where both educational level and age are important predictors of a sense of civic obligation.[26]

One further important query is in order. Can we be sure that we can trust our respondents' self-reports? Maybe they are exaggerating their feelings of duty to vote, perhaps as a result of what survey methodologists term 'social desirability bias'. We will get a chance to look at this in Chapter 7, when we are able to compare what our respondents had to say about voting with what they actually did (based on our checks of the actual marked-up electoral registers). The punchline is that the evidence supports the conclusion that minorities, like the white British, do indeed succumb to social desirability bias, and some minorities appear to succumb in somewhat greater proportions. However, the evidence that social desirability bias is at work could also be quite informative in its own right. People will only succumb to social desirability bias if they are indeed aware of the norm, and hence are anxious to avoid giving the interviewer the impression that they (the respondents) fail to adhere to the norm. At the very least, then, social desirability bias strongly suggests that people are aware of the norms that they feel they should be following.

Why do we find this higher level of civic duty among migrants than among white British, and without the striking educational and age differences found among the majority group in Britain? There are several possible answers: apart from social desirability bias, it could well be that enthusiasm for democracy is greater among migrants than it is among established British citizens because the latter take democracy for granted and have perhaps become rather cynical. While there is no doubt a great deal wrong with British democracy, as the Parliamentary expenses scandal amply demonstrated, there is not (yet) the widespread corruption that prevails in even the most democratic of the origin countries.[27] It is also likely, as we argued in Chapter 2, that migrants who come to Britain are a relatively selective group of people who have come to Britain out of choice. They are likely to be both dynamic and positive in their orientations. (While many of our adult migrants have been here quite some time, of course, we find no relationship whatsoever between time spent in Britain and feelings of duty to vote, unlike the situation with political interest. Hence it is reasonable to suppose that the patterns described above apply to the migrants at the time of their arrival in Britain.)

Generational differences

So far we have been focusing exclusively on the first generation who migrated as adults. Several of the arguments we have considered might be expected to apply most powerfully to the first generation and to have weaker impact as we move to the one point five and second generations. Our central expectation is that, across generations, there will be a gradual convergence with the white British as the legacies of home-country experiences and socialization weaken, ties with the homeland weaken, and exposure to British institutions and experiences increase.

More specifically, we might expect a sense of duty to vote to weaken across generations, especially among the young, as they mix with their young British compatriots and come to share their cynicism. We also expect interest in homeland politics to decline as later generations acquire British citizenship and adopt a British (or dual) identity. Conversely, interest in and knowledge of British politics may be expected to increase. However, this may move at different rates for different groups. Even though our evidence so far suggests that informal ethnic social capital has no effect on commitment to democratic norms, it is still possible that rates of generational change will be slower in more cohesive communities with higher levels of bonding social capital. Do low levels of political interest persist among the communities of Bangladeshi or Pakistani background, for example?

We begin by looking at changing patterns across generations for all minorities combined, using the distinction between first, one point five and second generations described in Chapter 2. This provides us with the headline results, which are shown in Table 3.3. We also look at the patterns among a sample of 'quasi-parents' (as we did in Chapter 2), so that we can explore change between parental and filial generations. And, given the youthful profile of our second generation minorities, we also make some comparisons with younger members of the majority group.

The most striking results in Table 3.3 are the *declining* levels of interest in homeland politics and in duty to vote, where the first-generation figures were higher than the white British ones. This contrasts with the *increasing* level of political knowledge, where the first-generation figures had been lower than

Table 3.3. Generational differences in political orientations and knowledge
Cell percentages

	Ethnic minorities				White British	
	1st generation	Quasi-parents	1.5 generation	2nd + generation	All	Age 18–45
Agree every citizen's duty to vote	**92**	**90**	**88**	**81**	78	66
Disagree family/friends think voting waste of time	**78**	**75**	**70**	68	70	67
Interested in homeland politics	**35**	**24**	**19**	10	–	–
Interested in British politics	38	36	41	37	41	33
Knowledge of British politics (mean scores)	2.5	2.5	**2.7**	**2.7**	2.9	3.0
N	*1313*	*332*	*449*	*997*	*2761*	*1021*

Notes: The percentages are for 'agree' or 'strongly agree' about duty to vote, 'disagree' or 'disagree strongly' for norms of voting, 'a great deal' or 'quite a lot' of interest in homeland and British politics. Quasi-parents defined as respondents born abroad who were aged fifty-five or over in 2010 and had been resident in Britain for twenty-five years or more. For columns 1 to 3, figures in bold are significantly higher than the overall ethnic minority expectation. Chi^2 (duty) = 67.4, p < 0.001; (family/friends) = 48.2, p < 0.001; (interest in homeland) = 146.3, p < 0.001; (interest in British politics) = 5.9, p > 0.05 (all with 2 df).
Sources: BES 2010, EMBES 2010, weighted data

among the white British. In short, we find a clear pattern of convergence. Interest in British politics, on the other hand, shows no significant change, but in this case the first-generation figures were not all that different from white British ones to start with.[28]

As always, we need to be somewhat cautious in our interpretation of the trends shown in Table 3.3, because the second generation tend to be considerably younger than the white British comparison group (the average age of the second generation being thirty-two years and that of the white British being fifty-one). Since age is strongly associated with feelings of duty to vote, and interest and knowledge of British politics among the white British, it is important to take this into account when making comparisons. We have therefore added a further column to Table 3.3 showing the white British levels for people of roughly comparable ages to the second generation, namely those aged eighteen to forty-five. As we can see, feelings of duty to vote are substantially lower among younger white British than among older British people. When we compare the second-generation minorities with their white British age-peers, we see that on balance the second generation are more committed to the duty to vote, and at least as politically interested and almost as knowledgeable. This provides a highly positive picture, with no indication of apathy, disengagement, or withdrawal on the part of second-generation minorities.

A second major issue is whether these rates of convergence with British mores have proceeded at the same rates for all minority groups alike. One possibility is that some groups, especially the minorities of Pakistani and Bangladeshi background where there are stronger ethnic communities, will have shown a lesser tendency to converge towards the majority profile, perhaps retaining a focus on homeland politics across generations. We do find, in fact, some mixed evidence that people of Pakistani background are more likely to retain an interest in homeland politics across generations, although this is not replicated among people of Bangladeshi background. Nor do we find any significant differences in rates of generational change in their interest in British politics, and so on. In general, the story is that rates of generational change are much the same for most groups and for most outcomes.[29]

Positive beginnings followed by convergence

The headline story, then, is that minorities show positive orientations towards British political life. The first generation (the adult migrants) express higher levels of agreement with the duty to vote than do white British citizens, although they have somewhat lower interest in British politics and lesser political knowledge. Overall, there is very little sign of the levels of apathy and disengagement that have been found among migrants in some other countries. And while the adult migrants show quite high levels of interest in the politics of their home country, this is temporary, and declines both across generations and the longer people remain in Britain.

A second headline is that across generations there is clear evidence of convergence with British norms. The sense of civic duty declines from its initially high level to one closer, but still above, the white British average, while political knowledge and interest increase towards, but do not quite reach, white British levels.

Nor do we see much sign that ethnic bonding and so-called separate lives have negative effects. Indeed, one of the most striking results is that members of ethnic or cultural organizations actually have a greater interest in British politics, and a greater feeling of an obligation to vote, than do non-members. While we cannot be sure of the causal processes, at the very least we can be confident that ethnic organizations are not deflecting people away from British politics or norms of participation. Our results also call into question some of the claims made by politicians about the need for minorities to learn and adopt British values. At least with respect to the democratic norm of turning out to vote, it would appear that the reverse might be the case, and that British politicians should not be complacent about the extent of commitment to British values on the part of younger white people. Our results also call into question the concerns that have been raised about the difficulty of incorporating Muslim groups into British political life.

Appendix: Supplementary tables

Table 3.A1. Significant associations with interest, knowledge, and duty: first generation (adult migrants)
Correlation coefficients

	Interest in homeland politics	Interest in British politics	Knowledge of British politics	Duty to vote
Years in Britain	−0.25	–	0.14	–
British citizen	−0.21	–	0.10	–
Family in origin country	0.19	–	–	–
Ethnic identification	0.14	−0.09	–	–
Reason for migration—fleeing persecution	0.07	–	–	–
Reads daily newspaper	0.25	0.29	–	–
Educational level	0.23	0.24	0.13	0.06
Associational bonding	0.22	0.17	0.12	0.12
Fluency in English	0.16	0.25	0.16	–
British practices	0.14	0.24	0.16	0.06

Political Orientations: Home or Away?

Reason for migration—to study	0.20	0.12	–	–
Associational bridging	0.10	**0.17**	–	–
Ethnic media	**0.11**	0.10	–	–
Female	**−0.15**	**−0.14**	**−0.14**	–
Reason for migration—family reunion	−0.17	−0.18	–	–
Other language at home	−0.06	−0.17	−0.11	–
Informal bonding social capital	−0.07	−0.11	−0.05	–
Non-white percentage in area	−0.07	**−0.08**	−0.10	–
Democracy in origin country	–	−0.07	–	0.06
Attends church regularly	–	–	–	**0.09**

Notes: Figures in bold indicate a coefficient that remains significant in a full ordered logit model. Correlations not shown when non-significant in a bivariate analysis.
Source: EMBES 2010, weighted data. N (minimum) = 1131

Table 3.A2. Test of differences between generations: OLS regressions Coefficients

	Interest in homeland politics	Interest in British politics	Knowledge of British politics	Duty to vote
Constant	3.74	2.13	0.69	3.21
Ethnic group				
Indian (reference)	0	0	0	0
Pakistani	−0.07	**−0.15**	−0.08	0.06
Bangladeshi	**−0.34**	**−0.22**	−0.14	0.04
Black Caribbean	**0.25**	0.04	0.03	**−0.27**
Black African	**0.41**	**0.31**	−0.08	**−0.15**
Interactions with generation				
Generation	**−0.84**	0.11	**0.24**	**−0.22**
Generation*Pakistani	0.24	0.17	0.12	0.01
Generation*Bangladeshi	0.34	−0.02	0.13	0.05
Generation*Black Caribbean	0.24	0.11	0.01	0.17
Generation*Black African	**0.32**	−0.15	−0.04	0.16
Controls				
Age (ln)	**−0.24**	**0.27**	**0.48**	**0.27**
Female	**−0.24**	**−0.22**	**−0.17**	**0.07**
Highest qualification	**0.12**	**0.15**	**0.14**	**0.03**
London resident	**0.29**	**0.09**	**0.15**	−0.06
% non-white	**−0.20**	**−0.25**	**−0.23**	**−0.11**
R^2	0.11	0.08	0.08	0.03
N	2605	2605	2605	2603

Notes: Figures in bold are significant at the 0.05 level. Generation is a contrast between the first generation (coded 0) and the one point five/second + generations combined (coded 1).
Source: EMBES 2010, unweighted data

Table 3.A3. Test of differences between parental and filial generations: OLS regressions Coefficients

	Interest in homeland politics	Interest in British politics	Knowledge of British politics	Duty to vote
Constant	2.46	2.70	1.14	2.77
Ethnic group				
Indian (reference)	0	0	0	0
Pakistani	−0.16	−0.10	0.09	−0.01
Bangladeshi	0.09	0.19	0.03	0.12
Black Caribbean	0.17	0.01	0.08	−0.12
Black African	−0.01	−0.03	−0.20	−0.21
Interactions with generation				
Generation	−0.57	−0.08	0.04	−0.16
Generation*Pakistani	0.52	0.12	−0.03	0.07
Generation*Bangladeshi	−0.24	−0.35	0.23	−0.10
Generation*Black Caribbean	0.24	0.14	−0.03	0.04
Generation*Black African	0.77	0.21	0.22	0.22
Controls				
Age (ln)	−0.01	0.13	0.35	0.33
Female	−0.17	−0.18	−0.13	0.17
Highest qualification	0.12	0.18	0.20	0.06
London resident	0.37	0.08	0.03	−0.03
% non-white	−0.26	−0.36	−0.33	−0.22
R^2	0.08	0.06	0.08	0.04
N	1231	1231	1213	1229

Notes: Generation is a contrast between the quasi-parental generation (coded 0) and the 2nd + generation (coded 1).
Source: EMBES 2010, unweighted data

Notes

1. See Diehl and Blohm (2001), Table 2.
2. See, for example, Anwar (1979) on the 'myth of return'.
3. See Doerschler (2006), Tables 2 and 3. We replicated Doerschler's questions in the EMBES questionnaire.
4. See Morales and Pilati (2011), p. 106.
5. See, for example, Bloemraad (2006) who compares Canada and the USA.
6. See Clarke et al., (2004), p. 251.
7. In Britain, the turnout in 2010 for the voting age population was 65.1 per cent compared with 72.6 per cent in Mauritius in 2010, 56.5 per cent in India in 2009, and 49.6 per cent in Jamaica in 2007 (although Jamaica had had much higher turnout rates in the 1970s and before). Source: International IDEA. Mauritius and Jamaica also score 10.0 on the Polity IV score of democracy, the same as the United Kingdom, while India scores 9.0.

8. Response codes for both questions were 'a great deal', 'quite a lot', 'some', 'not very much', 'none at all'. Respondents who were born in Britain were asked about their interest in their mother's and father's country of birth (as appropriate).
9. Studlar (1986) also commented briefly on Asians' relative lack of political knowledge with a high level of 'don't know' responses.
10. See Diehl and Blohm (2001), Table 2.
11. The correlation between interest in British and interest in origin-country politics was 0.33. That between knowledge of British politics and interest in British politics was 0.27, while that between knowledge of British politics and interest in homeland politics was not surprisingly much lower at 0.09. But all three correlation coefficients were statistically significant at the 0.01 level.
12. Rice and Feldman (1997) have suggested that the civic culture of European-origin minorities in the USA is very similar to the civic culture of citizens currently living in those European countries. Similarly, in the case of Australia, Bilodeau, McAllister, and Kanji (2010) found that immigrants who had experienced authoritarianism in their country of origin, although quite supportive of democracy, were more likely than other immigrants and the Australian-born population to support forms of political systems that were non-democratic. Other scholars have reported a relationship between democracy in the country of origin and participation in the country of destination, although findings are somewhat mixed. See Bueker (2005), Maxwell (2010a), André et al. (2009), and Aleksynska (2011).
13. See Clarke et al. (2009), Table 8.4.
14. There are a number of tricky methodological issues here. When one is testing for a great number of potential drivers there is a real risk of discovering 'false positives' (as they are called in medicine), that is cases where the associations are statistically significant but should be disregarded (since by chance alone we expect to find one in twenty relationships to be significant. There is also the issue, when testing simultaneously for a number of drivers, that some may work indirectly via other ones; for example education may influence language fluency and so in turn affect political interest, but education may appear to be insignificant when it is included in a comprehensive model along with language. We therefore report both the simple correlations and the associations that remain statistically significant when all variables are simultaneously included in a multivariate model. One further issue is whether these processes work differently among different ethnic minorities. In particular we might wonder whether patterns among South Asian groups, or among Muslims, differ from those among blacks. We therefore checked the correlations separately for each of our five main groups. While there was some variation, which is hardly surprising given sampling error, the major patterns on which we focus in the text were all replicated in each of the five groups.
15. This is measured with the item on membership of an ethnic or cultural organization (eq42).
16. This measure is derived from the items on membership of other voluntary organizations (eq43) combined with measures of the ethnic composition of those organizations (eq45).

17. This is measured with the item on the ethnic composition of one's friends (eq46_1).
18. See footnote 14 above.
19. Canadian research has suggested that, the longer people have stayed in the new country, the more they adapt to destination-country politics (White et al. 2008). This research suggested that political orientations learned in the country of origin were not resistant to change, and that resocialization into Canadian political norms was the most common model. DiSipio (2001) has found similar results in the USA.
20. See Morales and Pilati (2011), Table 5.4.
21. Verba et al. (1995) provide a much-cited discussion of the civic voluntarism model.
22. Our results on informal bonding social capital are diametrically opposed to those of Morales and Pilati (2011, Table 5.4). There are two potential reasons for the difference. First, while their research was carried out in London as well as in other European cities, the London sample is only a small proportion of their total and it is quite possible that their results are being driven by those from other countries. Secondly, and perhaps more importantly, their measures of interest appear to be relative ones. In particular their model 3 compares people who are only interested in home-country politics with those who are only interested in residence-country politics. So their findings are not necessarily inconsistent with our findings on absolute levels of interest. It is also striking that the variance explained in Morales and Pilati's model 3 (which has the best pseudo R^2 of their three models at 0.081) is a great deal lower than ours.
23. Heath, Rothon, and Ali (2010) present a more general discussion of minorities' acceptance of British values, using alternative data sources, and found minorities to be generally supportive of these values.
24. See Clarke et al. (2004), p. 251.
25. We have scored origin countries according to the Polity IV classification (Marshall and Jaggers 2011). This classification assigns annual scores (since 1946) ranging from −10 (fully institutionalized autocracy) to +10 (fully institutionalized democracy). Scores from −5 to +5 are regarded as 'anocracies' (with democracies scoring 6 and above and autocracies −6 and below). Many of the countries from which the migrants came in fact have had rather fluctuating democratic histories, with periods of democracy interspersed with military coups and periods of autocratic government. And, of course, the migrants themselves are of different ages and had varying periods in the countries of origin before emigrating to Britain. We have therefore classified origin countries according to their average scores for the decade preceding the mean date for the arrival in Britain of the migrants from the relevant country. Polity IV scores were not available for Barbados and Grenada, and for these countries we have used other sources.
26. For example, among the white British we find (as have other researchers) that age and education are both strongly related to feelings of a duty to vote (see Table 3.A2). Higher levels of education are often found to be related to a stronger sense of civic duty, probably owing to socialization processes, while our interpretation of the association with age is that it reflects a generational process. See Clarke et al. (2004) and Clarke et al. (2009) for more detailed investigations of this. That is to say, older generations socialized in earlier periods at a time when turnout itself was much

higher than it is today would have learned a stronger sense of duty to turn out and vote. Strikingly, however, we find no sign of age differences in the commitment to civic duty among our first-generation migrants.
27. On Transparency International's index of perceptions of public sector corruption, the UK scores much more highly at 7.8 (which is itself well below the scores of the Nordic countries) compared with the scores of 5.1 for Mauritius, 3.3 for Jamaica and 3.1 for India.
28. Among the British population as a whole there appears to be a long-term decline in the duty to vote, especially among young people. Hence it would be wrong to think that there is a stable British pattern to which minorities are converging. See Butt and Curtice (2008) and Curtice (2012).
29. Specifically we tested for interactions between generation and ethnic group on the four outcomes of interest in home country politics, British politics, political knowledge and duty to vote. Table 3.A2 shows the results when we contrast the first generation with the one point five and second + generations combined, and Table 3.A3 shows the results when we compare the quasi-parental generation with the second + generation. We do not control for mediating variables in these analyses but for the main potential-confounding variables, namely age, gender, educational level, region (contrasting London with the rest of the UK), and non-white density in the neighbourhood (in order to take account of differential sampling fractions). There are some differences of detail between the two sets of analyses, with the sample size being considerably lower in the analyses involving the quasi-parental generation and hence fewer statistically significant coefficients.

4
The Ethnic Minority Agenda(s)

One of our central questions is whether minority interests are excluded from the political market place. But in order to answer this we have to begin with the prior question whether minorities actually do express different interests and concerns from those of the majority group. After all, if minorities share the same political concerns, and want the same kinds of policies, as other British citizens, then the question of exclusion from the political marketplace will not arise. Indeed, our expectation is that many concerns, for example, about the recession, and the need to reduce unemployment and control inflation, will be shared right across British society. On such issues there is a broad consensus on goals, and voters' major concerns are to judge the capabilities and competence of rival parties to resolve these key problems of the day. To paraphrase Harold Clarke and his colleagues, 'the key question is not *what* should be the objective, but *how* to achieve it, and *who* is best able to do so'.[1] We assume that minorities will be part of this broad consensus.

There are also more ideological issues associated with the main social cleavages in British society, such as those based on social class, where voters typically hold contrasting rather than consensual views. On these issues the question is *what* should be the objective as well as *how* to achieve it. Previous research has shown that in contemporary British politics voters distinguish at least two cross-cutting ideological dimensions: one that reflects economic 'left-right' preferences about the extent to which the state should intervene in the economy (and society), rather than leaving matters to the free play of market forces; and a second that measures preferences for liberal rather than authoritarian approaches to dealing with criminals, censorship, civil liberties, and the like.[2] Where do minorities stand on these two ideological dimensions? Do they adopt similar views to their white British peers in similar socio-economic positions? Or is there a distinctive ethnic angle on these mainstream issues, with minorities being relatively united around left-wing or liberal policies, as they are in the USA?

The Ethnic Minority Agenda(s)

In addition to these two enduring ideological divisions within the British public, two other issues have been highly salient in recent general elections—the wars in Iraq and Afghanistan (which were particularly prominent in 2005), and the issue of immigration (prominent in 2010). Some minorities might well have distinct views on these issues; for example, Muslims might well be particularly opposed to the Iraq war (and there is evidence that they were in 2005).[3] This was a matter of concern across all social groups during the course of the 2005–10 Parliament, but it was especially so for Muslim voters, many of whom felt that the war meant UK troops were involved (wilfully or accidentally) in the deaths of Muslim civilians in a Muslim country. Non-Muslim minorities, however, might well be more akin to the majority group in their views.

Minorities might also be more supportive of immigration into Britain than is the majority group, although we would not expect the differences to be all that great. Given their high unemployment rates, minorities might not be particularly keen on high levels of immigration from, say, Eastern Europe increasing the competition for the limited number of jobs available in Britain. On the other hand, minorities such as those of Pakistani or Bangladeshi background, for whom family reunion continues to be an important channel of immigration (as we saw in Chapter 2), might be supportive of immigration, while recent arrivals from Somalia and other war-torn countries of Africa might be supportive of asylum-seekers. On Afghanistan and immigration, therefore, minorities might have rather different views on average from the majority, although we could hardly say that these issues are excluded from the mainstream agenda. Indeed, they are hotly debated; and as we shall see, minorities are not without white British allies on these issues.

In addition to these mainstream ideological divisions, there are potentially some specific ethnic issues which might unite minorities and divide them from the majority group. This is where questions of political exclusion are most likely to arise. Previous scholars have distinguished two main types of ethnic issues—those concerning equality of opportunity and treatment, which might be shared by all minorities insofar as all minorities experience prejudice and discrimination, and those concerning the preservation of cultural practices, on which particular minorities might have distinctive views that set them apart both from other minorities and from the majority. Paul Statham, for example, has investigated the claims put forward by organizations representing minorities in Britain.[4] He shows that black groups have tended to mobilize along racial lines, and have targeted state bodies 'with claims which appeal to the principle of redress for racial discrimination' (Statham 1999, p. 24). In contrast, South Asian minorities have mobilized politically along lines of religion, national, and ethnic origin for cultural rights. Examples here would be the Sikh campaigns for the right to wear turbans,[5] or Muslim groups' campaigns following the Salman Rushdie affair, pressing for the extension of the blasphemy laws to cover Islam as well as Christianity.[6] A key question for us is whether there is in fact a single pan-ethnic agenda on any of these issues, or whether, alternatively, there is a multiplicity of distinct ethnic agendas.

Most important issue facing the country

We begin by looking at the answers to the long-running question of what people think the most important problems facing Britain are. Here we expect to find a broad consensus on the part of both minorities and the majority. Past research by Donley Studlar, for example, found that the issues identified by minorities as being of the greatest importance were those also considered to be most important by the general population, and that any distinctive interests of minorities often had a relatively low priority among those groups themselves, as well as being of negligible importance to the general population. He argued that race-specific issues did not dominate the political priorities of non-whites, and concluded that 'There is no such thing as a distinctive nonwhite political agenda' (Studlar 1986, p.176).[7]

We asked a similar question in our 2010 surveys to the one drawn on by Donley Studlar thirty years ago. We asked respondents in both the main BES and in the Ethnic Minority BES:

> *Now, I'd like to ask you a few questions about the issues and problems facing Britain today. As far as you're concerned, what is the single most important issue facing the country at the present time?*

This was an open-ended question, which means that respondents named the issue or problem that they thought was important without being prompted by the interviewer. Answers were then coded by the interviewer into a set of pre-codes. Unfortunately there was one important difference in the BES and EMBES pre-codes: the financial crisis appeared in the BES list of pre-codes but not in the EMBES list. This means that some of the differences between the two surveys might be attributable to coding practices. In Table 4.1, therefore, we show the distribution of responses given by minority respondents to the main BES, as well as those from the EMBES data. We do not attempt to distinguish individual minorities at this stage, given their small numbers in the BES.

As we can see from the BES data, there are a considerable number of significant differences between the majority group and the minorities in what they take to be the most important issue facing the country. The biggest difference concerns unemployment, to which minorities attach much more

Table 4.1. Most important issue facing Britain today
Column percentages

	White British	Minorities (BES)	Minorities (EMBES)
State of the economy	39	31	23
Financial crisis	23	17	2
Immigration	11	5	8
Unemployment	6	20	25
War in Iraq/Aghanistan/on terror	4	1	8
Law and order	2	4	6
NHS	2	1	3
Taxes	1	3	2
Inflation/prices	1	1	4
Education	1	1	5
My standard of living	1	0	2
Other	8	11	8
None	0	2	1
Don't know	2	3	4
N	2643	277	2784

Notes: Figures in bold indicate statistically significant (at the 5% level) differences between the white British and minority respondents in the BES data. Chi^2 (for the minority/majority comparison in the BES) = 48.1 (13 df), p<0.001.
Sources: BES 2010, EMBES 2010, weighted

importance. Correspondingly, minorities attach less importance to the more abstract issues of the state of the economy and to the financial crisis. The other notable difference is that minorities attached somewhat less importance to immigration. There was also a slight difference in the proportions saying that no issues were important or that they did not know what was important (which may reflect the lower political knowledge that we reported in Chapter 3).[8] The EMBES data shows similar patterns, although rather larger differences from the white British figures (possibly because of the coding differences mentioned above). In more detailed analysis we found that there were very few significant differences between the five main minority groups in their priorities, although not unexpectedly people of Pakistani and Bangladeshi background attached greater importance to the wars in Iraq and Afghanistan than did other groups. We return to the war in Afghanistan later in this chapter.

These patterns are not, in fact, all that different from those found by Donley Studlar over twenty-five years ago. For example, in his analysis of 1983 Gallup data, he found that minorities rated unemployment as a more important problem than did the majority group. He attributed this difference in priorities to minorities' greater risks of being unemployed, which as we saw in Chapter 2 remains true today. So one reasonable interpretation of Table 4.1 is the same as Studlar's: minorities have somewhat different priorities, reflecting their different socio-economic positions and interests, but they prioritize the same sorts of issues as the majority, with the same four issues occupying the top four places in both lists (albeit in different orders).[9]

However, it must be said that the set-up of the question asked in all these surveys is bound to lead the interviewee to focus on *common* rather than on ethnic-specific questions, since the introduction specifically talks about the issues and problems 'facing Britain today'. This not unnaturally leads interviewees to focus on common problems on which there is a broad consensus on goals. This still leaves open, however, the question of whether there are some, more ideological, issues, where minorities take up different stances from the majority.

Ethnic differences on mainstream ideological issues

Turning to the more ideological issues that figure on the mainstream political agenda, we begin by looking at two questions that tap the left/right and liberal/authoritarian dimensions which have tended to dominate British politics in the last fifty years. We have one question, asked in both the BES and EMBES, about views on government spending versus tax cuts (a classic left/right issue) and another question on reducing crime versus protecting the rights of the accused (a classic liberal/authoritarian issue). We asked:

> *Now, another issue. Using the 0 to 10 scale on this card, where the end marked 0 means that government should cut taxes and spend much less on health and social services, and the end marked 10 means that government should raise taxes a lot and spend much more on health and social services, where would you place yourself on this scale?*
>
> *Some people think that reducing crime is more important than protecting the rights of people accused of committing crimes. Other people think that protecting the rights of accused people, regardless of whether they have been convicted of committing a crime, is more important than reducing crime. On the 0 to 10 scale, where would you place yourself on this scale?*

To be sure, in the particular political context of the 2010 general election, with governments having to cut expenditure in order to reduce the budget deficit, spending more on health and social services was not really a serious political alternative. However, these questions had been asked in identical format in previous election studies, and to maintain comparability over time we kept them unchanged. Moreover, our respondents (both in EMBES and in the BES) recognized that the Conservatives were more inclined towards cutting taxes than were Labour, and most were able to place themselves and the parties on this scale.[10]

Given that most minorities, apart from those of Indian background, are economically disadvantaged compared with the white British, we might expect to see minorities taking up relatively left-wing positions on this dimension, as they appear to do in the USA: Shaun Bowler and Gary Segura, for

The Ethnic Minority Agenda(s)

example, show that minorities in the USA, especially African-Americans, tend to be more in favour of government intervention and expenditure on issues of redistribution and provision of public services.[11]

We also expect that minorities will tend to be more liberal on civil liberties issues, tending to take the side of the accused rather than that of the police. This is because minorities have historically had greater difficulties with the police, and indeed the Macpherson enquiry into the murder of Stephen Lawrence concluded that the police exhibited institutional racism.[12] We also know that young men from minority backgrounds, especially young black men, are heavily over-represented in prison.[13] Closely related is the issue of detention without trial for those suspected of terrorist offences, where we might expect Muslims to be especially concerned, as they might feel particularly vulnerable to unjustified arrest on suspicion of terrorism.

To simplify and standardize the presentation, in Table 4.2 we report the proportions who placed themselves on the 'progressive' (left or liberal) side of the debate on each issue, that is who supported greater spending on health

Table 4.2. Attitudes to spending/tax cuts, civil liberties, immigration, and Afghan war by ethnic group
Percentage favouring the 'progressive' side of the debate (cell percentages)

Ethnic background	Spend more on health and social services rather than cut taxes	Protect rights of the accused rather than reducing crime	Disagree putting suspected terrorists in prison without trial	Disagree sending asylum-seekers home	Disapprove of war in Afghanistan	N
White British	49	15	33	39	64	2761
Indian	33	24	47	34	46	586
			Muslims 68		Muslims 60	
Pakistani	33	20	75	41	68	665
Bangladeshi	32	20	63	43	59	271
Black Caribbean	42	23	52	59	56	603
Black African	43	24	52	74	51	530
			Muslims 67		Muslims 62	
Mixed white/black	46	18	49	58	61	80
All ethnic minorities	37	22	57	50	56	2775
Majority/minority difference	+12	−7	−24	−11	+8	

Notes: For the scale items on spending/tax cuts and civil liberties, the percentages are those who place themselves to the left of the mid-point. For the items on detention without trial, asylum-seekers and the Afghanistan war, they are for those who disagree or disagree strongly with the statement. Figures in bold are ones where there is a significant difference from the white British percentage. Chi^2 for spending/tax cuts = 148.6, for civil liberties = 43.2, for prison without trial = 153.9, for asylum = 299.2 and for Afghanistan = 116.3 (6 df), $p < 0.001$ for all analyses.
Sources: BES 2010, EMBES 2010, weighted data

and social services, and who thought that protecting the rights of the accused was more important than cutting crime.

We also asked a second question (in the mailback questionnaire) on a more concrete civil liberties issue, namely the detention of suspected terrorists without trial. We asked our respondents to indicate how much they agreed with the statement that:

> *The government has the right to put people suspected of terrorism in prison without trial.*

This had been a highly contentious issue in the last Parliament. Following the London bombings of 2005, the Labour government had proposed raising the maximum period of detention that the police can hold a suspect without bringing a charge from fourteen to ninety days. This was defeated in the House of Commons in one of the biggest parliamentary rebellions of New Labour's period in office (and the first defeat that Tony Blair had suffered as prime minister). A twenty-eight day period of detention was subsequently passed. When he became prime minister, Gordon Brown attempted to increase the period to forty-two days, but after narrowly getting the proposal through the House of Commons it was defeated in the Lords, and abandoned.

We also asked a number of questions about immigration and the war in Afghanistan. Immigration had become a particularly contentious issue in the run-up to the election (following the very large increases in net immigration that had occurred over the previous few years), and many people felt that the Labour government had allowed immigration to rise far too much, without considering or understanding the views of the public, most of whom were unhappy with the policy. The war in Afghanistan had also been a source of continuing discontent, with the rising level of casualties and growing pressure to bring British troops home. We report the results of the following two questions (answers to related questions, given in supplementary tables at the end of the chapter, showing very similar patterns):

> *How much do you agree or disagree with this statement? Most asylum-seekers who come to Britain should be sent home immediately.*
>
> *Please indicate whether you strongly approve, approve, disapprove, or strongly disapprove of Britain's involvement in the war against the Taliban in Afghanistan.*

Table 4.2 shows many significant differences between minorities and the white British, and also between the different minorities, although the patterns are rather complex and vary from issue to issue. First, on the tax cuts versus spending question we find, as Rafaella Dancygier and Elizabeth Saunders did when analysing the 1997 ethnic minority survey, that minorities are in general less supportive of government spending than is the majority group.[14] In this respect they appear to be less left wing than the majority, which contrasts strangely both with their greater support for Labour and with their greater

The Ethnic Minority Agenda(s)

emphasis on unemployment when answering the 'most important issue' question.[15] One possible explanation might be that minorities have typically come from countries where there is neither a strong labour movement nor a comprehensive welfare state. They do not, therefore, come with the same expectations of, or commitment to, welfare spending as the white British majority group, who have grown up with and value highly a generous welfare system. In contrast, migrants may compare the welfare system that they find in Britain with the relatively meagre welfare states in their countries of origin. The British welfare state might seem a big improvement, and hence minorities may not see the need for the British government to spend even more on welfare. Minority and majority frames of reference may thus be rather different.[16]

Moving next to the question on protecting the rights of the accused, minority responses fit more straightforwardly with our expectations: we find that minorities generally are more supportive of the rights of the accused, although like other British citizens most of our respondents feel that reducing crime is what is important. Interestingly, there are no significant differences between any of the different minority groups on this rather abstract question about civil liberties, although differences do emerge in the related but much more concrete question on detention without trial, with Muslims unsurprisingly being more concerned about these particular violations of civil liberty than are non-Muslim groups.

Third, we see much bigger differences on the question of asylum-seekers. The black Africans, especially those from countries which had seen state repression or civil war (such as Somalia, the Congo, and Zimbabwe) are much more likely to disagree with the proposition that all asylum-seekers should be sent back immediately. The South Asians, in contrast, are even less supportive of asylum-seekers than are the white British. There is clearly no shared ethnic minority position on asylum. This finding is not unique to the question of asylum: the same general pattern also holds for our other questions on immigration.

Finally, we see that minorities overall are less hostile to the war in Afghanistan than are the white British, although unsurprisingly the Muslim groups—not only those with Pakistani or Bangladeshi backgrounds but Indian and black African Muslims as well—are significantly more hostile. In contrast, (non-Muslim) Indians are significantly less hostile than are the white British. So, as with the question of asylum, Afghanistan is an issue where there are greater divisions between minorities than there is between the majority and the average minority respondent.

So what are we to make of this? On government spending, civil liberties, and the war in Afghanistan we cannot make a convincing argument for a distinctive ethnic minority agenda, since the majority/minority differences are not all that large. Moreover, the average minority position tends to be on the same side of the debate as the majority position; for example, on the civil liberties question, the typical minority position is clearly on the side of cutting crime, just like the typical majority position. There is a difference of degree but not a difference in direction. The same holds true with the war in Afghanistan. The majority group and most minorities are all effectively pushing in the same direction—to get British troops home. The only one of these mainstream issues where there are clearly groups pushing in opposite directions is detention without trial, where Muslims are pushing for policies that would go in the opposite direction to the majority group's preferences.[17]

The headline, then, is that there are substantial differences between the various minority groups in attitudes to most of these mainstream issues, although not in any consistent manner. Thus the black groups are significantly more progressive than the South Asians on government spending; the black African groups, especially those from the Congo, Somalia, and Zimbabwe, are significantly more progressive on asylum; while the various Muslim groups, but not non-Muslim South Asians or blacks, are significantly more progressive on the war in Afghanistan. Ethnic minorities do not show a united front on these mainstream issues, although on the war in Afghanistan and detention without charge there is a united Muslim stance.

Redress for racial discrimination

We now turn to the issues that Paul Statham's work on the claims-making of minorities suggests as the most likely set of issues on which to find a distinct ethnic minority agenda. We begin with claims 'which appeal to the principle of redress for racial discrimination'. We asked one question in the same format as those on tax cuts versus greater spending and on protecting the rights of the accused versus reducing crime. We asked:

> Using the 0 to 10 scale on this card, where the end marked 0 means that government should make every effort to improve opportunities for black and Asian people, and the end marked 10 means that there is no need for government to take action to improve opportunities for black and Asian people, where would you place yourself on this scale?

The first column of Table 4.3 provides powerful evidence that the provision of equal opportunities for minorities does constitute a distinct and pan-ethnic minority claim that unites all minorities, and contrasts markedly with the view of the white majority, with a 50 percentage-point gap between the average views of the majority and the minorities. To be sure, there is some modest variation between different minorities, with the black groups tending to be even more anxious to improve opportunities than the South Asian

Table 4.3. Attitudes to minority opportunities and affirmative action by ethnic group Percentage favouring the 'progressive' side of the debate (cell percentages)

Ethnic background	Improve opportunities for minorities	Give priority to minorities	N
White British	20	1	2761
Indian	65	26	586
Pakistani	71	28	665
Bangladeshi	70	37	271
Black Caribbean	74	20	603
Black African	75	36	530
Mixed white/black	62	25	80
All ethnic minorities	70	28	2775
Majority/minority difference	−50	−27	

Notes: For the scale item on improving opportunities, the percentage gives those who place themselves to the left of the mid-point. For the item on giving priority, it is the percentage who agree or agree strongly with the statement. Figures in bold are ones where there is a significant difference from the white British percentage. Chi^2 for improving opportunities = 1543.2, for giving priority = 1010.9, 6 df, $p < 0.001$ for both analyses.
Sources: BES 2010, EMBES 2010, weighted data

groups, but in every case the overwhelming majority of all groups support improved opportunities. Here, moreover, it is clear that minorities are on the opposite side of the argument from the majority group.

In a sense, 'making every effort to improve opportunities for black and Asian people' is a relatively easy statement to agree with if you are black or Asian yourself, so we asked a more difficult question on affirmative action policies:

> *And how much do you agree or disagree with this statement:*
> *Black and Asian people in Britain who apply for jobs should be given priority, to try to make up for past discrimination against them.*

Affirmative action of the sort implied in this question is a fairly extreme policy which has never been strongly advocated in Britain, and might even be against EU law. Something approaching affirmative action was actually included in the Equality Act 2010 for women, although surprisingly not for ethnic minorities. That is, the Act allowed firms to appoint women in preference to men if they were in other respects equally suited for the job. In practice, ethnic minority groups have tended to ask for more modest interventions in order to promote equal opportunities, and so we do not expect to find great support for this policy even among minorities. The second column of Table 4.3 shows that this is indeed the case: only 28 per cent of our ethnic minority sample supported affirmative action. But even this figure contrasts very sharply with the white British figure, which was only 1 per cent. Moreover, there is no significant variation between the ethnic minority groups in their support for affirmative action.

Overall, then, while there is only modest support on the part of minorities for measures as strong as affirmative action, our evidence does show that redress for racial discrimination is a principle on which all minorities take a very similar stance, and which differentiates them sharply from members of the dominant majority group. There is general agreement among minorities on *what* the objective should be—namely equality of opportunity—although disagreement on *how* it should be achieved. This is an objective which all minorities share, and the majority/minority differences on these issues are much the largest of any included in our survey. They dwarf almost every other cleavage that can be found either in the BES or EMBES.

Measures to preserve ethno-religious culture

We now turn to various issues that fall under the rubric of cultural rights. In the mailback questionnaire we included a general question about arrangements to allow minorities to practise their culture and religion. We asked whether respondents agreed that:

> *There should be special rules in place for people of ethnic minority origin so they can practise their culture or religion at work and school.*

We also asked two more specific questions about provision for religious teaching and the wearing of traditional dress in schools:

> *There has been a lot of debate among teachers about how British schools should cater for children whose parents come from other countries and cultures. Do you think in general that schools with many such children should:*
>
> a. *Provide them with separate religious instruction if their parents request it*
> b. *Allow those for whom it is important to wear their traditional dress at school*

We also asked Muslim respondents about the introduction of Sharia law:

> *And looking at these statements about Sharia courts being introduced in Britain, which of these come closest to your view?*
> *Introduce Sharia law, that is traditional Islamic law, in all cases*
> *Introduce Sharia law, but only if penalties do not contravene British law*
> *Do not introduce Sharia law.*

Since these questions were all asked in the mailback questionnaire (or just of Muslims in the case of Sharia), the number of respondents is much lower than in the previous table, and we need to be more circumspect in drawing conclusions. We are also unable to make any comparisons with the white British on these items. Table 4.4 provides the details of attitudes towards these cultural provisions and towards Sharia law.

As we can see, there is much stronger support for these special cultural provisions at work and school among the groups of Pakistani and Bangladeshi

Table 4.4. Attitudes to introduction of culturally specific institutions and practices Percentage favouring the ethnic side of the debate (cell percentages)

Ethnic background	Minorities should be given special provisions at work	Schools should provide separate religious instruction	Schools should allow minorities to wear traditional dress	Introduce Sharia law in all cases	Introduce Sharia law only if consistent with British law	N Mailback/ Muslims
Indian	32 Sikhs 29 Muslims **60**	38 Sikhs 45 Muslims **67**	41 Sikhs 49 Muslims **85**	Muslims 13	Muslims 25	*202/70*
Pakistani	**63**	**68**	**74**	Muslims 19	Muslims 22	*230/611*
Bangladeshi	54	59	73	Muslims 20	Muslims 16	*94/252*
Black Caribbean	27	28	41	–	–	*218*
Black African	27 Muslims 33	37 Muslims **57**	40 Muslims **61**	Muslims 17	Muslims 21	*182/136*
All ethnic minorities	39	45	51	Muslims 19	Muslims 21	*976/1097*

Notes: Except for Sharia, the percentages are those who agree or agree strongly with the statement. Figures that are significantly higher than expectation are emboldened. The question on Sharia law was asked only of Muslim respondents. Chi^2 for special provisions at work = 89.5, for separate religious instruction = 89.2, for traditional dress = 94.1, 4 df, p < 0.001 in all cases. For the Sharia question Chi^2 = 13.7 (9df), p > 0.05.
Sources: EMBES 2010 face to face and mailback questionnaires, weighted

background than there is among the Indian or black groups.[18] For all three of these items there is a clear majority in the Muslim groups for special provision. While this question was not asked in the main BES, we suspect (given the responses of the non-Muslim groups) that this is a second question where Muslims are pressing in the opposite direction to the majority group. Interestingly, Indian Sikhs do not share this concern, despite the requirement on devout Sikhs to wear the five Ks. (The five Ks are Kesh (uncut hair), Kara (a steel bracelet), Kanga (a wooden comb), Kaccha (cotton underwear) and Kirpan (steel sword). Taken together, they symbolize that the Sikh who wears them has dedicated himself to a life of devotion and submission to the Guru.)

In contrast to this Muslim demand for cultural rights, there is no great support for the introduction of Sharia law 'in all cases'. There is, however, more support for Sharia 'if the penalties do not contravene British law'. This provides an interesting parallel with the low level of support for affirmative action: in both cases, we see that our respondents favour policies that go with the grain of British policy rather than against it. Incidentally, Sharia courts (strictly, Muslim Arbitration Tribunals) already and quite legally operate in Britain under the 1996 Arbitration Act, dealing with certain kinds of dispute resolution, but have to do so within the terms of British law.

Within-group divisions

As we observed at the beginning of this chapter, British society is highly stratified. We should certainly not treat the white British as a homogeneous group any more than we should treat minorities as homogeneous. Broadly speaking, within British society there is a social class cleavage, with the middle class and especially the more entrepreneurial sections of the middle class tending to be more supportive of free-market policies, and the working class supporting redistribution and greater state spending. The white British are also divided in their positions on the liberal/authoritarian dimension, although these positions are more closely linked to education than to social class, with the higher educated tending to take more liberal views.

In understanding the current political concerns of minorities, and their possible future trajectories, we need to check whether they too are stratified internally in their political concerns. It is quite possible that minorities' own socio-economic positions will divide their political interests in much the same way as they divide the interests of the majority group, and we might well expect this tendency to have strengthened in recent years as some members of all minorities have become economically successful, leading to the rise of South Asian and black middle classes. Do we find the same ideological cleavages within minority groups as we do among the majority group? Or are minorities more united around the particular issues that are important to them as a group? Does ethnicity trump class?

To help answer these questions, Table 4.5 highlights some key lines of socio-economic stratification comparing the magnitude of associated political cleavages within the majority and minorities respectively. We also look at Muslim/non-Muslim and at generational differences within the minorities, as there are important debates about whether second-generation minorities are converging with British patterns, as we saw in the last chapter, or reacting against them.

Considering first the majority group, we find that class and educational differences track each other fairly closely. Much the largest cleavages are apparent between graduates and people with low qualifications on the issues of detention without trial and asylum-seekers, university graduates having much more progressive views than the least educated members of the British public. In this sense, the white British appear to be polarized on these two issues, with a huge gulf in opinion between the most and the least educated members of society.

With one important exception, these cleavages are much reduced among the minority population. There are divisions, similar to those among the majority group, between highly and less-educated members of minority communities,

The Ethnic Minority Agenda(s)

Table 4.5. Socio-economic differences within the majority and minority ethnic groups on key issues
Net differences

	Unemployment	Detention	Asylum	Afghanistan	Affirmative action	Sharia
Middle/working class (majority)	−6	+20	+30	−12	0	–
Middle/working class (minorities)	−7	+1	+7	−6	−11	+3
Graduates/low qualifications (majority)	−5	+32	+43	−12	0	–
Graduates/low qualifications (minorities)	−3	+7	+14	−3	−15	+11
Owners/social housing (majority)	−4	+10	+16	−6	−2	–
Owners/social housing (minorities)	−7	+7	−13	−1	−12	−2
Muslim/non-Muslim (minorities)	+3	+16	−4	+17	+8	–
2nd/1st generation (minorities)	−3	+15	+3	+11	−14	0

Notes: A positive sign indicates that the first-named group is more 'progressive' than the second-named group, and vice versa. Statistically significant differences at the 0.05 level are emboldened. Comparisons are between the middle class and the working class; between those with tertiary education and those with low or no qualifications; and between home owners and those in social housing (renters from a local authority or housing association).
Sources: BES 2010, EMBES 2010 weighted

but they are only a pale reflection of the cleavages in the majority group. In other words, at least on these items, there is much less socio-economic division of opinion within minorities than within the majority group. Minorities are not yet internally stratified in the way that the white British are.

The one exception concerns affirmative action. Whereas the majority group are uniformly opposed to affirmative action to help ethnic minorities, we do see some divisions of opinion along socio-economic lines among the minorities themselves. The differences are relatively small, and we should not exaggerate their importance, but it is clear that minority individuals in more privileged socio-economic positions, who have done well despite the widespread racism in British society, are less inclined to support affirmative action policies.

Generational differences are also quite small, although it is again quite interesting that the second generation are somewhat less supportive of affirmative action than the first generation was.[19] In this respect there is the same kind of convergence with white British norms as we saw in Chapter 3. However, this convergence is not repeated with any of the other items. For example, the second generation is more concerned than the first about detention without trial and about the war in Afghanistan (although once we control for age and educational level the change is no longer significant). However, this is not a story of uniform radicalization across generations, since there is no change among Muslims on Sharia law.

Why do we find this lack of socio-economic polarization among the minority groups, and in particular lack of polarization between highly and less-educated minorities of the kind that is found among the white British? One possibility that we can quickly discount is that minorities who received their university degrees abroad were not socialized into the same set of liberal values that British higher education tends to inculcate. An absence of educational polarization remains even if we restrict our attention to minorities who have been through the British educational system.

Our preferred alternative account focuses on the nature of the social relationships between members of the different communities. Our interpretation is that the social distance between highly educated and poorly educated white British is much greater than that between minority individuals with different levels of education.[20] In this sense we really can talk of minorities as communities, whose members talk to each other and share common values. In contrast, the social gulf between different strata of white society is much greater. To stand a common catchphrase on its head, it is the different strata of white society who live parallel lives, apart from each other and apart from the mainstream (much as the Conservative prime minister Benjamin Disraeli wrote about over a hundred years ago in his novel *Sybil*).

All in it together?

In many ways Donley Studlar's argument from twenty-five years ago still holds true. Ethnic minorities in Britain do share the same political concerns as the majority about the state of the economy, the financial crisis, and unemployment. It would be surprising if it were otherwise, since minorities and most members of the majority, except perhaps the privileged financial elite, really are 'all in it together'. Minorities are faced, probably even more so than most members of the majority, by the economic hard times brought about by the financial crisis and the irresponsibility of the banks. To be sure, minorities placed a higher priority on unemployment than did the majority, but this too is entirely unsurprising. There is a great deal of evidence that minorities have higher unemployment rates than the white British, reflecting the ethnic penalties they encounter in the labour market. But this does not amount to a separate agenda. A better way of viewing it would be that minorities are likely to press more strongly, but in the same direction, as other British citizens who have also suffered from the aftermath of the recession. On other mainstream issues too, such as crime and the war in Afghanistan, minorities differ somewhat from the majority (and sometimes from each other) in their precise positions, but are essentially pressing in the same direction as other British citizens.[21]

But there are a few issues where some minorities are pressing in the opposite direction to the majority, and hence where issues of representation may well arise. First, there is the controversial issue of detention of terrorist suspects, where Muslims are clearly on the opposite side from most members of the majority group. However, even here Muslim views are not especially different from those of white British university graduates, who are also strongly in favour of protecting civil liberties. Therefore Muslims are not without influential allies. The same is true of asylum, although on this issue it tends to be black groups from war-torn countries of Africa rather than Muslims who are most concerned. Here, too, even if their views are unpopular with the British public generally, they are shared by the highly educated, who are pretty effective at getting their concerns into the public arena. So while these are not issues on which 'we are all in it together', they are issues on which some ethnic minorities are in it together with some white British elites.

Ethno-religious cultural concerns distinguish Muslim groups from other minorities. Unfortunately, we do not have any data from white British respondents on such issues, although we suspect that the picture might be quite similar to that on detention of terrorist suspects: there would not be a great deal of sympathy from the majority of the British public for Muslim concerns, but the educated elite might well turn out once again to be influential allies in support of multicultural policies for accommodating Muslim concerns.

But our main new finding is that there is indeed a distinct and dramatic majority/minority difference on the issue of equal opportunities for ethnic minorities. This is an issue that unites the different minorities, and where within-group differences based on class or other socio-economic interests are tiny compared with the overall majority/minority difference. This is not in itself at all surprising given the evidence we reported in Chapter 2 on ethnic penalties and exclusion in the labour market—exclusion which, it should be remembered, applies to well-educated Blacks and Asians, not just to the disadvantaged. What is much more remarkable, at least to the authors of this book, is that such a minimal proportion of the white British share this concern with equal opportunities. One might have thought that equality of opportunity was a fundamental British value; and so it may be in abstract. But it is quite remarkable that not even the educated elite are allies on this rather fundamental aspect of equality of opportunity. Moreover, it is not as though minorities themselves are pressing for policies that go against the grain of British legislation. There is no great support among minorities for the stronger forms of affirmative action that have been implemented in the USA. On this issue all minorities are in it together, but alas they appear to be abandoned by the white British on this most British of all issues.

Appendix: Supplementary tables

Table 4.A1. Multiple regression of attitudes to selected issues: BES respondents only
Regression coefficients

	Unemployment most important issue	Spend more on health and social services rather than cut taxes	Protect rights of accused rather than cut crime	Disagree with sending asylum-seekers home	Disapprove of war in Afghanistan	Improve opportunities for minorities
Ethnic minority	**0.41**	**−0.44**	0.30	0.22	0.03	**2.01**
Female	0.01	**0.29**	**−0.20**	0.03	**0.32**	0.05
Age (ln)	**−0.39**	**0.66**	**0.38**	0.04	**0.30**	**0.19**
Married	−0.04	−0.07	−0.12	−0.07	−0.07	**−0.10**
Education	**−0.07**	0.02	**0.20**	**0.22**	−0.08	**0.31**
Middle class	−0.11	**−0.21**	−0.17	0.16	−0.12	0.03
Working class	**0.28**	**−0.34**	−0.07	−0.12	0.01	−0.14
Unwaged (ref)	0	0	0	0	0	0
Owner	−0.06	0.17	−0.19	−0.03	−0.07	**0.08**
LA/HA renter	0.13	0.25	−0.09	**−0.20**	0.03	**−0.12**
Other tenure (ref)	0	0	0	0	0	0
Income	−0.020	−0.010	0.004	0.00	**−0.012**	−0.004
Christian	0.07	0.04	−0.07	−0.05	**−0.20**	**−0.12**
Muslim	0.20	0.30	**−0.56**	0.34	**0.44**	1.38
Other religion	0.30	0.18	−0.02	−0.14	−0.17	0.37
No religion (ref)	0	0	0	0	0	0
Constant	0.14	2.94	2.14	2.23	2.53	2.36
R^2	0.06	0.03	0.01	0.12	0.06	0.09
N	2912	2905	2910	2909	2911	2903

Notes: OLS regressions except for importance of unemployment, which is a probit model. Coefficients significant at the 0.05 level are in bold.
Source: BES 2010, robust standard errors

Table 4.A2. Percentages adopting left-wing views on left/right questions
Cell percentages

	White British (BES)	Minorities (BES)	Minorities (EMBES)	Significance of majority/minority difference
Disagree there are fair shares for ordinary working people	66	42	45	0.001
Agree one law for rich and one for poor	63	52	52	0.05
Disagree no need for strong TUs	62	68	57	NS
Disagree private enterprise best	22	26	22	NS
N	1581	134	975	
Cronbach's alpha	0.58	0.37	0.39	

Notes: Significant differences between majority and minorities in the BES are emboldened. The levels of significance in column 4 are for comparisons within the BES.
Sources: BES 2010 and EMBES 2010 mailback questionnaires

Table 4.A3. Percentages adopting libertarian views on civil liberties
Cell percentages

	White British (BES)	Minorities (BES)	Minorities (EMBES)	Significance of majority/minority difference
Disagree young people should show more respect	11	11	9	NS
Disagree censorship needed	24	15	13	0.05
Agree allow protest	69	59	60	0.05
Agree people should be more tolerant	44	39	40	NS
Agree undemocratic parties should not be banned	22	22	19	NS
Disagree detention without trial for terrorists	33	47	56	0.001
N	1597	133	935	
Cronbach's alpha	0.58	0.33	0.21	

Notes: Significant differences between majority and minorities in the BES are emboldened. The levels of significance in column 4 are for comparisons within the BES.
Sources: BES 2010 and EMBES 2010 mailback questionnaires

Table 4.A4. Percentages adopting progressive views on immigration
Cell percentages

	White British (BES)	Minorities (BES)	Minorities (EMBES)	Significance of majority/minority difference
Disagree immigrants increase crime	31	34	45	NS
Agree immigrants good for economy	29	56	63	0.001
Disagree immigrants take jobs	24	53	52	0.001
Agree immigrants enrich culture	35	46	56	0.01
Disagree immigrants increase risk of terrorism	23	40	48	0.001
Disagree immigrants threaten language	33	43	64	0.05
N	1605	136	945	
Cronbach's alpha	0.84	0.73	0.69	

Notes: Significant differences between majority and minorities in the BES are emboldened. The levels of significance in column 4 are for comparisons within the BES.
Sources: BES 2010 and EMBES 2010 mailback questionnaires

Table 4.A5. Percentages adopting progressive views on Afghanistan
Cell percentages

	White British (BES)	Minorities (BES)	Minorities (EMBES)	Significance of majority/ minority difference
Disagrees war good in long run	65	61	49	NS
Agrees war threatens own safety	34	37	29	NS
Disagrees moral case for war	49	46	36	NS
Agrees war damages British interests	49	53	51	NS
Disapproves of war	64	66	54	NS
N	2643	277	2700	
Cronbach's alpha	0.70	0.65	0.64	

Notes: Significant differences between majority and minorities in the BES are emboldened. The levels of significance in column 4 are for comparisons within the BES.
Sources: BES 2010 and EMBES 2010 mailback questionnaires

Notes

1. See for example Clarke et al. (2004). Political scientists tend to refer to these consensual issues as 'valence' or 'performance' ones, following the distinction introduced by Butler and Stokes (1969), p. 189.
2. See for example Heath et al. (1994), Heath et al. (1999), Clarke et al. (2004), Sanders (2006).
3. See, for example, Curtice et al. (2005).
4. See also Koopmans and Statham (1999).
5. In 1967, Wolverhampton's Transport Committee had banned Sikh busmen from wearing turbans on duty. There was a long-running campaign to overturn the ban, supported both by the Transport and General Workers Union and the Indian High Commission. Sohan Singh Jolly threatened to burn himself to death in protest, and other Sikhs promised to follow suit. The Transport Committee eventually agreed to remove the ban 'in the interests of race relations'. (BBC News 9 April 1969)
6. Salman Rushdie's novel *Satanic Verses*, published in 1988, was widely felt by Muslims to be blasphemous, for example using the derogatory name Mahound for the prophet. A *fatwā* ordering Muslims to kill Rushdie was issued by Ayatollah Khomeini of Iran (although later withdrawn in 1998). For a detailed account of the issues involved see Modood (2005).
7. For a more detailed discussion of past rival accounts as to whether there is a distinct ethnic agenda see Saggar (2000), chapter 6.
8. In general, for all the items reported in this chapter we find slightly higher levels of 'don't know' responses on the part of minorities.
9. However, it is unclear that minorities' greater concern with unemployment simply reflects their greater risks of being unemployed. In more detailed analysis of the BES data (shown in Table 4.A1 at the end of the chapter) we find that, although the importance attached to unemployment is indeed associated with one's socio-

economic position, this fails to account for minorities' greater concern about unemployment.

10. However, we should note that minorities felt somewhat less at ease with the terms 'left' and 'right' than did the majority group, and were probably also less at ease with the somewhat abstract questions on tax cuts versus spending and cutting crime versus protecting rights of the accused, and were more likely to respond 'don't know'. Thus on the tax cuts versus spending question, 8 per cent of minorities compared with 5 per cent of white British responded 'don't know'. On the cutting crime question, the figures were 15 per cent and 2 per cent respectively, and even on the equal opportunities question, the figures were 5 per cent for minorities and 4 per cent for the white British. In the mailback questionnaire, 65 per cent of minorities said that they never used the terms 'left' and 'right', compared with 58 per cent of the white British. As the supplementary tables also show, the reliability of scales to measure left/right and liberal/authoritarian values is substantially lower among minorities. However, it is important to recognize that this lack of reliability does not apply in the same way to the issues of war in Afghanistan and of immigration, on which minorities do have reliable and robust views. Tables 4.A3–4A5 show the details.
11. See Bowler and Segura (2012), chapter 5.
12. The 1999 Macpherson report was an investigation into the murder of Stephen Lawrence. It found that the recommendations of the 1981 Scarman report had been ignored, and famously concluded that the police force was institutionally racist.
13. For detailed evidence see EHRC (2010) and the supporting research papers cited by the EHRC.
14. See Dancygier and Saunders (2006), Table 1. Cf. Davis and Robinson (2006).
15. We asked some further items covering different aspects of the left/right dimension in the mailback questionnaire. Again, we found a rather similar picture (with results for the ethnic minority respondents to the main BES and those in EMBES being reassuringly similar). There was either no significant difference between the majority and the minority, or the majority was more left wing than the minority. See Table 4.A2 at the end of the chapter for details.
16. This is a rather different explanation from Dancygier and Saunders' argument. We feel that their argument—that minorities' greater support for tax cuts is owing to the positive selection of migrants—is not wholly persuasive, as there appears to be no clear relationship between the degree of selectivity of the minority and their level of support for tax cuts. For example, one of the most highly selected groups is the black African minority, but this is actually a group that comes closest to the white British in their responses. Dancygier and Saunders' interpretation should surely also apply to the USA where migrants have also been positively selected and it is puzzling therefore why minorities in the USA tend to be more in favour of government spending. In contrast, the US welfare state is much less generous than the British one, and is not a major focus of national pride in the way that the British welfare state, especially the National Health Service, is.

17. We have an open mind over the merits of the directional and proximity theories of vote choice, but it will surely be important whether minorities are on opposite sides of any issue from the majority or are on the same side but more or less lukewarm. On the debate over these directional and proximity approaches see Rabinowitz and Macdonald (1989) and Lewis and King (1999).
18. This pattern appears to be quite long standing, and was also found by Saggar using the 1997 EMBES. See Saggar (2000), Table 6.3 and the related discussion.
19. The change between the first and second generations is statistically significant at the 0.001 level after controlling for age, gender, and educational level. We also find significant interactions, with the change being smaller among black Caribbeans and black Africans than among Indians. If we use our measure of parental generation in place of the first generation, the change is also significant at the 0.01 level although the interactions are no longer significant.
20. We can test this idea by looking at intermarriage, which is probably the best indicator of social distance. See, for example, Blossfeld and Timm (2003).
21. Sobolewska (2005), however, has shown that there are some issues, especially on Europe and foreign policy, which minorities are not especially bothered about. Minorities do not have opposed views on these issues—they simply do not see them as a priority or take no interest in them (which amounts to much the same thing).

5
Representation of Ethnic Minority Concerns

In Chapter 4 we showed how minorities share the same concerns as the majority on mainstream issues, such as the financial crisis and the economy, although they place somewhat greater emphasis on unemployment. On a number of other issues, such as immigration and asylum, detention without trial, and the war in Afghanistan, there are substantial differences between minorities, and no united front. But there is a united minority concern with redress for racial discrimination. Moreover, this is the one minority concern where there is no significant set of white British allies. This, then, is clearly the issue where minority concerns are most likely to be excluded from the mainstream political agenda.

Previous research by Donley Studlar and Zig Layton-Henry on minority access to the political agenda in Britain concluded that 'Nonwhite access to the British political agenda remains minimal and problematic. While overt hostility toward nonwhites may have diminished over the years, indifference to their situation is still the norm among both elites and masses, but especially the latter' (1990, pp. 286–7). They suggest a number of reasons for this neglect, some of which we have already encountered. They highlight, for example, the overlap of non-white and mainstream agendas; differences between minorities in their agendas; the need for, but declining number of, liberal white allies (who have turned their attention to other issues); the weakness of non-white representative organizations and lack of any lasting umbrella organization; fragmented responsibility within government for race-related issues; and the risk of white backlash. They also noted that the main effective ways of getting ethnic minority concerns onto the political agenda have been official enquiries, such as Lord Scarman's report on the Brixton riots and Sir William Macpherson's report on the Stephen Lawrence murder investigation.

In rather similar vein, in a persuasive article reviewing developments up until 1983, Jim Bulpitt (1986) argued that the 'centre' has generally followed a strategy of maintaining its own autonomy, by which he meant insulation from citizens' (both white and black) demands, and offloading race issues onto the 'periphery', by which he meant local councils and quangos. His basic view was that there had been a long-standing elite consensus, with a desire to focus on high politics (such as foreign affairs, defence, and macro-management of the economy), and to keep race off the agenda as much as possible through a bipartisan policy: 'The substance of this consensus was simple: limits on immigration were necessary [in order to appease popular disquiet], but these were to be accompanied by efforts to reduce race discrimination and deprivation' (Bulpitt 1986, p. 31).

On these accounts, a crucial problem for both main parties is the risk of a white backlash. Given the long-standing hostility to immigration on the part of whites, particularly the less educated, who constitute a large proportion of Labour voters, and the potential for defections to the racist parties of the far right, both main parties but especially Labour thought that they risked losing more white votes than they would have gained black votes if they unequivocally expressed support for minority concerns. As Marian Fitzgerald has argued, closer Labour identification with ethnic minority interests in the 1980s was perceived, both inside and outside the party, as part of the extremist image which harmed its electoral prospects.[1]

A somewhat different perspective, which goes some way to explaining minority support for Labour, has been provided by Anthony Messina. He agrees that there was indeed an elite consensus in the 1950s and 1960s designed to keep race off the agenda, because of tensions within each of the main parties. But this consensus was broken in the late 1970s by the Conservatives under Margaret Thatcher, who was the first leader of the party to articulate concerns over immigration—with her famous speech about the risks of Britain being 'swamped by people with a different culture'.[2] Anthony Messina plausibly argues that this was in part a response to fears that the Tories might lose votes to the far right National Front, which had made worrying gains in the two 1974 elections. At the same time, the Labour Party, perhaps also partly out of electoral calculations—the growing presence of minority Labour voters and activists within the party—proposed quite radical reforms to tackle racial discrimination and unequal opportunities. There was thus throughout the late 1970s and 1980s a clear distinction between the two main parties in their approach to race, just as there was on so many other political issues in the period.

We begin by reviewing the party manifestos for the period from 1974 onwards. We do not suppose for one minute that the average voter reads the manifestos or is aware of their detailed content. Nor do manifestos give any clear indication of what parties will actually do when in office: governments often quietly abandon some of their more radical manifesto promises once they get into office (for example, the Thatcher government's abandonment of its promise to end the entry concessions to husbands and male fiancés, which were introduced by Labour in 1974). Some of the major pieces of government action or legislation, such as the Iraq and Afghanistan wars and proposals for detention without trial, were never anticipated in the manifestos. But the manifestos do provide statements of intent that tend to be reflected in the material circulated by parties through their local election leaflets or party election broadcasts, and they do enable us to assess whether the elite consensus persists. We can also compare the story told by the manifestos with the parties' records of passing legislation to help minorities once in office. In a sense, this tells us whether the parties live up to their pre-election promises.

Another angle on representation is to look at the extent to which parties are representative in the sense that the profile of their MPs matches that of their electors, and specifically whether there is any under-representation of ethnic minorities in the House of Commons. We can think of this as 'symbolic' representation. The number of ethnic minority candidates put forward by each party, and whether they are selected for winnable seats, may tell us something about how serious the parties are about ethnic issues. To be sure, there is no guarantee that ethnic minority MPs will be able to persuade their party to enact minority-friendly proposals, but the presence of minority candidates is at least a symbol to the electorate of what the party stands for. And our own evidence from the survey suggests that minority electors believe that more minority MPs would make a difference.

Finally, we will review our own survey evidence on the perceptions of the electors themselves, both minority and majority, on the differences between the parties in the extent to which they look after minority interests. As sociologists often like to emphasize, it is not the 'objective' reality that necessarily influences how individuals behave but their perceptions and definition of the situation. As William I. Thomas and Dorothy Swaine Thomas phrased it, in one of the most cited aphorisms of sociology, 'If men define situations as real, they are real in their consequences' (1928, p. 572).[3] How, then, do British citizens perceive the parties, and where they stand on ethnic issues?

Party manifestos 1974–2010

Our first focus is on the promises that the main parties have put forward in their manifestos to address minority concerns, and in particular to redress the racial discrimination that minorities continue to experience, since we believe this to be the issue which is most likely to be excluded from mainstream policymaking. Given the nature of the elite consensus, and ethnic minority interest in this issue, we also need to look at immigration policy. In Figure 5.1 we therefore summarize the main passages in each of the three main parties' manifestos which bear on racial discrimination or immigration. (The detailed

	Conservative	Labour	Liberal Democrat
Oct 1974	Promises positive policies to help minorities, coupled with strict immigration controls.	Promises to strengthen legislation protecting minorities and to reform nationality law, but nothing explicit.	No mention of ethnic inequalities or migration, but commitment to sex equality.
1979	Affirmation of equal opportunities for ethnic minorities, but good community relations linked to stricter control of immigration.	No new proposal for redress of racial discrimination but promises to take a lead in the public sector.	Proposes a single Anti-Discrimination Board to protect rights of minorities and other groups.
1983	Affirmation of equal opportunities for ethnic minorities, but good community relations linked to stricter control of immigration.	Explicitly promises positive action to overcome racial inequality and measures to overcome prejudice.	Proposes UK Commission of Human Rights, positive action on race equality and non-discriminatory citizenship and immigration legislation.
1987	Affirmation of equal opportunities for ethnic minorities, but good community relations linked to absence of 'reverse discrimination'; emphasizes need for ethnic minorities to participate in British culture.	Promises to promote racial equality, for example through contract compliance; promises to tackle racial hatred but also stresses immigration control.	Proposes UK Commission of Human Rights, positive action on race equality and non-discriminatory citizenship and immigration legislation.
1992	Affirmation of equal opportunities for ethnic minorities; emphasizes need for ethnic minorities to participate in wider community; new proposal for additional help with English language.	No explicit mention of redressing racial discrimination but proposes strengthening anti-discrimination law generally (singling out age discrimination).	Proposes to establish UK Commission of Human Rights, reinforce race equality legislation, and reform citizenship and immigration legislation so that it is non-discriminatory and encourage multiculturalism in schools.
1997	No explicit mention of redressing racial discrimination, but does promise action against racial harassment; firm immigration linked to good race relations.	No explicit mention of redressing racial discrimination but some general remarks on ending discrimination more generally (singling out disability).	Proposes UK Commission of Human Rights, action against discriminatory policing and non-discriminatory immigration legislation.
2001	No explicit mention of redressing racial discrimination, but does offer endorsement of a multicultural society.	No explicit mention of redressing racial discrimination but some general remarks on ending discrimination more generally and tackling the ethnic employment gap.	Proposes Equality Act and Equality Commission and non-discriminatory immigration rules.
2005	No explicit mention of redressing racial discrimination, but endorses diversity while linking its benefits to immigration control.	Explicit commitment to tackling racial discrimination and single Equality Act and Commission; proposes to introduce points system for immigration and English language tests.	Proposes single Equality Act and Equality and Human Rights Commission, though focus is on LGBT issues more than race.
2010	Endorses equality of opportunity in general terms but no explicit mention of redressing racial discrimination; emphasizes need for minorities to embrace British values and need to reduce immigration (with new language test).	No new proposals to tackle racial discrimination but promises to enforce equality act more generally (singling out gender inequality); emphasizes immigration controls.	New proposal to tackle racial discrimination by requiring name-blind job application forms.

Figure 5.1. Summary of manifesto commitments on immigration and redress for racial discrimination

Notes: In 1974 and 1979, we summarize the Liberal manifesto. In 1983 and 1987, the passages come from the SDP-Liberal Alliance (an electoral pact between the newly formed Social Democratic Party and the Liberal Party), and from 1992 onwards, from the Liberal Democrat Party manifesto.

passages themselves are provided in Figure 5.A1 We restrict ourselves to the 1974–2010 period in order to keep the task manageable, and not to test the reader's (and publisher's) patience.

Figure 5.1 begins in 1974 at the end of the bipartisan era. The Conservative manifesto in particular exemplifies the classic formula of limits on immigration coupled with efforts to ameliorate racial discrimination. The Labour and Liberal manifestos, on the other hand, have little to say about redress of racial discrimination, and are thus consistent with the thesis that minority concerns were marginalized at this time (although, in fairness to the parties, all three manifestos were dominated by the economic crisis then engulfing Britain).

After 1974 we can see major differences between the three parties, and a strong line of continuity in the commitments of all three main parties. Not a single Conservative manifesto from 1979 onwards explicitly promises to tackle racial discrimination in the way that the 1974 manifesto had done. True, all the Conservative manifestos uphold the classic liberal principle of equality of opportunity, but they come forward with no new proposals for making a reality of equality of opportunity for ethnic minorities, and they almost always couch their liberal message in general terms rather than singling out racial inequality. Where there are proposals for overcoming inequality, they tend to adopt a colour-blind approach, as with Enterprise Zones. Moreover, good community relations are explicitly linked to strict control of immigration in the 1979, 1983, 1987, 1997, and 2005 manifestos. To be fair, in 1987, 1992, and 1997 there are explicit commitments to dealing with racial hatred, and help with learning English is mentioned in a number of manifestos. However, the 1987 manifesto also implicitly attacks multiculturalism and 'linguistic and cultural ghettos', while the 2010 manifesto emphasizes the sharing of core British values, and proposes a language test for family reunion. Labour and Liberal Democrat manifestos, in contrast, never criticize minority culture and values in this way.

Labour makes explicit commitments to tackle racial discrimination in its manifestos for 1979, 1983, 1987, and 2005. While there was a conspicuous absence of explicit commitments in the 1992, 1997, and 2001 manifestos, even in these years there were more general, albeit vaguer, commitments—perhaps a deliberate attempt to shake off the party's extremist image by backpedalling on its commitment to minorities. But the 2005 manifesto does return to explicit commitments, following the Cabinet Office's Strategy for Race Equality and the report of the National Employment Panel.[4] Moreover, none of the Labour manifestos in this period explicitly proposed to limit immigration, although the 2005 manifesto did propose to introduce an Australian-style points system, while the 2010 manifesto went further in the direction of restricting immigration and access to citizenship. So, overall, it would be wrong in our judgement to say that non-white access to Labour's agenda was minimal, although the emphasis given to tackling racial discrimination varies greatly from manifesto to manifesto, with the strongest commitments in 1983, but backpedalling in 1992, 1997, and 2001. There has also been a revived Labour emphasis on the control of immigration in 2005 and 2010, moving back to the elite consensus that scholars had identified for the earlier period.

The other striking feature of Figure 5.1 is that the Liberal Democrats are throughout explicit about their support for various minority-friendly policies, both on tackling racial discrimination and on non-discriminatory immigration policies, with many concrete proposals. Recurrent themes are the proposals to introduce a unified Equality Commission and a single Equality Act (both of which were actually implemented by Labour). This in turn raises the question why minorities do not support the Liberal Democrats in greater numbers. Possibly the party's emphasis on dealing with gender, gay, lesbian, and disability discrimination at the same time as race discrimination might be thought to weaken the force of their arguments, and to raise doubts about the priority attached to redressing racial discrimination.

Our reading of these manifestos, then, is that there was a clear, albeit varying, difference between the Conservative and Labour parties over this period, with Labour demonstrating a markedly greater commitment to tackling racial discrimination, and the Conservatives demonstrating markedly greater opposition to immigration. The manifesto evidence is thus in line with Anthony Messina's account of a breakdown of the previous elite consensus, and does not really support the more pessimistic accounts of the marginalization of ethnic minority concerns. However, it could be argued that in 2010 there was not really all that much difference between the Labour and Conservative manifestos. Perhaps the elite consensus is re-emerging. But taking the period as a whole, there are strong continuities in the positions of all three parties, both tone and emphasis of the Conservative and Labour manifestos being distinctly different at many of these elections.

What parties say in their manifestos and what they actually do when they eventually get into office can be very different. It is noticeable that the explicit Liberal Democrat promise in 2010 to require name-blind job applications did not become part of the coalition agreement. We need to check what parties actually did in government, and not simply look at their promises. Therefore we have checked the main legislation that has been passed on immigration, citizenship, and redress of racial discrimination over the post-war period. We also, to indicate what life has been like for minorities in Britain, report the unemployment rates for minorities and white British since 1974. (Data for earlier periods is not available.)

As we can see in the timeline below in Figure 5.2, there is considerable continuity in the extent to which Labour has been the party enacting legislation to tackle racial discrimination, whereas the Conservatives have predominantly enacted legislation to reform and restrict citizenship and immigration.

As we can see, every single measure designed to tackle racial discrimination has been passed by Labour. In contrast, Conservative governments have enacted a series of measures designed to restrict immigration, although so too did the Labour governments of 1964–70 and New Labour while in office from 1997 to 2010. So as with the manifestos, the story is not entirely straightforward: it is not a simple story of elite consensus, since the Conservatives have never initiated measures to redress discrimination—although, to be fair, we must also recognize that they never attempted to repeal Labour's

Representation of Ethnic Minority Concerns

		Immigration and citizenship legislation	Racial discrimination legislation	Median annual net migration rate	Ethnic minority unemployment rate
1945–51	Labour governments under Clement Atlee	British Nationality Act 1948 created the status of Citizen of the United Kingdom and Colonies, giving free right to enter the UK to 800 million citizens (as well as right to vote, if resident in the UK)		Not available	Not available
1951–64	Conservative governments under Winston Churchill, Anthony Eden and Alec Douglas-Home	Commonwealth Immigrants Act 1962 – requiring migrants to have employment vouchers before entry		Not available	Not available
1964–70	Labour governments under Harold Wilson	Commonwealth Immigrants Act 1968 passed to control entry of refugee East African Asians	1965 Race Relations Act forbids discrimination on the "grounds of colour, race, or ethnic or national origins" in public places. 1968 Race Relations Act. Extends provisions to cover employment and housing	Not available	Not available
1970–1974	Conservative government under Edward Heath	Immigration Act 1971 replaces 1962 and 1968 Acts. Tightens controls but Asians expelled from Uganda in 1972 allowed to enter Britain.		Not available	Not available
1974–1979	Labour governments under Harold Wilson and Jim Callaghan		1976 Race Relations Act and formation of Commission for Racial Equality. Act introduces concept of indirect discrimination, and outlaws all forms of discrimination in employment	–19,000	4.5% compared with white 3.4%
1979–1997	Conservative governments under Margaret Thatcher and John Major	British Nationality Act 1981 created new categories of British nationality that would not have right of abode. British Nationality (Hong Kong) Act 1997 allowed citizenship to certain British nationals in Hong Kong (designed to deal with problems arising after Hong Kong returned to China).		+36,000	11.8% compared with white 7.8%

Figure 5.2. Discrimination and immigration legislation 1951–2010
Sources: annual net immigration rates—ONS; unemployment rates—pooled GHS and LFS, generously estimated for us by Yaojun Li

| 1997–2010 | Labour governments under Tony Blair and Gordon Brown | Immigration and Asylum Act 1999 reforms asylum process to ensure that most cases will be decided within six months and replaces welfare benefits for asylum seekers with vouchers.

Nationality, Immigration and Asylum Act 2002 extends power to detain asylum seekers, provides for accommodation centres, creates a 'white list' of safe countries - citizens of these countries who have their asylum applications rejected cannot remain in the UK while they mount an appeal.

Borders, Citizenship and Immigration Act 2009 designed to strengthen border controls and changes residence rules for acquisition of citizenship | 1998 Human Rights Act gives effect in UK law to the rights contained in the European Convention on Human Rights.

2000 Race Relations (Amendment) Act extends 1976 Act and places duty on public bodies to promote race equality

2006 Racial and Religious Hatred Act made it an offence to stir up hatred against persons on racial or religious grounds

2006 Equality Act creates unified Equality and Human Rights Commission and outlaws discrimination on the grounds of religion or belief

2010 Equality Act consolidates and extends previous legislation on race, sex, disability discrimination etc | +171,000 | 7.2% compared with white 4.0% |

Figure 5.2. Continued

measures. But equally we need to recognize that Labour administrations have often been Janus-faced, looking both ways at once, and attempting to restrict immigration while simultaneously trying to promote equality of opportunity.

It is useful to set this legislation in context. There was typically net outward migration under the Wilson/Callaghan administration of 1974–9 (no doubt reflecting Britain's economic difficulties after the 1974 oil shock), so the absence of any restrictive immigration legislation in this period is hardly surprising. In contrast, there were very high net inward rates of migration under New Labour (owing in part to EU enlargement), so the series of acts to make entry from outside the EU more difficult is understandable. The absence of any legislation to help minorities during Margaret Thatcher's and John Major's Conservative administrations is perhaps less understandable, since minorities had fared very badly during the two recessions of the early 1980s and 1990s, with marked disparities in unemployment rates. To this can be added the 1981 Brixton riots and Lord Scarman's report on them, which highlighted problems of racial disadvantage and inner-city decline, warning that urgent action was needed in order to prevent racial disadvantage becoming an 'endemic, ineradicable disease threatening the very survival of our society'. His recommendations were, however, largely ignored.

So on balance this is a picture of basically supportive, albeit sometimes Janus-faced, Labour administrations and more restrictive and/or neglectful Conservative ones. As we shall see, our respondents took much the same view as ours.

Symbolic representation: number of candidates and MPs

While our focus in this chapter is primarily on the extent to which ethnic minority interests and concerns are incorporated into the policy agendas of the main political parties, we propose to digress briefly and look at what is sometimes termed 'descriptive' or 'symbolic' representation, that is to say at the extent to which the parties select ethnic minority candidates for Parliament. We doubt whether there is any simple relationship between the proportion of a party's MPs who are from ethnic minorities and the party's commitment to addressing minority grievances,[5] but our respondents tended to agree that getting more black and Asian people into Parliament 'would improve things for ethnic minorities' (62 per cent agreement overall) and that 'Black and Asian MPs can better represent Black and Asian interests than White MPs can' (46 per cent agreement).[6] And it must be said that the figures shown in Table 5.1 do provide some unambiguous evidence of progress, especially on the Conservative side.

There were three Asian MPs in the late nineteenth and first half of the twentieth century—Dadabhai Naoroji (Liberal), Mancherjee Bhownagree (Conservative), and Shapurji Saklatvala (Communist), all three incidentally being Indian Parsis. But the post-war period saw no minority MPs until 1987, when Diane Abbott, Keith Vaz, Bernie Grant, and Paul Boateng were all elected as Labour MPs. Labour continued to dominate until 2005, when they returned thirteen out of the total of fifteen minority MPs. As we can

Table 5.1. Numbers of ethnic minority candidates and MPs 1979–2010

	Conservative		Labour		Liberal Democrat		Total	
	Candidates	MPs	Candidates	MPs	Candidates	MPs	Candidates	MPs
1979	2	0	1	0	2	0	5	0
1983	4	0	6	0	8	0	18	0
1987	6	0	14	4	9	0	29	4
1992	8	1	9	5	5	0	22	6
1997	9	0	13	9	17	0	39	9
2001	16	0	21	12	29	0	66	12
2005	41	2	32	13	40	0	113	15
2010	45	11	50	16	44	0	139	27

Sources: Rallings and Thrasher (2007), with authors' own figures for 2010

see from Table 5.1, however, Labour's long-standing advantage was much reduced in 2010 as the Conservatives selected a considerable number of minority candidates for winnable seats. Maria Sobolewska has argued that this was part of the wider Conservative efforts to soften the party's image and to appear more socially inclusive.[7]

By 2010, moreover, the overall number of candidates, although not of MPs, had become more proportional to the size of the ethnic minority electorate. Assuming that around 8 per cent of the electorate were from ethnic minorities, forty to fifty candidates for each party looks reasonable, since there are 650 seats up for election (649 if one excludes the Speaker, or 631 if one excludes the Northern Ireland seats as well). However, ethnic minority candidates tend to be selected for less winnable seats, and so the proportion of minority MPs (27 out of 650) was still well short of being representative, at only 4 per cent of the House of Commons.[8]

Moreover, while all three main parties now have roughly equal numbers of minority candidates, one might wonder whether Labour ought not to have a larger proportion, reflecting its much greater dependence on minority votes. Thus in 2010 we estimate that almost 15 per cent of Labour voters were from ethnic minorities, whereas only 3 per cent of Conservative voters and 5 per cent of Liberal Democrat voters were members of our five main minority groups. This suggests that, if MPs were to be representative of a party's voters, over 30 out of the 254 Labour MPs elected should have been from ethnic minorities, 10 out of the 305 Conservative MPs, and 3 out of the 57 Liberal Democrat MPs. On this reckoning, therefore, it was actually the Conservatives who were most in line with their voters in 2010.

However, candidates were disproportionately South Asian rather than black in both the Conservative (31 South Asian and 10 black candidates) and the Labour parties (36 South Asian and 7 black). Given that black voters are even more likely than South Asian voters to support Labour, the unrepresentativeness of Labour MPs becomes even more marked. (Among the Liberal Democrats the figures were 28 South Asian and 13 black candidates, which is closer to the population proportions of these two pan-ethnic groupings.)

It is doubtful, however, whether voters themselves are aware of these distinctions and of what the 'correct' figures should be. Also, given the high-profile character of some Labour MPs, such as Diane Abbott, David Lammy, and Keith Vaz, the public perception may well be that Labour has better ethnic minority representation. Certainly, the majority (57 per cent) of our respondents rightly believed that Labour had the most ethnic minority MPs, although a surprisingly large proportion (34 per cent) did not know whether this was true or not.

So once again the story is not entirely straightforward. Just as Labour historically had been the party most likely to enact legislation for the redress

Representation of Ethnic Minority Concerns

of racial discrimination, so it has been in recent decades the party most likely to return ethnic minority MPs. But in 2010, neither Labour's policy representation nor its symbolic representation was as distinctive as it had been in the past. In effect, there was a measure of convergence between the parties, with the Liberal Democrats ahead in terms of policy representation and the Conservatives ahead on symbolic representation.

Perceptions of party positions on the ethnic agenda

We now turn to our respondents' perceptions of party positions on race issues. To what extent is our interpretation of the parties' stated policies on race reflected in our respondents' perceptions? In particular, were they aware that the difference between Labour and Conservatives was perhaps reduced in 2010, as the similarity in the manifestos (and increase in Conservative MPs) seemed to suggest? Citizens' perceptions, not academics' assessments, are likely to be the key to understanding minorities' sympathies and loyalty to the parties. What did minorities themselves feel about their representation?

In Chapter 4, we reported our respondents' own positions on three central issues—cutting taxes versus increasing spending on health and social services, cutting crime versus protecting the rights of the accused, and making every effort to improve opportunities for blacks and Asians versus no need to do so. We also asked our respondents where they thought the three main parties stood on these central issues. In Table 5.2a, we report the proportions of our ethnic minority sample who perceived each party as taking a 'progressive' view (that is, left of centre) on each issue, and in Table 5.2b, we report the white British percentages.

While there are several interesting differences of detail, the broad outlines are pretty clear both white British and ethnic minorities were much more likely to think that Labour was more progressive on opportunities for minorities than was the Conservative Party. Both white British and ethnic minorities

Table 5.2a. Perceptions of party positions: ethnic minorities
% perceiving the party as adopting a 'progressive' position

	Labour Party	Conservative Party	Liberal Democrat	Labour/ Conservative gap
Spend rather than cut taxes	42	32	28	10
Protect rights of the accused	18	18	16	0
Improve opportunities for minorities	60	35	40	25

Notes: 'Don't know' responses included in the base but refusals excluded.
Source: EMBES 2010, weighted data. Minimum N = 2772

Table 5.2b. Perceptions of party positions: white British
% perceiving the party as adopting a 'progressive' position

	Labour Party	Conservative Party	Liberal Democrat	Labour/ Conservative gap
Spend rather than cut taxes	48	40	43	8
Protect rights of the accused	37	18	28	19
Improve opportunities for minorities	46	19	32	27

Notes: 'Don't know' responses included in the base but refusals excluded.
Source: BES 2010, weighted data. Minimum N = 2754

also shared the perception that, in 2010, the gap between the parties on equal opportunities for minorities was much larger than the gap on the other two issues of government spending and protecting the rights of the accused, with the Liberal Democrats generally perceived as coming somewhere in between the two main parties.[9]

We also asked ethnic minorities (but not the white British) the same question about party positions in our 1997 survey.[10] On equal opportunities for blacks and Asians, the gap between the perceived Labour and Conservative positions was slightly larger, at 30 percentage points compared with the 25 point gap in 2010. So essentially we have considerable continuity in perceived party differentials, just as there was considerable continuity on manifesto positions. In contrast, on the tax cuts versus spending question the gap was much larger in 1997—35 points compared with the meagre 8 point gap in 2010. This, of course, is in line with the convergence between the parties on the left/right dimension over the New Labour years, as the party moved to the centre ground of British politics in order to appeal to middle Britain.[11] So while our analysis of manifestos and MPs might suggest that the parties had converged on race in 2010, our respondents continued to see a major difference between the parties.

We also asked a second set of questions about the extent to which the main parties look after the interests of blacks and Asians, and of other groups. We asked:

> *Some people say that political parties look after the interests of some groups and are not so concerned about others. How well do you think that the Labour Party looks after the interests of the following groups? [The question was then repeated for the Conservative and Liberal Democrat parties.]*

This question is not specifically about policy positions, and answers to a large extent depend on what respondents define group interests to be. We cannot assume that black and Asian interests will necessarily be defined in terms of redress for racial discrimination. Answers are also quite likely to reflect respondents' perceptions of the parties' records in office rather than their manifesto promises. These questions might thus go some way to addressing the concern that parties' actual practice in government may not always match their rhetoric.

As with the previous questions on policy positions, there is considerable consensus between both majority and minorities (and between the different minorities) on which groups the parties look after and how big the differences are.[12] All groups alike see Labour as much more concerned than the Conservatives about the interests of the unemployed, the working class, trade unions, and blacks and Asians, and the Conservatives as much more concerned about the interests of the middle class and, especially, of big business. There are again some differences of detail, with the white British having a somewhat more polarized view of the parties than do ethnic minorities. Some of the

Table 5.3a. Perceptions that the parties look after group interests very or fairly well: ethnic minorities
Cell percentages

	Labour Party	Conservative Party	Liberal Democrats	Labour/Conservative Gap
Unemployed	73	23	36	50
Blacks and Asians	70	25	35	45
Working class	76	36	45	40
Women	73	40	39	33
Trade Unions	60	27	30	33
Pensioners	63	33	36	30
Middle class	71	54	44	17
Big business	60	65	40	−5

Notes: 'Don't know' responses included in the base but refusals excluded.
Sources: EMBES 2010, weighted mailback questionnaire. Minimum N = 908

Table 5.3b. Perceptions that the parties look after group interests very or fairly well: white British
Cell percentages

	Labour Party	Conservative Party	Labour/Conservative Gap
Trade Unions	69	27	42
Unemployed	75	41	34
Blacks and Asians	80	59	21
Working class	63	42	21
Women	63	59	4
Pensioners	43	42	1
Middle class	57	74	−17
Big business	55	80	−25

Notes: 'Don't know' responses included in the base but refusals excluded. Question not asked about Liberal Democrats in the main BES.
Source: BES 2010, weighted data. Minimum N = 1605

differences may well be down to the role of party identity in shaping people's perceptions of their 'own' party. But for our purposes the key point is that there is clear agreement, reflecting the party manifestos and the historical record when in office, that Labour is much more concerned with ethnic minority interests than are the Conservatives.

As with perceptions of the parties' policy positions, there is considerable continuity with 1997 in respect of black and Asian interests. In 1997, the gap perceived by minority respondents was 47 percentage points, compared with the 45 point gap that we see in 2010. Moreover, just as with the taxes versus spending question, there were changes between 1997 and 2010 in perceptions of how much the parties looked after the interests of the unemployed (a 66 point gap in 1997 falling to 50 in 2010), the working class (a 65 point gap in 1997 falling to 39 points in 2010), and trade unions (a 53 point gap falling to 33 points). So once again we see continuity on race but convergence on class.[13]

Overall, then, our analysis of the party manifestos and party record is closely in line with our respondents' perceptions. Our analysis suggested that historically the Conservatives and the Labour Party have differed substantially in what they promise for minorities, and minorities' perceptions are likewise that the parties differ substantially in how much they look after black and Asian interests. In both cases, the differences are long-standing and stable ones, unlike many other aspects of party policy and practice: whereas minorities have indeed recognized that the parties have converged on class issues, they continue to see a major difference between the parties on race—despite the increase in 2010 in the number of Conservative MPs, and the absence of any firm commitments from Labour to tackle racial discrimination.

Does this mean, then, that our original concern that minority interests might be excluded from the mainstream agenda was misplaced? This certainly looks to be the case if we take minorities' own perspective: 70 per cent of minorities felt that Labour looks after their interests very well or fairly well. This compares with the working class, of whom only 61 per cent felt that Labour looks after their interests well; similarly 69 per cent of trade unionists and 61 per cent of the unemployed (including people on other state benefits) felt that Labour did so. We must be cautious, since these perceptions may be coloured by party loyalties, but it would certainly be difficult to conclude that minorities feel more excluded from the mainstream agenda than do other disadvantaged groups. This is not what we or previous commentators had expected to find. On the other hand, it certainly remains true that minorities are under-represented in the number of MPs they have in the House of Commons; and on the Labour side, despite having the largest number of minority MPs, the mismatch between the profile of its supporters and the profile of its MPs is surprisingly large.

Table 5.4. Minority feelings about their representation
Percentage agreeing

Ethnic background	Own political party needed to deal with minorities' special problems	N	No party represents my views reasonably well	N
Indian	19	241	28	585
Pakistani	27	196	29	666
Bangladeshi	21	69	29	270
Black Caribbean	22	201	**43**	594
Black African	20	212	25	521
Mixed black/white	20	37	41	93
All ethnic minorities	22	956	30	2775

Notes: 'Don't know' responses are included in the base but refusals excluded. Chi^2 for 'own political party' = 6.6 (5 df), p > 0.05, for 'no party represents' = 38.9 (5 df), p < 0.001. Emboldened figure is significantly higher than expectation.
Sources: columns 1 and 2—EMBES 2010 mailback; columns 3 and 4—EMBES 2010 face to face; weighted data

As a final check, we have two further relevant questions which directly ask about representation. One asked

Would you say that any of the parties in Britain represents your views reasonably well?

And the second asked whether respondents agree that

Until ethnic minorities have their own political party/parties, their special problems will never be dealt with effectively

The pattern in Table 5.4 is more or less the obverse of the pattern in Table 5.3a. Whereas in Table 5.3a around 70 per cent of our ethnic minority respondents felt that Labour looks after black and Asian interests very or fairly well, we now find that around 30 per cent feel no party represents their views reasonably well, with 22 per cent feeling that minorities need their own political parties in order to deal effectively with their special problems. Once again, this is a similar pattern to the one we found in 1997.[14] And just as there were few differences between ethnic minorities in their perceptions of Labour, there are similarly few differences between minorities in their feelings of representation—with the one important exception of black Caribbeans.

It is of some interest to investigate what considerations led respondents to feel unrepresented or to feel that a separate minority party was required. Were these feelings linked to particular ethnic or religious concerns, such as the war in Afghanistan, asylum, detention without trial, or positive action to redress racial discrimination? Or are they linked to more general feelings of ethnic identity, as has been suggested in the US context, or to feelings of relative deprivation (a concept which we will be exploring in more detail in the next chapter)?

The details of these analyses are shown in Table 5.A1 in the appendix to this chapter. There are a number of intriguing differences between the analyses of these two different indicators of feelings of lack of representation. But perhaps more important are the similarities. It turns out that strength of ethnic identity, and feelings of what Garry Runciman has termed 'fraternal relative deprivation', are both significantly related to feelings that one is not represented. The sentiment that a separate party is needed in order to address minorities' special problems effectively is also quite strongly related to desires for affirmative action policies. Our interpretation is that it derives from the belief that existing parties do not effectively represent minorities' special problem of securing redress for discrimination.

In contrast, the sentiment that 'no party represents my views' appears to reflect a more general disillusionment with and disengagement from British politics, and is not specifically related to any particular issues. Instead, it is related to lack of political interest: the less interested one is, the more likely one is to feel that one is unrepresented by any of the parties. People who are more integrated into the ethnic community through informal bonding social capital are actually less likely to feel unrepresented, as are church members. We shall return to these indications of disillusionment in later chapters, especially in Chapter 10.

So these analyses provide a useful corrective to the more optimistic story of representation that our earlier analyses told. While most of our sample feel reasonably well represented by the main political parties, especially by Labour, there are a substantial number of dissenters who are perhaps disillusioned by the mainstream parties. Unfortunately, we cannot carry out similar analyses of the white British, since these questions were not asked in the main BES. But we suspect that similar dissenters are almost certainly present among the majority population too, some turning away from politics altogether, others turning to smaller parties such as Respect, the Greens, UKIP, or the Far Right. In other words, while the overall picture is a remarkably positive one, very similar to the positive picture from Chapter 3, important challenges remain for the main political parties, especially over key concerns of the black and Asian populations, such as redress for discrimination, inequality of opportunity, the war in Afghanistan, and detention without trial.

Representation—up to a point

Contrary to our initial expectations, we have found it difficult to sustain the thesis that minority concerns, particularly those over redress for racial discrimination, have been excluded from the mainstream political agenda. While there are undoubtedly tensions within the parties, worries over a white backlash, and a fair amount of backpedalling in 2010 (or at best a failure to advance), nevertheless there is a continuing theme of Labour manifestos proposing measures to combat discrimination, of Conservative manifestos proposing stricter controls on immigration (and failing to propose specific measures to combat discrimination), and the Liberal Democrat manifestos (and Labour in 2005) advocating a single Equality Commission and a single Equality Act to remedy gender, disability, and other forms of discrimination, as well as racial discrimination.

As we emphasized earlier in the chapter, we should not place too much reliance on party manifestos. The rhetoric of the manifestos may well not be reflected in a party's practice should it win the election and get into government, at which point parties may attempt to follow the kind of statecraft, preserving their own autonomy and passing tricky issues to quangos or local authorities, of the kind described by Jim Bulpitt. But it is striking that our ethnic minority respondents' perceptions of the parties' stances are very similar to our account of the parties' manifesto statements. Two thirds or more of our minority respondents perceive substantial differences between Conservative and Labour policy positions on equal opportunities for minorities, and perceive substantial differences in the extent to which the three main parties look after the interests of blacks and Asians. We cannot therefore conclude, as Zoltan Hajnal and Taeku Lee concluded in the US context, that there has been a failure of political parties to represent the minority electorate. In the British context, it appears that at least one of the parties, Labour, has engaged with the concerns of the ethnic minority electorate, partly perhaps as a result of struggles within the party from minority activists and their allies.[15] Labour also has a record of passing legislation aimed at redressing racial discrimination, although this legislation has not been as successful in practice as we might have wished.

Moreover, there are striking parallels with the sentiments of the working class, the unemployed, and trade unionists about the extent to which the main parties look after their interests. If ethnic minorities are not adequately represented, this is something they share with other disadvantaged groups in society.

To be sure, we must not overlook the finding that around a quarter of minorities feel that they are not represented. There is dissent, and it appears to be greater in the second generation. Not all minorities feel adequately represented, and some of their members are inclined either to more radical separatist solutions or to opt out. And we must not forget that there is also under-representation—especially on the Labour side—in terms of the number of MPs from ethnic minority backgrounds. Again, this is an under-representation that minorities share with other disadvantaged groups in British society.

Appendix: Supplementary tables

Table 5.A1. Regression analyses of representation (ordered logit for separate party, logistic for no party)
Regression coefficients

	Separate party	No party represents my views
Ethnic group (ref = Indian)		
Pakistani	0.04	0.30
Bangladeshi	−0.35	0.50
Black Caribbean	−0.21	0.01
Black African	**−0.60**	0.00
Mixed White/Black	−0.08	0.13
Demographics		
1.5 generation	0.04	**0.43**
2nd generation	0.33	**0.84**
Female	0.09	−0.06
Married	0.05	−0.12
Age (ln)	−0.26	**0.41**
Education	−0.03	−0.06
Middle class	0.05	**0.28**
Working class	0.20	0.20
Owner	−0.01	0.01
LA/HA tenant	0.20	−0.02
Christian	−0.22	**−0.49**
Muslim	−0.20	**−0.59**
Other (ref none)	−0.42	**−0.50**
Integration		
Fluency in English	0.08	**0.31**
Other language at home	0.14	0.01
Ethnic identity	**0.11**	**0.17**
Informal bonding capital	0.01	**−0.24**
Associational bonding capital	0.03	0.03
Associational bridging capital	0.08	0.08
Politicization		
Political interest	0.00	**−0.22**
Interest in origin country politics	0.06	0.05
Political knowledge	**−0.17**	0.04
Reads daily newspaper	0.03	−0.16
Uses ethnic media	0.09	−0.03
Attitudes to issues		
Asylum	−0.02	0.05
Afghanistan	0.02	0.04
Affirmative action	**0.25**	−0.08
Unemployment	0.00	−0.21
Discrimination		
Individual	−0.05	0.20
Fraternal relative deprivation	**0.13**	**0.16**
Non-white percentage	0.51	**0.63**
Index of Multiple Deprivation (ln)	−0.07	0.04
Constant	—	−5.06
(Pseudo) R^2	0.15	0.11
N	866	2530

Notes: Figures in bold are significant at the 0.05 level (estimated with robust standard errors). Detention without charge and Sharia do not have significant coefficients (not shown here because their inclusion reduces the N substantially).
Source: EMBES 2010, mailback for 'separate party', main questionnaire for 'no party'

	Conservative	Labour	Liberal Democrat
Oct 1974	In many urban areas, in particular, social harmony depends on the white and the coloured communities living and working together on equal terms and with equal opportunities. A Conservative government will pursue positive policies to promote good race relations. This means, among other things, seeking remedies for the problems faced by coloured people, especially adolescents, in employment and in education (for example, in the teaching of the English language). The Government must take the lead and set an example, but local authorities, employers, trade unionists and voluntary organisations have an important part to play. Better community relations, however, depend also on reassuring people that immigration is being kept down to the minimum. In the interests of good race relations, and for the benefit of immigrants already in Britain, as well as for the wider community, a Conservative government will follow a policy of strictly limited immigration.	A Labour Government set up the Law Commission machinery to overhaul the whole body of our laws, some of which are out of date and irrelevant. In the interests of a wider, more just and effective democracy we shall seek to: • give real equality to women; • strengthen legislation protecting minorities; • reform the law of nationality and citizenship;	
1979	The rights of all British citizens legally settled here are equal before the law whatever their race, colour or creed. And their opportunities ought to be equal too. The ethnic minorities have already made a valuable contribution to the life of our nation. But firm immigration control for the future is essential if we are to achieve good community relations. It will end persistent fears about levels of immigration and will remove from those settled, and in many cases born here, the label of 'immigrant'. …. We will encourage the improvement of language training in schools and factories and of training facilities for the young unemployed in the ethnic communities. But these measures will achieve little without the effective control of immigration. That is essential for racial harmony in Britain today.	Labour has already strengthened the legislation protecting minorities. The next Labour Government will continue to protect the community against discrimination and racialism. We will: Give a strong lead, by promoting equality of opportunities at work throughout the public sector. Help those whose first language is not English. Monitor all Government and local authority services to ensure that minorities are receiving fair treatment. Consider what measures may be necessary to clarify the role of the Public Order Act and to strengthen and widen the scope of the Race Relations Act.	Britain is a diverse and multicultural society and Liberals rejoice in its richness, which owes much to the peoples of many different ethnic origins and cultures who have chosen to live here. We defend their right to maintain and develop their own traditions. Minority groups must be allowed to practise and advocate their beliefs, provided this does not reduce the freedom of others. We will protect and defend the rights of minorities by: a comprehensive law out-lawing discrimination on grounds of race, sex or political belief with enforcement through a single Anti-Discrimination Board.
1983	We are utterly opposed to racial discrimination wherever it occurs, and we are determined to see that there is real equality of opportunity. The Conservative Party is, and always has been, strongly opposed to unfairness, harassment and persecution, whether it be inspired by racial, religious or ideological motives. To have good community relations, we have to maintain effective immigration control. Since 1979 , immigration for settlement has dropped sharply to the lowest level since control of immigration from the Commonwealth began more than twenty years ago. By passing the British Nationality Act, we have created a secure system of rights and a sound basis for control in the future; and we will continue to pursue policies which are strict but fair. We shall encourage greater opportunity for all those who live in our inner cities, including our ethnic minorities. Our small business schemes are helping to bring firms back into the city centres, and the Enterprise Zones we have set up are already bringing new life to some of the hardest-hit places in industrial Britain.	The next Labour government will lead a political offensive against racial disadvantage, discrimination and harassment, and we have set out our proposals in *Labour's Programme 1982*. To encourage equality and reduce discrimination, we will greatly expand funding to ethnic minority projects. We will also encourage local authorities, in selecting projects under the Urban Programme, to provide for greater ethnic minority participation. We will also: Stimulate a wide range of positive action programmes to ensure that ethnic minorities receive a fair deal - in employment, education, housing and social services: and encourage the keeping of ethnic records, in order to assess the needs of ethnic minorities and take steps to meet them. Launch a major public education initiative aimed at eliminating prejudice. Strengthen the existing Race Relations Act - in particular, to enable us to deal more effectively with racialist literature, speeches and marches, and to remove the exception for seamen recruited abroad. Appoint a senior minister to lead the offensive against racial inequality.	We shall create a *UK Commission of Human Rights* to help people bring proceedings under the Bill of Rights to secure compliance with its provisions. This will incorporate the existing Equal Opportunities Commission and Commission for Racial Equality and will deal with discrimination on grounds of sex or race; The Alliance believes that *sex and race equality* are fundamental to our society; they will be promoted by positive action in relation e.g. to public employment policies which will be monitored in central and local government. Anti-discrimination legislation will be actively enforced; *Nationality and immigration:* we believe the British Nationality Act 1981 to be offensive and discriminatory. We will revert to the simple concept that all those born in Britain are entitled to British Citizenship. There should be objective tests for citizenship and a right of appeal against refusal. Immigration controls will be applied without discrimination on grounds of sex, race or colour, and rules on dependents will be revised to promote family unity;

Figure 5.A1. Manifesto statements on immigration and redress for racial discrimination

Notes: In 1974 and 1979, we give the Liberal manifesto. In 1983 and 1987, the passages come from the SDP-Liberal Alliance (an electoral pact between the newly formed Social Democratic Party and the Liberal Party), and from 1992 onwards, from the Liberal Democrat Party.

1987	Immigration for settlement is now at its lowest level since control of Commonwealth immigration first began in 1962. Firm but fair immigration controls are essential for harmonious and improving community relations.

We will tighten the existing law to ensure that the control over settlement becomes even more effective. ….

We want to see members of the ethnic minorities assuming positions of leadership alongside their fellow citizens and accepting their full share of responsibility. Racial discrimination is an injustice and can have no place in a tolerant and civilised society. We are particularly concerned about racial attacks. They require effective and sympathetic attention from the police and we have ensured that increasingly they receive it.

Progress towards better community relations must be on a basis of equality. Reverse discrimination is itself an injustice and if it were to be introduced it would undermine the achievement and example of those who had risen on their merits.

Immigrant communities have already shown that it is possible to play an active and influential role in the mainstream of British life without losing one's distinctive cultural traditions. We also want to see all ethnic minorities participating fully in British culture. They will suffer permanent disadvantage if they remain in linguistic and cultural ghettos. | All the people of this country - whatever their race, colour or religion - must enjoy the full rights of citizenship.

Our policies for employment, education, housing, health care, local government and much else will clearly be of benefit to people of the ethnic minorities as they will be to the whole community.

In addition, Labour will take firm action to **promote racial equality**, to attack racial discrimination and to encourage contract compliance and other positive means of ensuring equity for all citizens. We will strengthen the law on public order to combat racial hatred and take firm action against the growing menace of racial attacks. We will make prosecution easier in order to encourage the reporting of offences.

Labour's policy of **firm and fair immigration control** will ensure that the law does not discriminate on the basis of race, colour or sex. | We will establish a Human Rights Commission, which will take over the work of the Equal Opportunities and Racial Equality Commissions, and counter all discrimination on grounds of race, sex, creed, class, disability or sexual orientation. The Commission would be able to initiate action in the courts.

The Alliance accepts the need for immigration controls and for clear legal definition of British nationality, but also accepts that the law in this area is fundamental to individual rights and should be fair to everyone regardless of race and regardless of whether they are men or women. There should be effective rights of appeal against refusal of citizenship and referral to an independent body in cases of deportation, and immigration procedures should be revised so as to promote family unity without significantly affecting immigration totals, which remain lower than rates of emigration from Britain.

We will combat discrimination against black people in housing and employment and take positive steps through such measures as contract compliance to secure equal opportunities for racial minorities, and we will devote more police resources to dealing with racial harassment. |
| 1992 | Racial harmony demands restraint on all sides, and a tolerant understanding of the legitimate views of others.

Everybody, regardless of ethnic background, religious or personal belief, has the right to go about his or her life free from the threat of intimidation and assault. We are determined that everyone lawfully settled in this country should enjoy the full range of opportunities in our society. That requires openness on the part of the majority and, on the part of the ethnic minorities themselves, a determination to participate fully in the life of the wider community.

The Home Office invests £129 million in grants designed to encourage those running public services to ensure that people from ethnic minorities can enjoy the full range of public services - such as health, housing and social services. We believe that these grants would be more effective if responsibility was transferred to those Departments which can make best use of the money.

Racial and sexual discrimination have no place in our society. We have given the police stronger powers to deal with racial hatred. We will continue to ensure that the full force of the law is used to deal with racial attacks.

We will transfer the education share of the Home Office's 'Section 11' money to the Department of Education, to focus help on those from ethnic minority backgrounds who need additional English language teaching. | Anti-discrimination law will be strengthened and we will consider as part of that law outlawing discrimination in employment on the grounds of age. | We will
• Fight discrimination by incorporating the European Convention on Human Rights into UK law and then extending it into a full UK Bill of Rights. This will reinforce existing protection in British courts against discrimination on the grounds of sex, race, age, disability, religion or sexual orientation. We will set up a Commission on Human Rights to assist individuals to take legal action in cases of discrimination or other breaches of the rights guaranteed in the Convention.

• Protect the rights of ethnic minorities. We will reinforce legislation to ensure equal opportunities for all, in housing, employment, education and training, especially in inner-city areas. PR will greatly increase the possibilities of participation in the political process. We will repeal the 1981 Nationality Act, reform immigration legislation to make it free from racial discrimination and restore the right of entry to British passport holders. We will push for the extension of EC race discrimination legislation and ensure that the rights of black and Asian British citizens are respected throughout the EC. We will encourage changes to the education system which place a positive value on a pluralist, diverse and multicultural society. |

Figure 5.A1. Continued

Representation of Ethnic Minority Concerns

1997	Tolerance, civility and respect have always been hallmarks of our nation. It is thanks to them that we have an excellent record in race relations. Everybody, regardless of colour or creed, has the right to go about his or her life free from the threat of intimidation. We are taking tough action to tackle harassment. Under proposals in the Protection from Harassment Act 1997, it will be a crime to behave in a way which causes someone else to be harassed. The maximum penalty will be 6 months in prison. Firm, but fair, immigration controls underpin good race relations. We will ensure that, while genuine asylum seekers are treated sympathetically, people do not abuse these provisions to avoid normal immigration controls.	We will seek to end unjustifiable discrimination wherever it exists. For example, we support comprehensive, enforceable civil rights for disabled people against discrimination in society or at work, developed in partnership with all interested parties.	Despite progress over recent years, members of ethnic minorities are too often denied equal opportunities and have to face racism and discrimination on a daily basis. Diversity, pluralism and a multicultural society are sources of strength for Britain. We will: Strengthen action against discrimination. We will create a new Human Rights Commission, combining the Commission for Racial Equality and the Equal Opportunities Commission. We will give statutory force to the Commission for Racial Equality's Code of Practice in employment, and ensure that Britain plays a leading role in strengthening anti-discrimination legislation throughout the European Union. Ensure equal opportunities for all. We will require local authorities and housing associations to ensure equal opportunities in housing allocation. We will expand access to mother-tongue teaching, for both adults and children, where this takes place through self-help and community groups. Free immigration laws from racial discrimination. We will ensure that immigration policy is non-discriminatory in its application. We will reform current immigration laws so as to enable genuine family reunions. We will restore benefit rights to asylum seekers and ensure that asylum claims are dealt with swiftly. Increase ethnic minorities' confidence in the police. We will encourage the recruitment of ethnic minorities into the police force and require action to be taken against discrimination within the force. We will tackle any discriminatory use of police powers, such as stop and search, and enhance police action to deal with racial attacks. We will encourage the use of aggravated sentencing for racially motivated crimes.
2001	Tolerance is one of Britain's historic virtues. A strong society is built on respect for all people - whatever their race, religion, gender or sexual orientation. "Britain is made up of many ethnic communities. Conservatives believe that we are richer and stronger for it."	We also need to ensure that the barriers to work are pulled down by delivering on our obligation to tackle discrimination so that all people can make the most of their talents. We will build on the Action Teams for Jobs model, which is targeting 40 of the most severely disadvantaged areas, to tackle the employment gap for ethnic minorities, and devote £45 million to provide stepping stones into employment for the hardest to employ.	We will combat discrimination on the grounds of race and in all its other forms. We will: Strengthen the fight against discrimination with an Equality Act. This will fight unfair discrimination on whatever grounds, including race, sex, religion, sexual orientation, disability, age or gender identity. A new Equality Commission will be able to investigate potential breaches of the Act and take action in its own name. The Commission will also have responsibility for Children's Rights, through a Children's Rights Commissioner. We will also create a separate Human Rights Commission to safeguard human rights. **Support recent European anti-discrimination legislation.** We will back measures under Article 13 of the Treaty of Amsterdam on anti-discrimination. This includes race and employment legislation and action.

(*Continued*)

				Immigrants are too often labelled as a problem for British society. Britain has benefited hugely from immigration, in the same way that many Britons who have emigrated have benefited from their experience. There are practical as well as humanitarian reasons for treating immigrants decently. The shortage of skilled workers in many fields means they have an important contribution to make to British society. We will: **Protect people fleeing from persecution** by dealing with asylum applications fairly and more quickly, which will also minimise any opportunities for anyone to exploit either the system or asylum seekers. We will introduce fair benefits for asylum seekers to replace the demeaning voucher system. We will review the failing dispersal system, end any unnecessary restrictions on asylum seekers undertaking voluntary work and review restrictions on paid work by asylum seekers in their first six months. Recognising pressures on host communities, we will ensure that local services are adequately compensated for the cost of supporting asylum seekers. We will work with other countries to ensure that responsibilities are sensibly shared, and to seek a system which discourages illegal trafficking in people. **Free immigration laws from discrimination.** We will ensure that immigration policy is non-discriminatory in its application. We will reform current immigration laws so that families are not divided. We will also regularly review immigration policy, separate from our asylum obligations, including an assessment of skills needs of the country in an increasingly global economy.
2005	Britain has benefited from immigration. We all gain from the social diversity, economic vibrancy and cultural richness that immigration brings. But if those benefits are to continue to flow we need to ensure that immigration is effectively managed, in the interests of all Britons, old and new. This Government has lost effective control of our borders. More than 150,000 people (net) come to Britain every year, a population the size of Peterborough. Labour see "no obvious upper limit to legal immigration".		We will implement the National Employment Panel's report on measures to promote employment and small business growth for ethnic and faith minorities. We will take forward the Strategy for Race Equality to ensure that we combat discrimination on the grounds of race and ethnicity across a range of services. The Equalities Review reporting to the Prime Minister in 2006 will make practical recommendations on the priorities for tackling disadvantage and promoting equality of opportunity for all groups. In the next Parliament we will establish a Commission on Equality and Human Rights to promote equality for all and, tackle discrimination, and introduce a Single Equality Act to modernise and simplify equality legislation. We need skilled workers. So we will establish a points system for those seeking to migrate here. More skills mean more points and more chance of being allowed to come here. We will ensure that only skilled workers are allowed to settle long-term in the UK, with English language tests for everyone who wants to stay permanently and an end to chain migration.	Liberal Democrats will pass an Equality Act which will tackle all forms of discrimination including on the grounds of sexual orientation. Public bodies will take a positive duty to tackle inequality and discrimination against lesbians, gay men, bisexuals and transgender people, in the same way as they are required to promote race equality and tackle race discrimination. The Act would not just apply to the public sector. It will end discrimination in the provision of goods and services. ...The current Labour Government blocked the Lib Dem Peer Anthony Lester's attempt to introduce this Act in the last Parliament. Liberal Democrats will bring together as the Equality and Human Rights Commission the various bodies involved in upholding and promoting the rights of different groups within society. This will have, amongst other responsibilities, a role in advising both the public and private sector on equality issues as well as being the guardian of equal rights.

Figure 5.A1. Continued

Representation of Ethnic Minority Concerns

		Where there has been evidence of abuse from particular countries, the immigration service will be able to ask for financial bonds to guarantee that migrants return home. We will continue to improve the quality and speed of immigration and asylum decisions. Appeal rights for non-family immigration cases will be removed and we will introduce civil penalties on employers of up to £2,000 for each illegal immigrant they employ.	
2010	By promoting equality and tackling discrimination, our policies, like recognising civil partnerships as well as marriage in the tax system and helping disabled people live independently, will give everybody the chance to play their part. This way, we can make Britain fairer and safer; a country where opportunity is more equal. Immigration has enriched our nation over the years and we want to attract the brightest and the best people who can make a real difference to our economic growth. But immigration today is too high and needs to be reduced. We do not need to attract people to do jobs that could be carried out by British citizens, given the right training and support. So we will take steps to take net migration back to the levels of the 1990s – tens of thousands a year, not hundreds of thousands. In addition, we will promote integration into British society, as we believe that everyone coming to this country must be ready to embrace our core values and become a part of their local community. So there will be an English language test for anyone coming here to get married.	New legislation and the Equality and Human Rights Commission will ensure that people are not held back at work because of their gender, age, disability, race and religious or sexual orientation. The new Equality Act will be enforced, promoting fairness across our society. The public duty to promote equality of opportunity is being extended. We will encourage employers to make greater use of pay reviews and equality checks to eliminate unfair pay gaps, including inequalities in pay between men and women. Our new Australian-style points based system is ensuring we get the migrants our economy needs, but no more. We will gradually tighten the criteria in line with the needs of the British economy and the values of British citizenship, and step up our action against illegal immigration. There will be no unskilled migration from outside the EU. Skilled jobs are now advertised here first for four weeks with more vacancies going to local workers, and public procurement will in future give priority to local people. The points-based system will be used to control migration with limits for high skilled workers and university students We know that migrants who are fluent in English are more likely to work and find it easier to integrate. So as well as making our English test harder, we will ensure it is taken by all applicants before they arrive.	Liberal Democrats want to build a society where everyone has the opportunity to get on in life. Most businesses do a great job of supporting their employees, but there is more to do to tackle discrimination on the grounds of gender, sexuality, age, race, religion or disability. We want to give employees fair opportunities to make the best use of their talents, and greater control over their working lives and conditions. Women are still paid less than men. It can be hard to juggle work and family life. People from Black, Asian and Minority Ethnic communities are still more likely to suffer discrimination. And there are far too many barriers to work for people with disabilities. **We will change this by:** • Requiring name-blind job application forms to reduce sex and race discrimination in employment, initially for every company with over 100 employees (p 30)

Notes: In 1974 and 1979 we give the Liberal manifesto. In 1983 and 1987 the passages come from the SDP-Liberal Alliance (an electoral pact between the newly-formed Social Democratic Party and the Liberal Party), and from 1992 onwards from the Liberal Democrat Party.

Notes

1. See Marian Fitzgerald (1987).
2. Quoted in *The Times*, 31 January 1978. For further discussion see Messina (1989), p.122.
3. For an entertaining discussion of this aphorism or theorem, see Robert K. Merton's piece on 'The Thomas theorem and the Matthew effect' (1995).
4. The Cabinet Office report was prepared by a team led by Shamit Saggar, who had also directed the 1997 ethnic minority election survey.
5. Saalfeld and Kyriakopolou (2011) provide a very interesting exploratory study of the behaviour of BME MPs in the House of Commons. They find that BME MPs have asked a large number of minority-related questions in the House, although in other respects (such as their votes in the Division Lobbies) their behaviour has not been especially distinctive.

6. See also Saggar (2000), chapter 8, for a more detailed examination of the questions in the 1997 survey.
7. See Sobolewska (2013).
8. James Hampshire (2012) however has estimated that ethnic minorities now constitute 11 per cent of the electorate and that there would need to be seventy-one BME MPs in order to reflect this proportion accurately. He is also provides a detailed account of the reasons for ethnic minority under-representation in Parliament.
9. The mean perceived difference between the Labour and Conservative positions on these three measures was +0.58 for tax cuts *versus* spending, -0.27 for reducing crime *versus* protecting rights of the accused and +1.34 for improving opportunities for blacks and Asians.
10. While the perception of the size of the gap between Labour and the Conservatives was very similar among white British and ethnic minority respondents, it is perhaps a little surprising that the minorities tended to place all three parties as being more progressive on equal opportunities than the white British did. We do not have an immediate explanation for this.
11. For a detailed examination of the rise of New Labour and its electoral strategy see Heath et al. (2001).
12. Since this question on perceptions of representation of group interests was asked in the mailback questionnaire, which had a poor response rate in EMBES, we have also checked results for the ethnic minority respondents in the main BES. The patterns were reassuringly similar. We also checked for differences between ethnic minorities in their perceptions of the parties, but in general differences were small and non-significant.
13. We need to be somewhat cautious in interpreting changes in perceptions, since perceptions can be coloured by respondents' party preferences. That is to say, respondents who view a particular party favourably are more likely to perceive that party as looking after the interests of all groups alike.
14. See Saggar (2000), table 8.2 for details of the patterns in 1997, although the 1997 question wording was slightly different.
15. For detailed discussions of minorities' historical engagement with the Labour party, see Fitzgerald (1987) and Shukra (1998).

6

Partisanship

In this chapter we move on to consider minorities' patterns of allegiance to the political parties. To what extent do minorities' perceptions of the parties which we described in Chapter 5 translate into support and allegiance? Political scientists have traditionally made a distinction between electors' more enduring psychological attachments to particular parties (termed 'party identification') and their actual vote choice at a particular election, which may be influenced by a variety of contingent short-term factors.[1] We shall follow this distinction, and in this chapter will focus on psychological attachments to the parties, turning to vote choice in Chapter 8. Hence, in this chapter we ignore short-term influences on party support, such as Gordon Brown's leadership of the party and Labour's performance in dealing with the economy, and focus on longer-term influences.

There are two important but clearly different questions about minority attachment to the established political parties. The first, about which we know very little in Britain, asks whether minorities are more or less likely than the majority group to feel attached to any party at all. US research by Zoltan Hajnal and Taeku Lee shows that recent migrant groups such as Latinos and Asian-Americans have much lower levels of attachment to either of the main US parties than do white Americans. They attribute this in part to low levels of political interest and knowledge on the part of minorities, but more importantly to the failure of US political parties to engage with the concerns of the minority electorate. In other words, exclusion of minority concerns from the political agendas of mainstream parties leads to lack of psychological attachment to those parties. Does the same hold true in Britain? If Zoltan Hajnal and Taeku Lee's argument, and our findings in Chapter 5, are correct, we would expect that minorities in Britain would actually have quite high levels of party attachment, since most feel that their interests actually are being represented, notably by Labour. Thus our findings at the conclusion of Chapter 5 about perceptions of representation ought to be mirrored by findings in this chapter on patterns of party identification.

The second question concerns the particular party to which minorities are attached. On this we have considerable evidence from the past that minorities in Britain have historically shown very high levels of support for the Labour Party—roughly double the level of support found among white British voters—and as we shall see later in this chapter, this remained true in 2010. Furthermore, when analysing the 1997 results, Shamit Saggar and Anthony Heath argued that 'The evidence presented... shows that there was little that was new in minority voting patterns in 1997. A bold line of continuity ran through these patterns. Labour maintained its virtual monopoly of the allegiances of this group of the electorate' (1999, p. 121). We expect this bold line of continuity to remain true in 2010 given Labour's big lead over the other parties in looking after black and Asian interests.

It will hardly be surprising, then, if we find that ethnic minorities tend to support the Labour Party rather than either of the other main parties. There are, however, two specific puzzles that we shall attempt to explore in this chapter: why is Labour partisanship so much more prevalent among minorities than it is among the working class or trade unionists? And, why are some minorities more supportive of Labour than others?

The first puzzle is essentially about the magnitude of minority support for Labour, rather than its existence. If minorities supported Labour to the same extent as the working class supports Labour, there would be nothing to get excited about. After all, according to Chapter 5, the perception that Labour is more supportive than the Conservatives of working-class interests is similar to the perception that Labour is more supportive than the Conservatives regarding black and Asian interests. And yet, as we shall see, the magnitude of black and Asian support for Labour far exceeds that of the working class. Why are ethnic minorities so much *more* supportive of Labour than the other groups that Labour is perceived to represent?

The second puzzle is about the differences between minorities in their support for Labour. There have been suggestions in the past that blacks were generally even more supportive of Labour than were South Asians. Thus Shamit Saggar and Anthony Heath noted some variation between ethnic minorities in 1997, with voters of black Caribbean and black African background having higher rates of support for Labour than did the various South Asian groups. Indians in particular had the highest level of support for the Conservatives of any of the ethnic minorities, although still falling far short of the support among white British voters. As Shamit Saggar has suggested, the more entrepreneurial members of some successful minorities, such as Indians, might be starting to find that elements of Conservative policy now hold more attractions for them.[2] More recently, at the 2005 general election, voters of Pakistani and Bangladeshi background appeared to be less inclined to support Labour than they had been previously, and more inclined towards the Liberal

Democrats, almost certainly because of their opposition to Labour's wars in Iraq and Afghanistan.[3] In 2010, these differences between minorities were once again evident, as we shall shortly see. Explaining these differences is clearly of interest in its own right. These differences might also give us some pointers as to why minorities are so supportive of Labour.

Theoretical approaches

Broadly speaking, there are a range of approaches to explaining partisanship. The first kind of approach, which has been dominant in recent political science attempts to understand party preferences generally, is essentially an individualistic one, focusing on the particular interests and ideological positions of the individuals within the electorate. This is the kind of approach developed by the economist Anthony Downs, who saw electors as rational egoists (aiming to maximize their own individual welfare), analogous to consumers in the marketplace choosing between different products. On this account, voters will prefer the party which they believe to be most likely to implement policies advancing their own individual welfare. Downs assumes that this will be the party whose position on the central issues came closest to the individual voter's own policy preferences, in other words the party which provides the best fit to the voter's preferences.[4] So we could try to explain minority support for the Labour Party by the extent of fit between the parties' and minorities' positions on the issues to which minorities give highest priority. Given the evidence in Chapters 4 and 5, minority support for Labour would be explained by Labour's support for policies to redress discrimination, the Conservatives' silence on this, and their opposition to immigration; and so on.

While it may be a useful starting point, we do not really expect this kind of explanation to succeed in fully explaining the very high level of minority support for Labour in 2010, given the apparent lack of fit between Labour's positions on issues such as detention without trial, the war in Afghanistan, and the vagueness of their promises on redress of discrimination (as well as the puzzling lack of fit on tax cuts and government spending). In addition, as we noted earlier, it is hard to see why the fit with respect to policy positions would be any greater for minorities than it is for the working class or trade unionists.

A somewhat more promising variant of Downs' approach, however, emphasizes not just the fit with respect to current policy positions but instead the whole history of the citizen's experience of the party. Mo Fiorina once famously wrote that

> Citizens are not fools. Having often observed political equivocation, if not outright lying, should they listen carefully to campaign promises?... In order to ascertain whether the incumbents have performed poorly or well, citizens need only calculate the changes in their own welfare. (Fiorina 1981, p. 5)

His argument was that voters judge what parties have actually done for them in the past, updating their tallies as they go along, giving more weight to recent experiences but still attaching some importance to past experiences. This is still an instrumental and egocentric view of voters, in the same spirit as Downs' work, but offering a more promising account of minority support for Labour. Given the long history of Labour legislation to protect minorities' interests, and the history of Conservative opposition to immigration and failure to tackle discrimination, this offers a promising way forward if current policy positions are an insufficient explanation.

A third approach moves away from an egocentric approach towards what political scientists have termed a sociotropic approach to understanding party support. For example, some research on the electorate as a whole has found that it is not the voter's individual experience of their personal finances, economic situation, or unemployment under the previous government which is most strongly associated with their party preferences. Instead, it is their perceptions of how well a party has looked after the overall finances of the society and the overall unemployment rate that is most crucial.[5] This kind of sociotropic or collectivist thinking has been suggested as being particularly important for minorities.[6] The idea has been developed most forcefully by Michael Dawson to account for African-American support for the Democratic Party in the USA.[7] Dawson developed the notion of a black utility heuristic: 'It is much easier for an individual African American to determine if a given government policy is good or bad for the racial group—an evaluation often provided by black political and economic elites—than to determine the ramifications of a given policy for oneself as an individual' (Dawson 1994, p. 57). In other words, whatever their individual situations, all African-Americans are powerfully affected by the racism and prejudice that characterizes US life, and hence they experience what Michael Dawson terms linked fate. The fact of being black is thus the major determinant of an African-American's life chances, and hence it is individually rational to vote on the basis of black group interest.

Whether race is actually the dominant factor in the lives of blacks and Asians in Britain could be debated. Certainly, our evidence in Chapter 2 showed that some Asian groups have achieved occupational levels similar to those of the white British, and educational levels that surpass those of their white contemporaries. However, the research that Anthony Heath and others have carried out on the labour market experiences of ethnic minorities does show that all minority groups in Britain experience some degree of ethnic penalty, and in that sense minorities do in practice experience a degree of linked fate.[8] That is to say, even the most successful minorities do not obtain income or occupation that is fully commensurate with their qualifications and experience. There is thus a shared component, arising we believe from racism and discrimination, which affects ethnic minorities in the British labour market whatever their individual positions. This shared ethnic penalty provides a basis for a shared political agenda. In the terminology of Garry Runciman's relative deprivation theory, there might therefore be a shared feeling of 'fraternalistic relative deprivation'.[9] Relative deprivation is a somewhat different concept from linked fate: its focus is on whether people are deprived relative to what they feel they ought to be getting. It thus has a moral or normative connotation. It is likely to have particular resonance in a country like Britain where the principle of equality of opportunity is enshrined in public discourse, but where minorities do not have the same opportunities in the labour market as their white British peers.[10] Relative deprivation is in essence a concept focusing on people's perceptions of social injustice— perceptions that they are not receiving the benefits or opportunities to which they are morally entitled.

Garry Runciman's use of the adjective 'fraternalistic', somewhat like Michael Dawson's adjective 'linked', emphasizes that these feelings of deprivation are shared among members of the group. It thus brings into focus collective experiences, and goes beyond the purely individualistic accounting of economists like Antony Downs. This kind of approach used to be applied to understanding working-class support for Labour in Britain. In Butler and Stokes' classic study of the British voter, they argued that some working-class voters supported Labour simply because it was seen to be 'the party of the working class', and that such voters were following a psychological bond between themselves and their class community. As Butler and Stokes argued:

> The individual's response to the political norms of his class milieu can also help to keep the classes politically distinct without perceptions of class interest necessarily being involved. However important the perception of interests may have been in creating the political divergence of classes in the first place or in sustaining them in the longer run, anything so pervasive as the norm of Labour voting in the working class... is likely to be accepted by many members of the class simply because it is there... it would be absurd to see perceived class interests in all class voting as it would be to infer such interests from class differences in the time of dinner or the rituals of mourning. (Butler and Stokes 1969, pp. 87–8)

Butler and Stokes, then, suggest that many people follow group norms of support for a particular party without necessarily having any clearly articulated perceptions of class interests or specific class-based policy preferences. They would not have been at all surprised at the failure of statistical models that try to predict class voting on the basis of individual attitudes towards party policies.[11] Similarly, we should not perhaps be surprised if individualistic explanations of ethnic minority support for Labour fail, given the evidence of strong group solidarity among ethnic communities.

While this approach to understanding class voting in Britain has fallen from favour, largely because class communities and their associated normative cultures have largely disappeared as traditional heavy industries and mining have declined, it may still have some considerable applicability to understanding ethnic minority support for Labour. As we saw in Chapter 2, ethnic minorities in Britain typically exhibit high levels of ethnic solidarity, and indeed they show much higher levels of solidarity than does the contemporary working class (Heath et al. 2008).

The key point about these group-based explanations is that one's party allegiance is expected to be linked to one's social milieu—to the norms and sentiments of the people one mixes with and respects—as well as to one's own individual interests or past experiences. In other words, it is a theory of social influence. This approach further suggests that people who are more firmly embedded socially within the group, or who feel a stronger sense of solidarity with the group, will be more likely to follow group norms and sentiments, while those who are more peripheral to the ethnic group (or more acculturated into the ways of life of the majority group) will be less likely to follow the norms of the minority group.[12]

A closely related expectation is that the stronger the attachment to the group the weaker will be the influence of the other cross-cutting interests that the citizen might recognize. Thus, if there is a fraternal sense of relative deprivation, then we should see the same political allegiances of minority group members irrespective of what side of the class divide they are located in.[13] Ethnicity (at least for people who are embedded in the minority culture and community) should trump class.

Our central questions, therefore, in this chapter are how minorities differed in 2010 in their level and direction of party allegiance, and how any such differences can be explained. In particular, do we find any evidence of group processes keeping minority patterns of party allegiance distinct from those of the majority? We begin with a descriptive account of patterns of ethnic minority party allegiance in 2010. We then turn to the egocentric approach, focussing on individual characteristics and experiences. Next we add our measures of fraternalistic relative deprivation before finally investigating group processes.

Patterns of partisanship

We begin by showing in Table 6.1 the distribution of party identification or partisanship, and of non-partisanship, among different segments of the white British electorate and among our ethnic minority groups.

The first important point is that only one fifth of ethnic minorities overall are non-partisans, a level that is almost identical to the figure for white British. The proportion who do not identify with any party is slightly higher among people of Bangladeshi origin and those of mixed black/white heritage (who tend to be younger). However, in general the differences are relatively small. There is no sign here of the kind of large-scale failure to identify with any party that Zoltan Hajnal and Taeku Lee found for Latinos and Asian-Americans in the USA.[14] On this criterion, therefore, all the main British ethnic minorities exhibit rather high levels of partisanship. This is, of course, consistent with the story that we told in Chapter 5, where we found that most minority members felt that their views were represented reasonably well, and most disagreed that a separate minority political party was needed in order to deal with their special problems effectively.[15] We suspect that this may be, as we argued in Chapter 5, because of the success of Labour in establishing itself as 'the' party that represents minority concerns, just as it used to be 'the' party of the working class, before the advent of New Labour and its move to the centre ground.

The second observation is that ethnic minority allegiance to the Labour Party is double that found among white British (61 per cent versus 28 per cent), and

Table 6.1. Partisanship by ethnic group, 2010
Row percentages

	None	Labour	Conservative	Liberal Democrat	Other	N
White British	22	28	31	13	6	2726
TU members	21	37	22	16	5	496
Working class	22	33	27	12	6	945
Tenants in social housing	26	40	14	11	9	365
Ethnic minorities						
Indian	18	54	17	10	1	571
	Hindus 18	Hindus **42**	Hindus 27	Hindus 12	Hindus 1	
	Sikhs 10	Sikhs **71**	Sikhs 14	Sikhs 4	Sikhs 1	
Pakistani	18	53	9	16	4	662
Bangladeshi	24	59	8	8	1	267
Black Caribbean	18	69	7	6	1	582
Black African	17	73	4	6	1	515
Mixed black/white	24	57	8	10	1	92
All ethnic minorities	19	61	9	10	1	2735

Notes: Refusals are excluded but 'don't know' responses are included in the category 'none'. Within ethnic groups other than Indian, religious differences were small and non-significant. Figures in bold are those which are significantly higher than the white British average. Chi^2 = 867 (24 df), p < 0.001.
Sources: BES 2010, EMBES 2010, weighted percentages

is also very substantially higher (by 20 percentage points or more) than Labour allegiance in the white working class (33 per cent), among trade unionists (37 per cent), or among tenants in social housing (40 per cent). This is a quite different pattern from Table 5.3, which showed small differences in the extent to which minorities, the working class and trade unionists perceived Labour to be looking after their interests.

There is also considerable variation between minority groups. Thus, Labour allegiance is lowest among Indian Hindus (42 per cent) and highest among Indian Sikhs (71 per cent), black Africans (73 per cent), and black Caribbeans (69 per cent). People of Pakistani background also show a higher level of support for the Liberal Democrats (16 per cent) than do most other groups, while Indian Hindus show relatively high levels of support for the Conservatives, closer to those of white British (27 per cent compared with the white British 31 per cent). So there is quite considerable variation between the different groups for us to explain. We turn to this in the next section.

Socio-economic differences, policy differences and relative deprivation

One line of argument is that some of the differences in partisanship between minorities, and between minorities and the majority, can be explained by their socio-economic characteristics, such as their social class positions. After all, as Shamit Saggar noted, Indians have been economically the most successful minority. Surely it is not entirely a coincidence that they also show the highest level of support for the Conservatives. However, past British research has suggested that this is at best a very small part of the story, although with the growing economic success of the Indian community it is certainly worth revisiting.[16] In addition to social class, it is worth looking at other indicators of socio-economic position of the kind that are typically associated with Labour support in Britain, such as housing tenure (especially social housing) and trade union membership.

Table 6.2 shows the size of the net differences in Labour partisanship within our main groups. For example, the figure of 12 points in the top left cell of the table shows that, among the white British, Labour support was 12 points lower in the middle class than it was in the working class, other things being equal. (These net differences have been estimated from models that control simultaneously for all three sources of cleavage.)

Among the white British we find that belonging to the working class, to a trade union, and living in social housing are significantly associated with Labour partisanship. (There are also some small differences according to educational level and main source of income.) In other words, the white

Partisanship

Table 6.2. Socio-economic differences in Labour partisanship within the main ethnic minorities and majority group
Difference in probability (percentage point gap)

	White British	Indian	Pakistani	Bangladeshi	Black Caribbean	Black African	All ethnic minorities
Middle class/working class	−12	−13	−17	+12	0	−8	**−8**
Non-member/TU member	−12	−15	+7	+16	−1	−5	**−7**
Owners/renters in social housing	−11	0	−2	−5	+5	+1	−4
N	2719	562	654	260	572	500	2686

Notes: Base includes respondents with no party identification. The net differences in probability are the average marginal effects for the relevant contrasts. Significant differences at the 5% level are emboldened. A positive sign indicates that the first-named group exhibits greater Labour partisanship than the second-named group, and vice versa.
Sources: BES 2010, EMBES 2010, unweighted

British electorate divides, albeit not very strongly, along socio-economic lines in its support for Labour. Given the evidence shown in Chapter 5 that Labour is widely seen to look after the interests of the working class and of trade union members, this is not at all surprising.

More interestingly, we find that these socio-economic cleavages are much less strong within the black (and Bangladeshi) minority groups than they are within the majority population. It is only really among the group of Indian heritage that we find significant differentiation along socio-economic lines more or less parallel to the stratification within the white British population.[17] It is striking that these socio-economic cleavages are virtually non-existent among the two black groups, where none of the differences reach statistical significance. For these groups it is clear that ethnicity does indeed trump social class.[18]

Given the small socio-economic differences shown in Table 6.2 within most minorities, it is hardly surprising that socio-economic situation fails to explain either the differences between minorities in their level of Labour allegiance, or the differences between minorities and the majority group (see Table 6.A2 in the appendix for details).[19] Moreover, even though the Indians are the group who come closest to the white British both in their levels of support for the Conservatives and in the way that they are internally stratified by socio-economic position, they nonetheless remain much more supportive of Labour than are their white British peers in similar class positions.

A slightly more promising approach focuses on the kind of policy preferences and agendas identified in Chapter 4, and more specifically the extent of fit between the individual's own preferences and her perception of party positions. This is essentially in the spirit of Antony Downs' account, where citizens are expected to support the party whose ideological position comes closest to their own. We can include the same range of policy issues that we discussed in Chapter 4, that is tax cuts versus government spending, cutting

Table 6.3. Attitudinal differences in Labour partisanship within the main ethnic minorities and majority group
Difference in probability (percentage point gap)

	White British	Indian	Pakistani	Bangladeshi	Caribbean	African	All minorities
Tax cuts vs spending	+13	+11	+3	−10	0	+8	+5
Importance of unemployment	+13	+7	+4	−1	+3	+7	+3
Civil liberties	+2	−10	−1	0	**−18**	−10	**−10**
Afghanistan	−3	+3	−6	**−15**	−4	**−14**	**−8**
Asylum-seekers	+3	+3	+2	−10	**+16**	+3	**+9**
Equal opportunities	+6	0	−1	**+10**	−2	**+12**	**+4**
Affirmative action	0	+7	+8	+2	+1	+6	**+6**
N	2707	552	640	250	560	490	2626

Notes: Base includes respondents with no party identification. The changes in probability are the differences in average marginal effects (at the 10th and 90th percentiles for continuous and ordered variables). Significant differences at the 5% level are emboldened.
Sources: BES 2010, EMBES 2010, unweighted

crime versus protecting the rights of the accused, unemployment, asylum, Afghanistan, affirmative action, and equal opportunities.[20]

Table 6.3 is in essence analogous to Table 6.2. It shows how much difference positions on these seven issues make to the probability of supporting Labour. Thus, the figure of 13 points in the top left-hand cell of the table shows that, among white Britons, the probability of supporting Labour was thirteen points higher if a citizen took a very progressive rather than a very regressive position on the tax cuts versus spending scale.

Table 6.3 is in many ways parallel to Table 6.2 on the socio-economic cleavages. Thus, among the white British, our two measures that belong to the classic left/right ideological dimension—tax cuts versus spending, and unemployment—are strongly and significantly related to Labour allegiance. But these left/right measures are not nearly so important among minorities. As with the socio-economic differences, people of Indian heritage are the ones who come closest to the white British profile. Among the other groups, the items belonging to the left/right dimension are never significant, and it is the other items, such as asylum, the war in Afghanistan, and equal opportunities, which differentiate between who does and who does not support Labour. The results are somewhat patchy, reflecting the small sample sizes, but in general ethnic minorities' ideological reasons for supporting Labour appear to be rather different from white British ones.[21]

Furthermore, exactly as with the socio-economic cleavages, the ideological dimensions covered in Table 6.3 do not go very far towards explaining the huge gap between majority and minority support for Labour, nor indeed for most of the differences between ethnic minorities. Detailed statistical analysis (see Table 6.A3) shows that inclusion of these issues still leaves huge differences in support for Labour to be explained. So we need to continue our search.

One possibility is that minorities follow a kind of black heuristic, of the kind suggested by Michael Dawson in his analysis of African-American political preferences. Thus, rather than supporting Labour because of its advocacy of specific issues such as government spending, minorities, or black groups in particular, might be guided by a fraternal sense of relative deprivation. Given that Labour has historically been the only party to implement legislation to redress the discrimination and unequal opportunities which minorities experience, a fraternal sense of relative deprivation is quite likely to be associated with support for Labour.

We asked several relevant questions, asking respondents whether they agreed for example that:

There is often a big gap between what people from my ethnic group expect out of life and what we actually get.

Non-white people don't have the same opportunities and chances in life as white people, as they are held back by prejudice and discrimination

We can think of these as measures of ethnic relative deprivation. They essentially measure the extent to which the ethnic group as a whole, rather than the individual member in particular, is held back by prejudice and discrimination. We constructed a combined scale of relative deprivation, using these two items together with two additional ones (see Appendix 2 for details of the scale). The pattern is shown in Table 6.4.

Here we see a consistent pattern for the black groups to feel strongly that their groups are held back by prejudice and discrimination. There is a clear divide between the South Asian and the black groups, with the South Asians typically falling below the overall ethnic minority mean and the black groups

Table 6.4. Ethnic group feelings of fraternal relative deprivation
Percentages agreeing/score

Ethnic background	Big gap between what my ethnic group expect and get	Non-whites held back by prejudice	Overall relative deprivation score	N
Indian	44	40	10.9	586
Pakistani	51	38	11.0	666
Bangladeshi	49	41	11.2	269
Black Caribbean	**67**	**58**	**12.8**	593
Black African	**63**	**53**	11.9	522
Mixed black/white	**69**	53	12.1	93
All minorities	53	45	11.4	2797

Notes: Refusals are excluded. Figures in bold are those which are significantly higher than the ethnic minority average. Chi^2 for 'big gap' = 88.6 (5 df), $p < 0.001$; Chi^2 for 'held back' = 64.4(5 df), $p < 0.001$.
Source: EMBES 2010, weighted

being significantly above. It should also be noted that this is entirely consistent with the objective evidence on ethno-religious penalties, reported in Chapter 2. These black/South Asian differences therefore suggest that these concerns do offer a potential for explaining the group differences in support for Labour. As we saw in Chapter 5, all groups alike see Labour as the party most likely to attempt to secure equal opportunities for minorities, but the black groups are typically considerably more concerned about this issue, and they also typically experience larger ethnic penalties in the labour market.

We therefore add our overall measure of relative deprivation to the analysis of Labour partisanship in Table 6.3, along with a measure of individual experiences of discrimination, in order to compare the importance of individual and collective experiences and concerns. As we can see, individual experience of discrimination has no significant association with Labour partisanship, while fraternal relative deprivation does have quite a strong relationship, confirming that the individualist/collectivist distinction is a valuable one for understanding minority political allegiance. However, if we include these new measures of individual and fraternal relative deprivation into a standard regression analysis of support for Labour, they make very little headway in explaining the variation between ethnic groups.

This must seem very surprising, given the significant differences between minorities shown in Table 6.4. One possibility for this disappointing finding is that our statistical models are themselves taking an individualistic approach to understanding party support. The key point is that an individualistic model looks for characteristics that predict why some individuals rather than others support a particular party; it then essentially estimates whether the prevalence of these characteristics in some groups can explain why the group as a whole is, in our case, more pro-Labour. In other words, it tests solely for compositional differences between groups. However, it is entirely possible that feelings of relative deprivation do not explain individual propensities to support Labour *within* a group but do explain variations *between* groups. These variations could, for example, be due to the operation of collective processes, such as the spread of shared norms and sentiments within the group. We shall look at this later in the chapter, but first we review the evidence on the idea of party identification as a running tally of experiences under Labour and Conservative governments.

Partisanship as a running tally of past experiences

As we described in the introduction, Mo Fiorina has developed a cogent theory of party identification as a running tally of retrospective evaluations of what life was like under different governments. This looks to have considerable

Partisanship

Table 6.5. Support for Labour in 2010 by year of arrival (first generation) and year of entry to the electorate (one point five and second generations)
Cell percentages

First generation (adult migrants)		1.5 and 2nd generation	
Year of arrival in Britain	% Labour	Year of entry to the electorate	% Labour
1997–2010 (N = 657)	58	1997–2010 (N = 647)	58
1979–96 (N = 267)	66	1979–96 (N = 594)	60
1974–8 (N = 59)	64	1974–8 (N = 112)	57
1970–3 (N = 45)	67	1970–3 (N = 40)	53
1964–9 (N = 64)	66	1964–9 (N = 27)	**78**
1951–63 (N = 99)	**74**		–

Notes: Base includes non-partisans. Figures significantly higher or lower than expectation are emboldened.
Chi^2 for the first generation = 12.9 (5 df), $p < 0.05$; Chi^2 for the 1.5/2nd generation = 5.7 (4 df), $p > 0.05$.
Source: EMBES 2010, weighted

potential for explaining the patterns of Labour identification. It seems very likely that it is Labour's past history of support for minority concerns rather than its modest and unpublicized current proposals which accounts for minorities' extraordinarily high levels of support for Labour.

A thorough test of the running tally approach would require a panel study which tracked the same people, and their evaluations of how well different governments had dealt with their concerns over time. This, unfortunately, is not open to us. However, one possible strategy is to compare levels and strength of Labour support among cohorts who have had more or less experience of what life was like under Labour and Conservative governments in Britain. Are ethnic minority citizens who have had more experience of Labour and Conservative administrations more pro-Labour than those who have only recently arrived in Britain, or only recently entered the electorate?

To address this question, we distinguish periods of entry according to the political complexion of the government in office, just in case there were particular formative periods, such as entering the British electorate during the 1974–9 Labour government, which passed the landmark 1976 Race Relations Act. Table 6.5 shows the levels of Labour support according to period of arrival for the adult migrants, and according to period of entry into the electorate for the one point five and later generations. We calculate Labour partisanship in the same way as in Table 6.1 above, so that the figures are directly comparable (that is, non-partisans are included in the base).

We find some support for Mo Fiorina's theory, with Labour partisanship being highest among the people who have been in the electorate for the longest time and have had most experience of life in Britain under different governments. For the adult migrants, Labour allegiance is significantly lower among those who arrived more recently, during the New Labour period of office.[22]

However, the most striking phenomenon is that even among the most recent, post-1997 entrants Labour support is far higher than anything we saw among the white British in Table 6.2. At 58 per cent, recent minority entrants into the electorate are much more supportive of Labour than are the white British working class, trade unionists, or tenants in social housing, whose support varies between 33 per cent and 40 per cent. This suggests that more must be going on than simply experience of life in Britain: minorities and recent immigrants who have only limited experience of what life has been like under Labour administrations still overwhelmingly give Labour their support.[23] We still have work to do.

Group identity and shared interests

While many new entrants will have had little direct experience themselves of what life has been like under Labour (or the Conservatives), they will in many cases be joining ethnic communities where there will be strong group traditions of Labour support. As Carole Uhlaner and Chris Garcia have suggested in the US context, since the conventional channel of parental socialization into party allegiance is largely missing among immigrants, contact with co-ethnics helps Latinos find the 'right' party.[24] Our idea is essentially the same: ethnic communities provide the cues to enable minorities to find the 'right' party.

Our key hypothesis, then, is that group norms and sentiments, rather than individual choices, can help to explain why minorities have levels of Labour allegiance that are so much higher than members of the majority group. To paraphrase Butler and Stokes, whom we quoted earlier, the individual's response to the political norms of her ethnic milieu can also help to keep ethnic minorities politically distinct without perceptions of ethnic interests necessarily being involved. However important the perception of interests may have been in creating the political divergence of ethnic groups in the first place or in sustaining them in the longer run, anything so pervasive as the norm of Labour voting among ethnic minorities is likely to be accepted by many members of the group simply because it is there. On this line of argument we might be able to explain differences between ethnic groups by the differences in the extent of group solidarity around the norm of Labour voting rather than in terms of individual attitudes. Or, to put the matter in a somewhat different way, the individual will be influenced not only by her own attitudes to key policies but also by the sentiments of the wider group in which she is embedded.[25]

To investigate this idea further, we first need to construct a measure of group norms and sentiments. Now we cannot directly measure group norms—except tautologically by inferring them from patterns of party support. And it may even be that the concept of norms is too strong: groups may not have anything as explicit as a norm that one should vote Labour but simply a widespread taken-for-granted assumption that Labour is the natural choice (hence our preference for the term sentiment rather than norm). One might perhaps talk of a pro-Labour culture within the group, or indeed of a collective Labour Party identification.

One way to tap this culture is to measure how far the attitudes and policy preferences of the group as a whole are aligned with Labour Party policy positions. In other words, we can use the degree of consensus within the group on Labour policy positions as an indicator or proxy for group sentiments and culture. Thus, we might expect that a pro-Labour culture would be weaker among Muslim groups, given their disapproval of Labour's adventures in Iraq and Afghanistan, but it might be stronger among refugee groups, given their approval of Labour's more generous policies and practices for asylum-seekers. We therefore construct our indicator of pro-Labour culture by constructing a measure of consensus within the group around the main issues covered in Table 6.3.[26] This method also has the advantage that we can apply it to the white British groups too. Using this method, we find that consensus on Labour positions tended to be strongest in the black groups, was rather weaker among the South Asian groups, and least prevalent among the white groups that we distinguished. While we were not able to replicate our measures exactly with the 1997 Ethnic Minority survey (since some questions such as those on Afghanistan were obviously not asked then), a similar approach to estimating pro-Labour sentiments produced a rather similar profile, with considerable continuity over time for our main ethnic groups. This gives us greater confidence that we are indeed measuring enduring community sentiments and culture.

Figure 6.1. shows how pro-Labour culture, measured in this way, relates to Labour partisanship. In order to obtain sufficient statistical power, we distinguish twenty-eight ethno-religious minority groups, together with five religious groups within the majority population. We chose religious affiliation as the criterion for subdividing ethnic groups, since these map quite well onto known social divisions within the broad ethnic groups, as in the case of Indian Sikhs, Hindus, and Muslims. Within the Pakistani and Bangladeshi groups we are able to distinguish between Sunni and non-Sunni Muslims, which is also likely to map onto ethnic subdivisions within these groups. Churches, such as Pentecostal churches, can also play a major role as a focus of community

The Political Integration of Ethnic Minorities in Britain

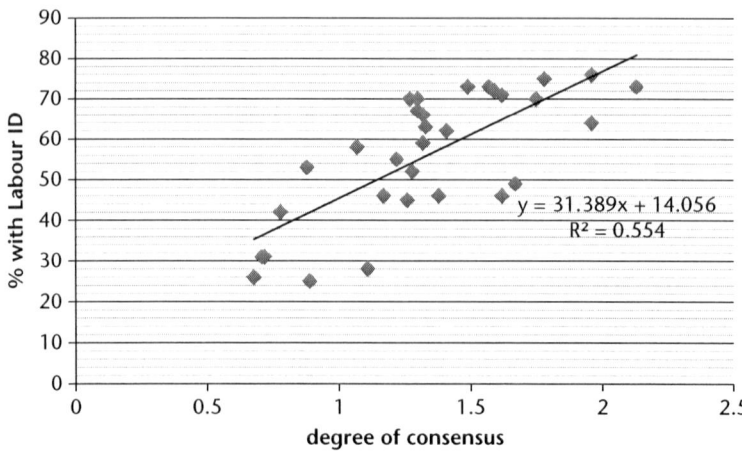

Figure 6.1. Ethno-religious group consensus on Labour policies and Labour partisanship
Sources: BES 2010, EMBES 2010

involvement within black Caribbean and black African groups, and indeed we found that pro-Labour sentiments were particularly prevalent among both black Caribbean and black African members of Pentecostal churches. It is arguable whether religious divisions are the major dividing lines within the white majority group, and we also experimented with alternatives such as the national identities of Scottish, Welsh, and English, and with class identities. In practice, we found low levels of consensus within the white majority whatever subdivisions we used, and for consistency we therefore adopted religious affiliation as the basis for creating subdivisions.[27]

We must emphasize that not all of the ethno-religious groups that we distinguish in this way are equally solidaristic. Some, such as the white groups, groups of mixed heritage, or the non-religious may indeed have rather low levels of within-group solidarity. But this is a key part of the explanatory mechanism rather than a weakness of the classification. We are unable to explore issues of group solidarity when comparing minorities with the majority group, since the main BES did not include the relevant measures of group solidarity. But we will pursue this in detail in the final part of the chapter, analysing variations between ethnic minorities (and dropping the white groups).

Figure 6.1 shows quite a strong relationship between the degree of consensus on Labour positions within an ethno-religious group and the level of Labour partisanship in that group. Broadly speaking, the black groups are towards the top right area of the figure and the white groups towards the bottom left area, with the South Asian groups neatly in between. This clearly suggests that the approach has some potential.

Our next step is to formally model the data. We run a multilevel model, with the individual respondents nested within the thirty-three ethno-religious groups. At the individual level, we include the characteristics that we have already reviewed in Table 6.3 above, while at the ethno-religious group level we include our measure of the group's consensus on Labour policies. The essential point here, of course, is that consensus is necessarily a property of a group, not of an individual. In effect, then, what we are testing is whether one's likelihood of being a Labour partisan is influenced not only by one's own attitudes to Labour policies but also by the degree of consensus within one's group. This is analogous to analyses in the sociology of education, which show that a student's attainment is associated not only with her own social class but also with that of the other students in the school.

Table 6.6 shows the results of the pooled multilevel analysis of the thirty-three ethno-religious groups (including people with no party identity in the base). The key points are, first, that individual attitudes towards the issues explain only a small proportion of the variation between the groups in Labour partisanship but, second, that the introduction in model 2 of our group measure of consensus on pro-Labour attitudes leads to a significant improvement in fit and, more importantly, explains almost three-quarters of the variation between the thirty-three groups. This, not surprisingly, is closely in line with the picture shown in Figure 6.1. In other words, our indicator of group sentiments and culture does a much better job than all the individual characteristics of explaining how our ethno-religious groups vary in their

Table 6.6. Multilevel logit models of Labour partisanship among majority and minority groups
Coefficient (standard error)

	Model 1	Model 2
Constant	−0.55 (0.30)	0.82 (0.19)
Level 1		
Tax cuts vs spending	0.07 (0.01)	0.08 (0.01)
Importance of unemployment	0.30 (0.08)	0.29 (0.08)
Civil liberties	−0.02 (0.01)	−0.02 (0.01)
Afghanistan	−0.09 (0.03)	−0.08 (0.03)
Asylum-seekers	0.06 (0.03)	0.05 (0.03)
Equal opportunities	0.05 (0.01)	0.04 (0.01)
Affirmative action	0.09 (0.03)	0.08 (0.03)
Level 2		
Extent of group consensus		0.46 (0.07)
Sigma u	0.53 (0.08)	0.27 (0.07)
Rho	0.08 (0.02)	0.02 (0.01)
Log likelihood	−3346.16	−3333.86
N1/N2	5328/33	5328/33

Notes: respondents with no partisan identity are included in the base. Sigma u for the empty model with no level 1 or level 2 predictors was 0.63 (0.09) and rho was 0.11 (0.03).

Sources: BES 2010 and EMBES 2010, unweighted

support for Labour. Moreover, we also find that our indicator does an even better job if we exclude non-partisans, that is if we simply contrast Labour partisanship with Conservative, Liberal Democrat, or some other party allegiance.

So far we have taken no account of group solidarity. Group norms and sentiments would be expected to have most force where there is strong group solidarity to reinforce them. As noted above, we did not collect the kind of data needed to measure solidarity within the white British groups. However, we can take solidarity into account when analysing the twenty-eight ethno-religious minority groups on their own. We therefore carry out parallel analyses to those in Table 6.6, beginning as before with our measures of individual attitudes towards the policy issues. We then add (individual-level) measures of fraternal relative deprivation and of bonding social capital. Individual feelings of fraternal relative deprivation, just as in Table 6.4, have a positive and significant association with Labour partisanship, but bonding social capital proves to be much the most powerful predictor. That is, the more embedded the individual is within the ethnic group, the more likely she is to be a Labour partisan.[28] We then finally add our measure of group culture, together with a group-level measure of relative deprivation (which proves to be quite highly correlated with the measure of group culture). As with Table 6.6, the inclusion of the measure of group consensus has a significant association with Labour partisanship, and also explains quite a lot of the level two variance. The group-level measure of fraternal relative deprivation plays a very similar role with similar explanatory power. Rather than attempting to treat them as distinct measures, our interpretation is that they are best understood as independent but complementary indicators tapping group culture and sentiments.

We then checked whether the relationship between group culture and Labour partisanship was stronger among people who were more embedded in their ethnic group, which is a key element of our theory of group processes. We found hints of this, but the picture becomes much clearer if we exclude the non-partisans. In other words, we obtain a clearer story if we look at the direction of party allegiance among those who actually have a party allegiance. One could indeed argue that group culture is likely to be particularly important in influencing *direction* of allegiance. This is where group sentiments give the most powerful cues as to which party is 'our' party, and we would expect that the more the individual is embedded within the group the more powerful the cues will become.

When we adopt this approach, the results change in important and interesting ways, and a comparison of the two approaches is shown in Table 6.7. As we can see, bonding has a much stronger relationship with partisanship if we include the non-partisans in the base. (This is, of course, entirely consistent

Table 6.7. Multilevel logit models of Labour partisanship among minority groups
Coefficient (standard error)

	Including non-partisans in the base	Excluding non-partisans
Constant	0.46 (0.27)	1.26 (.)
Level 1		
Tax cuts vs spending	0.03 (0.02)	0.02 (0.02)
Importance of unemployment	0.16 (0.10)	**0.28 (0.13)**
Civil liberties	**−0.05 (0.02)**	−0.04 (0.02)
Afghanistan	**−0.13 (0.04)**	**−0.15 (0.05)**
Asylum-seekers	0.06 (0.02)	0.04 (0.05)
Equal opportunities	0.02 (0.05)	0.02 (0.02)
Affirmative action	0.05 (0.06)	**0.10 (0.05)**
Fraternal relative deprivation	0.06 (0.05)	**0.13 (0.06)**
Bonding social capital	**0.26 (0.05)**	**0.16 (0.06)**
Level 2		
Group consensus	**0.15 (0.07)**	0.19 (0.10)
Group mean fraternal relative deprivation	**0.17 (0.08)**	**0.26 (0.11)**
Sigma u	0.21 (0.06)	0.31 (0.08)
Rho	0.013 (0.008)	0.027 (0.015)
Log likelihood	−1683.0	−1108.6
N1/N2	2625/28	2124/28

Notes: Measures of relative deprivation, bonding, group consensus and group mean relative deprivation are all standardized with mean 0 and standard deviation 1. Sigma u was 0.35 if the level-2 variables were dropped from the column 1 analysis, and was 0.50 if they were dropped from the column 2 analysis.
Source: EMBES 2010

with our findings at the beginning of the chapter, when we explored the drivers of non-partisanship.) When we look at the direction of partisanship, bonding remains significant, but the strength of association is markedly weaker.

When we focus on direction of partisanship, we find that individual feelings of fraternal relative deprivation become significant, and stronger in their effects. But, more interestingly, we find that the average level of fraternal relative deprivation within the ethno-religious group is highly significant, even after taking account of individual feelings, strongly suggesting that the feelings of fellow-group members are influential over and above one's own feelings. Finally, and perhaps most revealingly, we find that the strength of this group measure becomes greater if we narrow our sample to those with higher levels of bonding social capital. Thus, for the ethnic minority sample as a whole, the effect of fraternal relative deprivation is 0.26. If we exclude those with the lowest levels of bonding, the effect size increases to 0.42; restricting the sample further leaves it at 0.36; but subsequent restrictions to the most embedded individuals increase it to 0.50, 0.81, and finally to 1.83. (A similar but much less marked pattern occurs with group consensus.) In other words, group culture is particularly strongly related to Labour partisanship among the people who are most embedded within their group, and is much more weakly related to partisanship among those who are least embedded.

We should never draw strong causal conclusions from cross-sectional survey data of the kind we have used here. We also need to remember that there are important technical debates about the interpretation of contextual effects of the sort represented by our measures of group consensus and fraternal relative deprivation: there is a risk that unmeasured individual characteristics will influence one's choice of group (although we suspect that this will be more important in research on schools, where people are very likely to choose the school to which to send their children, whereas ethno-religious group membership is to a greater extent inherited rather than chosen). Nevertheless, the evidence here is certainly consistent with our argument that group sentiments and culture, combined with group solidarity, can account for the differences between blacks, South Asians, and white British in Labour allegiance with which we began this chapter.

Collective identities and sentiments

As all previous researchers have found at earlier British general elections, minorities show much higher levels of allegiance to Labour than do the white British, with black groups generally showing higher levels of Labour partisanship than South Asian groups. But these differences cannot be explained by differences in individuals' socio-economic status or political attitudes and ideology, and are present even among people who have quite recently arrived in Britain or only recently entered the electorate. Group sentiments and culture thus seem to be plausible explanations for the patterns of ethnic minority Labour allegiance, just as they were plausible explanations for the high levels of class voting that were once found in Britain in the days when Britain still had cohesive class communities.

While we must be careful not to over-interpret our findings, our analyses are consistent with a theory of group process. Our measures of group culture and sentiments, based on average feelings of fraternal relative deprivation and of consensus on Labour policy positions within the ethno-religious group, are strongly associated with group differences in Labour allegiance; and they appear to be more important among people who are more embedded within the ethnic group, exactly as one would expect if group processes were at work. They explain far more of the group differences in support for Labour than our measures of individual attitudes are able to.

While these group sentiments seem to be fairly stable over time, it is important not to treat them as immutable. Collective sentiments can evolve in exactly the same way as individual sentiments and partisanship can evolve. Indeed, it might be helpful to think of these collective sentiments as being analogous in many ways to individual partisan attachments, and having the same kind of dynamics. Mo Fiorina's theory of individual party identification as a running tally of experiences under previous governments can equally apply to collective party identifications. That is, adverse experiences under a government—such as the wars in Iraq and Afghanistan—may come to weaken pro-Labour collective sentiments. But the accumulated history of favourable action from Labour to address key minority concerns may nonetheless leave a legacy of favourable collective sentiments, although as we shall see in Chapter 8 it is not a legacy which can be taken for granted. Like other sorts of legacies, it can be consumed rather than reinvested.

Appendix: Supplementary tables

Table 6.A1. Logistic regression of no party identity (none versus any) coefficients

	Model 1	Model 2
Ethnic group (ref = Indian)		
Pakistani	0.13	0.13
Bangladeshi	0.41	0.41
Black Caribbean	0.28	0.28
Black African	−0.05	−0.05
Mixed white/black	0.28	0.28
Demographics		
1.5 generation	0.12	0.12
2nd generation	−0.22	−0.22
Female	−0.05	−0.05
Married	−0.20	−0.20
Age (ln)	0.28	0.28
Education	**0.09**	**0.09**
Middle class	0.11	0.11
Working class	−0.15	−0.15
Owner	−0.05	−0.05
LA/HA tenant	0.09	0.09
Christian	−0.31	−0.31
Muslim	−0.35	−0.35
Other (ref. none)	−0.19	−0.19
Integration		
Commonwealth not British citizen	0.35	0.35
Citizen of other country	**0.62**	**0.62**
Fluency in English	**0.22**	**0.22**
Other language at home	0.37	0.37
Ethnic identification	−0.02	−0.02
Informal bonding capital	−0.09	−0.09
Associational bonding capital	**−0.51**	**−0.51**
Associational bridging capital	−0.07	−0.07
Politicization		
Political interest	**−0.42**	**−0.42**
Interest in origin politics	−0.06	−0.06
Political knowledge	0.17	0.17

(Continued)

Table 6.A1. Continued

	Model 1	Model 2
Reads daily newspaper	−0.31	−0.31
Uses ethnic media	0.13	0.13
Discrimination		
Individual	0.02	0.02
Fraternal relative deprivation	0.01	0.01
Representation		
Separate party needed		**0.20**
No party represents me		**0.83**
Non-white percentage	**−0.46**	**−1.35**
IMD (ln)	0.03	−0.05
Constant	**−1.14**	1.05
(Pseudo) R^2	0.08	0.11
N	2558	869

Notes: Figures in bold are significant at the 0.05 level (estimated with robust standard errors). Attitudes to detention without charge and Sharia law were also explored, but did not have significant coefficients.
Source: EMBES 2010, mailback for model 2

Table 6.A2. Logistic regression of Labour identity—socio-economic characteristics coefficients

	Model 1	Model 2 + controls	Model 3 + interactions
Ethnic group (ref = white British)			
Indian	**1.04**	**1.33**	0.85
Pakistani	**1.05**	**1.24**	0.68
Bangladeshi	**1.15**	**1.23**	0.75
Black Caribbean	**1.61**	**1.61**	**1.11**
Black African	**1.72**	**1.82**	**1.31**
Mixed white/black	**1.00**	0.97	0.59
Socio-economic characteristics			
Female		−0.03	−0.04
Married		−0.01	0.01
Age (ln)		**0.23**	**0.26**
Education		**−0.08**	**−0.08**
Middle class		**−0.22**	−0.18
Working class		**0.17**	**0.19**
Unemployed, etc. (ref)		0	0
Income		−0.01	−0.01
TU member		**0.48**	**0.63**
Owner		0.11	−0.18
LA/HA tenant		**0.32**	**0.30**
Other tenant (ref)		0	0
Christian		0.07	0.04
Muslim		−0.06	0.17
Other		−0.11	0.03
None (ref)		0	0
Significant interactions			
Minority*TU member			−0.39
Minority*owner			0.51

	Model 1	Model 2 + controls	Model 3 + interactions
Minority*Christian			**0.48**
Constant	−0.83	−1.66	−1.57
(Pseudo) R²	0.14	0.16	0.17
N	5316	5316	5316

Notes: Don't know or no identity responses included in the base. Only significant interactions shown. Coefficients significant at the 5% level emboldened.
Sources: BES 2010 and EMBES 2010, unweighted

Table 6.A3. Logistic regression of Labour identity—issues Coefficients

	Model 1	Model 2 + controls	Model 3 + interactions
Ethnic group (ref = white British)			
Indian	**1.04**	0.86	**2.04**
Pakistani	**1.07**	0.88	**2.09**
Bangladeshi	**1.17**	0.91	**2.11**
Black Caribbean	**1.60**	**1.37**	**2.55**
Black African	**1.76**	**1.43**	**2.62**
Mixed	**0.97**	**1.36**	**1.95**
Issues			
Opportunities for minorities		0.04	0.04
Affirmative action		0.07	0.02
Tax cuts vs spending		0.08	**0.16**
Civil liberties		−0.02	0.01
Unemployment		**0.28**	**0.62**
Asylum		0.06	0.05
Afghanistan		−0.08	−0.05
Significant interactions			
Minority*tax cuts			**−0.13**
Minority*unemployment			**−0.46**
Minority*civil liberties			**−0.07**
Constant	−0.83	−1.39	−2.01
Pseudo R²	0.14	0.16	0.17
N	5298	5298	5298

Notes: Don't know or no identity responses included in the base. Only significant interactions shown. coefficients significant at the 0.05 level emboldened.
Sources: BES 2010 and EMBES 2010, unweighted

Notes

1. There is a huge literature on the precise concept and measurement of party identification. For our purposes, we treat party identification as whatever is measured by our standard question asked throughout the history of the British Election Surveys 'Generally speaking, do you think of yourself as Labour, Conservative, Liberal Democrat, or what?' Basically, this is a measure of the citizen's partisan self-concept, and it can be interpreted as a measure of support for or attachment or allegiance to a party.

2. See Saggar (2000), chapter 5.
3. See, for example, Curtice et al. (2005), Electoral Commission (2005).
4. See Downs (1957). Downs did not actually have a theory of party identification—it was not a concept he would have been familiar with—but a theory of party preference. However, he did have a concept of the individual's 'standing vote', which some have argued is close to partisanship.
5. The classic statement of this approach is by Kinder and Kiewiet (1981), although as usual among academics there has been considerable debate about the claim and some contradictory findings.
6. Donley Studlar (1986) for example has argued that most non-whites who support Labour do so out of general group interest rather than because of specific issue positions (1986, p. 176). Similarly, Anthony Heath and his colleagues argued that 'perceptions of group interests or processes of group identification are more plausible explanations [for minority support for Labour]' (Heath et al. 1991, p. 113).
7. For a more recent sociotropic account of African American party preferences see Wilson (2012).
8. See for example Heath et al. (2000), Heath and McMahon (2005), Heath and Li (2008), and Heath and Martin (2012).
9. See Runciman (1966), pp. 33-4.
10. The recent report of the All Party Parliamentary Group on Race and Community on Ethnic Minority Female Unemployment illustrates the resonance of these issues in British public life. See All Party Parliamentary Group (2012).
11. For example, Heath (1998) shows that the standard measures of fit between the voter's policy preferences and those of the parties are unable to explain class voting differentials. Instead, measures of the partisanship of friends and family are needed to account for class voting. See also Weakliem and Heath (1994).
12. For evidence in support of this argument from the 1997 survey see Dancygier and Saunders (2006). They concluded: 'We find strong evidence that identification with one's ethnic group leads immigrants to affiliate with the party that is dominant among the group. Second, ethnic minority concentration—and presumably increased contact with coethnics—is positively related to Labour partisanship' (2006, p. 975).
13. This kind of approach is essentially in the sociological tradition of Robert K. Merton's and Alice Rossi's (1950) theory of normative reference groups (which surprisingly is never referred to by Butler and Stokes). A modern social psychological version can be found in Tajfel's social identity theory (Tajfel 1978), and there are some similarities with Miller et al.'s (1981) political science theory of group consciousness. The approach can also easily be combined with the sociotropic perspective, as in Runciman's formulation of a fraternalistic sense of relative deprivation to explain collective action (1966, pp. 33-4).
14. See Hajnal and Lee (2011, Table 5.4). However, among the ethnic minority respondents to the main BES, the percentage with no identity was rather higher at 27 per cent. The figures were significantly higher among the mixed, Bangladeshi, and black Caribbean groups, while among Indians and Pakistanis it was the same as for the white British.

Partisanship

15. More detailed analysis (see Table 6.A1 in the appendix) indicates that the main drivers of identification are interest in British politics and, just as in Chapter 3, associational bonding capital. Unsurprisingly, the feeling that no party represents one's views is also very strongly (and negatively) related to party identification. And the main barrier to identification was lack of British citizenship. It is also rather interesting which variables are *not* associated with partisan identification: speaking a language other than English at home, interest in homeland politics, visits to one's country of birth, informal bonding social capital, and years since arrival in Britain fail to show any significant association with presence or absence of a party identification (and there was no sign that years since arrival had indirect effects mediated by the other variables in the model).
16. See, for example, Heath et al. (1991) and Sobolewska (2005).
17. Remember that we are including people with no partisan identity, so that the percentages used to calculate Table 6.2 are directly comparable with those in Table 6.1. If we excluded the non-partisans, the socio-economic cleavages would appear substantially larger, since disadvantaged social position tends to be associated with higher rates of non-identification.
18. See Heath et al. (2011) for further discussion of housing tenure and its relationship with vote among minorities.
19. Also, of course, as was shown in Chapter 2, minorities are no longer all that different from the majority in socio-economic position, so socio-economic position cannot explain much of the gap in Labour support.
20. We also investigated whether attitudes towards detention without trial and support for Sharia law helped to explain Labour support, but the inclusion of these variables substantially decreased sample size (since they were asked in the mailback and of Muslims respectively), and the coefficients were not significant.
21. For the three issues where we measured perceptions of party positions as well as the respondents' own positions, we can look at the 'fit' between the individual's position and that of the party. However, models that include measures of fit do not lead to any major differences in the coefficients.
22. More detailed analysis indicates that the major driver of these differences is in the proportion of non-partisans: recent entrants into the electorate are the ones who are least likely to have any party identity. We also find a significant tendency among Labour supporters for identity to be stronger among those who have had longest experience of life in Britain, again consistent with Fiorina's theory. An implication of Fiorina's running tally approach to party identification is that, if the positions of voters and of parties remain constant, then partisanship should strengthen over time and throughout the life-course: 'if the parties favour the same sides of various socioeconomic cleavages over time, and if citizens find themselves in the same socioeconomic circumstances over time, then one would expect most citizens consistently to evaluate the party as preferable to the other, which according to our model will produce a consistently strengthening party ID' (1981, p. 91). As Fiorina points out, this is contingent on the actual mobility experiences of the groups concerned, and hence might not apply to groups such as Indians who have experienced more upwards mobility. Among the adult

migrants, mean strength of Labour identity was 1.9 among those who entered during the New Labour period compared with 2.3 among those who entered in the earliest period. Among the later generations, mean strength was 2.1 among the most recent entrants to the electorate compared with 2.3 among those who had been in the electorate longest.
23. More detailed analysis shows that the Labour partisanship of these new entrants cannot be explained by their evaluations of how well Labour looks after the interests of blacks and Asians or by other individual characteristics and measures.
24. See Uhlaner and Garcia (2005). Bergh and Bjorklund (2011) have also suggested the value of a group-based explanation for Norway, but focus on voting for ethnic candidates and length of stay in Norway.
25. While this approach has some similarities with the classic Columbia approach, which emphasized the role of personal influence, group norms and sentiments are more than a simple matter of direct personal contacts. The central point is that the sentiment that Labour is the natural choice becomes widespread within the group, and becomes a taken-for-granted assumption within the group.
26. To construct the scale, we first identified what the Labour positions were. This could be done directly for the items on government spending, protecting the rights of the accused, and promoting equal opportunities, since we asked respondents for their perception of the Labour party's position. On asylum, we assumed that the Labour position was not to send asylum seekers home immediately; on Afghanistan, we assumed that the Labour position was that it was right to wage the war; and we also assumed that the Labour position was to preserve employment rather than to undertake austerity measures that would increase unemployment. We then estimated the proportion within each ethno-religious group who accepted the Labour position, or in the case of the scales who placed themselves in the same or a more leftist position than Labour. For example, in the case of the item on tax cuts versus government spending, most people perceive Labour as being the most leftist of the three parties (even under New Labour). So anyone who takes the same position as Labour on this item, or a position even further to the left, we define as holding pro-Labour attitudes on this issue. (Conversely, anyone who is to the right of Labour on this issue will be close to the Conservative or Liberal Democrat positions.) We can then calculate what proportion of the ethnic group shares a pro-Labour attitude on this issue. We then repeat this exercise for the other issues covered in Table 6.3, apart from affirmative action, and sum the proportions. We cannot really argue that support for affirmative action is currently a Labour policy (although it might have been in the 1980s). We also saw in Chapter 5 that support for affirmative action tends to be associated with the view that ethnic minorities need their own political party rather than one of the mainstream ones such as Labour.
27. One important issue is whether we are right to assume that group cultures are national, or whether different ethno-religious group cultures develop in different localities of the country. Unfortunately, our sample is not large enough for us to differentiate the groups by locality, but general checks on geographic variations in group culture were unable to detect significant regional variation.

28. We should however recognize that our measure of embeddedness strictly speaking refers to embeddedness within the broader ethnic group, not within the specific ethno-religious group used in the multilevel analysis. However, it may be that our respondents when answering these questions were thinking of their more specific social ties.

7
Eligibility, Registration and Turnout

In this chapter we turn from orientations, attitudes, and identities to political behaviour, starting with registration and participation in the 2010 General Election. In the following two chapters, we look at vote choice and other forms of political engagement. Participation in elections has often been regarded, from a normative standpoint, as fundamental in a democracy. While in theory low turnout might simply be a reflection of satisfaction with the operation of democracy, the usual assumption is that it more likely reflects either barriers to participation, lack of interest in elections, or disaffection and alienation from the political process. Lack of participation is therefore worrying for the health and legitimacy of democracy, since it means that the voices and viewpoints of many electors will not be heard in the political process.

There has been particular concern about the participation of migrants and minorities. In many countries migrants and minorities appear to have particularly low levels of turnout in elections, and in Britain too there has been some evidence that black electors have low levels of turnout.[1] As Ed Fieldhouse and David Cutts have argued, 'Inequalities in participation may be regarded as especially problematic if a minority group has distinctive political attitudes, preferences or interests. Low levels of participation may lead not only to a failure to represent these interests, but also undermine the legitimacy of the state in the eyes of the minority group' (Fieldhouse and Cutts 2008b, p. 333).

There are several possible barriers to participation, especially for the first generation. The first potential barrier is citizenship. To be eligible to vote in a British general election one needs to be either a British or a Commonwealth citizen. EU citizens are also eligible to vote in local and European elections, but are not eligible to vote in general elections (though we have very few EU citizens in our ethnic minority sample). The rules for eligibility for citizenship are also complex and have changed over time. Broadly speaking, however, anyone born in Britain before 1983 will have British citizenship automatically, while those born after 1 January 1983 (when the British Nationality Act 1981 came into force) will have British citizenship if one of their parents was either a British citizen or a legal resident. Among those born abroad (our first and one point five generations) from 1983 onwards, British citizenship could be acquired after five years' legal residence (three years for some categories). Before 1983, only three years' residence was required. However, the 2009 Borders, Citizenship and Immigration Act changed this: five years of residence now leads only to probationary citizenship, which can lead to full citizenship after earning a certain number of points, through such things as volunteering or civic activism. However, this will not have applied to the great majority of our respondents.

So, although Britain has been gradually making access to citizenship more difficult, for most of the relevant period it was fairly generous by international standards.[2] Britain is also more generous than many countries in allowing dual citizenship, which almost certainly makes it more acceptable for many migrants. Virtually all of the second-generation members of our sample had British citizenship. Aside from the legal requirements for citizenship, we also need to consider the reasons why people might want to become citizens. Most obviously, people who do not intend to remain long in Britain, and who see themselves as short-term residents, may not wish to acquire citizenship. In addition, citizenship does not bring many additional benefits (apart from voting rights and the protection of the British government when abroad) in comparison with the right of residence. Acquiring citizenship may indeed be largely a symbolic act, indicating a positive identification with Britain.

Assuming that one has either British citizenship or citizenship of a Commonwealth country, the next step is to register, and again there can be barriers, such as lack of fluency in the English language or lack of familiarity with British procedures (although translations of the relevant forms are designed to mitigate this). Having registered, there is then the issue of actually going to the polling booth. There has been a major literature on the reasons why people might or might not bother to go to the polls, and many of these reasons may also apply to the decision to register (although in law it is compulsory to return a household registration form).

A central puzzle in the literature on turnout is the so-called 'paradox of voting'—mentioned in passing in Chapter 3. The problem arises from the fact that an individual vote has an infinitesimally small chance of making a difference to the election outcome. A rational egoist, assuming his sole concern is to influence the election outcome in order to improve his own future welfare, will almost certainly decide not to vote, since the costs (such as the time foregone in going to the polling booth) will almost certainly outweigh the infinitesimally small benefits. In short, there is no point in voting. If everyone followed this logic, no-one would vote. But if no-one else voted, it would be entirely rational to vote oneself, since one would then be casting the only vote! And if there is no point in voting, there may not be much point in registering to vote either, aside from the legal obligation to register.[3]

To some extent, this paradox depends upon its starting point, which is a standard economist's view of rational self-interested behaviour. Alternative starting points do not lead to any paradox. As Brian Barry has pointed out, it makes perfect sense for a rational altruist to vote, since she believes that her vote is benefiting many other people.[4] Alternatively, one could argue that the point of voting is not so much to affect the outcome of the election but to signal to whoever wins the election that there is support for the policies advocated by a particular party—thus it makes perfect sense, even if one believes that the Conservatives are bound to win, to cast a vote for an alternative party in order to indicate to the winning party that they do not have such a sweeping mandate for their programme. Hence, it might be rational to vote for a minor party like UKIP, even if they have no chance of winning, if one wants to signal to the government that Euroscepticism needs to be taken more seriously. In this sense every vote counts, since worries about voters deserting the Conservatives for UKIP could well influence the Tory leadership to adopt a more Eurosceptic policy platform. The vote may thus not have changed the outcome of the election, but it may nonetheless have had a (tiny but not zero) effect on policy.

In somewhat similar vein, one of the strongest predictors of whether people will turn out and vote is their extent of commitment to a political party: people who are strongly attached to a particular party are more likely to turn out and vote than are those with weaker or no party allegiance. It might well also influence whether or not they will register to vote in the first place. In addition, if a party is seen as being 'the' party of a particular group (as we saw in the last chapter might be case for Labour and ethnic minorities), then strength of attachment to the ethnic group might also be related to registration and turnout: minorities who feel committed to their group might feel a greater wish to record a vote for their group's party.[5] Closely related to this might be mobilization by one's group: people who are more embedded within their ethnic group might be more susceptible to pressure or encouragement from fellow-members to register and vote. This has been suggested as a reason why South Asians might have higher rates of turnout than black British citizens, and David Cutts and colleagues have found that South Asian residential concentration is linked with higher turnout rates.[6] The kinds of group process that we discussed in Chapter 6 might also, therefore, affect registration and turnout.

A second line of argument is that a feeling of belonging and obligation to the political community as a whole, rather than to a particular party, might be an important influence on registration and turnout. In particular, a sense of citizen duty to vote has often been found to be one of the most powerful predictors of turnout, and, as we saw in Chapter 3, first-generation ethnic minorities in Britain express high levels of commitment to this duty. Conversely, a feeling of exclusion from the national community, perhaps as a result of experience of prejudice or feelings of relative deprivation, might lead to feelings of alienation, and lead to a rejection or lack of involvement in national rituals such as general elections.

A third line of argument emphasizes what political scientists term 'cognitive engagement'.[7] That is to say, cognitive factors such as knowledge, or its lack, about politics and interest, or lack of it, in British elections may serve to facilitate or inhibit registration and turnout. Closely related to cognitive engagement are other cognitive processes that might apply particularly to the first-generation minorities. Most obviously, lack of fluency in the English language is likely to be closely related to lack of political interest or knowledge, as well as to the capacity to understand and fill in the forms, and fluency has been found to be a particularly strong predictor of turnout among Asians and Latinos in the US.[8] There could also be more general processes of acculturation and acquiring familiarity with British practices—the longer migrants have been exposed to British media, for example, the more likely they may be to understand what the general election ritual is all about. US research has found that length of residence is one of the most powerful predictors of registration and turnout.[9]

Given the high levels of partisanship and group solidarity among ethnic minorities, their high levels of identification with British society, and the high level of reported feelings of duty to vote that we have described in previous chapters, we should expect to find quite high levels of registration and turnout. We do not expect to see the low levels of turnout reported in the USA or many European cities. That said, among the first generation barriers such as lack of citizenship, lack of English, and lack of interest in or knowledge about British politics might depress both registration and turnout levels somewhat. And in both generations experiences of exclusion and feelings of fraternal relative deprivation might be expected to depress electoral participation.

A major worry that affects all research on electoral participation is whether one can trust respondents' reports about whether they voted. Self-reports of turnout are notoriously biased upwards, since respondents to surveys tend to exhibit social desirability bias, over-reporting socially desirable behaviours such as voting in general elections. It has been suggested in the USA that minorities may be even more likely to over-claim than are members of the majority group.[10] Does this apply in Britain too? A particular strength of our research is that we can draw on validated measures of turnout (and of registration). By checking respondents' reports against the marked-up registers, we are able to obtain a much more accurate picture of registration and turnout.[11] It is only rarely possible in social science research to validate respondents' reports with objective external data, and validation of this sort is therefore especially important in order to give our research credibility.

The central research questions for this chapter, then, are first, whether ethnic minority patterns of citizenship, registration, and turnout differ across ethnic groups and generations, and from the white British. And second, what are the major influences? How important are barriers such as lack of fluency in English or lack of British citizenship? And does group solidarity and mobilization play a similar role in registration and turnout to the one that it plays in partisanship?

Documenting the differences

We begin with an overview of the major components that make up non-voting among ethnic minorities and the white British majority. We use the validated data rather than the self-reports, and we distinguish eligibility, registration, and turnout itself. Table 7.1 shows these components for first-generation migrants, the one point five generation, the second-plus generation, and the white British.

The big story here is that turnout was rather low at 53 per cent among the first generation, but then is considerably higher (at 63 per cent) in the second generation. This is still well short of overall white British levels (70 per cent), but much the same as the level for the eighteen–forty-fives. Lack of eligibility is only a minor component of non-voting, and only really for the first generation. The big story is about registration. Among those who are registered,

Table 7.1. Validated voting and non-voting
Column percentages

	Minorities			White British	
	1st generation	1.5 generation	2+ generation	All ages	Age 18–45
Not eligible/not a British or Commonwealth citizen	5	2	1	<1	<1
Eligible but not registered at the address	25	16	**20**	10	15
Registered at address but did not vote	17	**26**	17	20	24
Voted at sample address (including postal/proxy votes)	53	57	63	**70**	60
Total	100	100	100	100	100
N	1231	422	944	2578	997

Notes: Base excludes those whose records could not be traced for validation. Citizenship is based on the respondents' reports. Respondents who said they were neither British nor Commonwealth citizens were defined as ineligible unless the validated data showed that they had actually registered at the address. Figures in bold are significantly higher than expectation at the 5% level. Chi^2 = 271.8 (9 df), p < 0.001.
Sources: BES 2010, EMBES 2010 and electoral registers, weighted data

Eligibility, Registration and Turnout

minority turnout rates are not especially different from white British ones. But non-registration among minorities is double that among the white British, and shows only meagre sign of declining across generations. This is by no means a new finding: almost all previous research in Britain has shown lower registration rates among minorities than among the majority group.[12] Failure to register, in other words, is what accounts for the low turnout of the second generation. Among eligible electors who are registered, ethnic minority non-voting is not significantly different from white British non-voting. Hence, the key task is to understand registration. Before attempting to do so, however, we briefly review the evidence on citizenship and eligibility.

Citizenship and eligibility

In our sample, we find that 99 per cent of the second generation report that they have British citizenship. Even among the one point five generation 94 per cent report that they are British citizens, the main exceptions being recent arrivals from Sub-Saharan Africa. We therefore focus our analysis on the first generation, that is on those who arrived as adults. Table 7.2 shows their citizenship profile.

Table 7.2 shows rather high levels of British citizenship even in the first generation. To put this into context, Irene Bloemraad reports that, of those with eleven to fifteen years' residence, the citizenship rate was only 37 per cent in the USA compared with 83 per cent in Canada.[13] If we carry out the same calculation for Britain, we obtain a figure of 79 per cent with British citizenship—very close to the Canadian rate. Moreover, the British figure includes a substantial proportion of Indians who are not allowed dual

Table 7.2. Citizenship by ethnic group, adult migrants only
Row percentages

Ethnic background	British (including dual) citizenship	Commonwealth but not British citizenship	Other citizenship	N
Indian	51	**49**	0	313
Pakistani	**74**	25	1	306
Bangladeshi	**76**	22	2	117
Black Caribbean	**89**	8	3	165
Black African	58	29	**14**	349
Commonwealth	53	**44**	3	195
non-Commonwealth	66	6	**28**	154
All 1st generation minorities	62	33	5	1291

Notes: Figures in bold are significantly higher than expectation at the 5% level. Chi^2 = 266.3 (10 df), $p < 0.001$.
Source: EMBES 2010, weighted

citizenship by the Indian authorities. As we can see from Table 7.2, the Indians have much lower rates of British citizenship than other comparable groups. This low rate almost certainly reflects the disincentive effect of the Indian regulations, since people of Indian background who migrated from East African or from other countries outside India have much higher rates of British citizenship (84 per cent for the East African Indians and 79 per cent for the other diaspora Indians). However, black Africans also show a lower level of British citizenship, which is a bit more puzzling, as Nigeria, for example, does allow dual citizenship (although Kenya does not). Black Africans coming from non-Commonwealth countries also have lower rates of British citizenship.

In order to understand these variations, we explored relevant predictors. We focused on reasons for migration, the number of years spent in Britain, whether the respondent had arrived before the change in British citizenship law came into force in 1983, language spoken at home, and family in the origin country. (We also included the standard demographic controls—age, gender, marital status, education, social class, income, and housing tenure.) We should note that there is an important issue of causal direction in this kind of analysis. Since the acquisition of British citizenship may have happened at any point since arrival in Britain, it is possible that citizenship may influence integration into British society rather than the other way round. Without time-varying measures, we cannot be sure what is cause and what is effect, and we shall have to use our judgement. In general, we prefer to focus on more stable demographic attributes and those that are in principle before migration, such as reasons for migration, instead of more subjective ones (such as British identity), which are more likely to have changed over the course of the migrant's time in Britain.

Of the predictors that we considered, by far the most important was the number of years spent in Britain since arrival. This is hardly surprising, since one is not able to apply for citizenship until one has been resident for, usually, five years. This largely explains why the black Africans have lower citizenship rates, since they are the most recent arrivals (whereas migrants from the Caribbean have been in Britain longest). Reasons for migration were also important, with people who came for political reasons—especially those who said that they came for 'freedom'—being more likely to have become citizens; while those who told us that they came in order to study were less likely, probably reflecting an intention to return to their home country after completing their studies. Among other predictors, the most notable was housing tenure, where respondents who were in private renting or other non-standard types of housing were much less likely to have taken up British citizenship. This suggests that they were perhaps less established in Britain. (For full details see Table 7.A1.)

While these predictors do a fairly good job at explaining take-up of citizenship, we still find that Indians and black Africans from Commonwealth countries were less likely to have citizenship than were the other South Asian or black groups. This almost certainly reflects the citizenship rules of the country of origin rather than the barriers in Britain.[14] On the whole, despite the toughening up of the legislation in 1981, Britain has remained relatively generous in providing access to citizenship, and before the 2009 Borders, Citizenship and Immigration Act, Britain was one of the most generous countries in the developed world.[15] This generosity has been reciprocated by minorities who have taken up citizenship in large numbers. (Britain made more grants of citizenship than any other country in Europe in 2010, according to Eurostat 2012.)[16] Again, this is in line with our findings from Chapters 2 and 3, where we showed that ethnic minorities were highly committed to Britain and positive in their orientations.

Registration

So, unlike the situation in many other countries, access to citizenship has not in the past been a major barrier to political integration in Britain. How, then, do we account for the shortfall in registration?

Before turning to the data, we need to remember that at the time of our survey in 2010 Britain had a household system of registration, with heads of household being responsible for returning the registration form (though at the time of writing Britain is planning to move to an individual system). This naturally gives some scope for individual respondents to be unclear about whether they actually are registered or not. As we described earlier, we are able to check whether respondents were registered to vote: the registers of electors are available for public consultation after the election, and our interviewers checked these to determine whether the respondent was on the register at the address where they had been interviewed. We also asked the respondents themselves whether they thought they were registered, and if so where, and a small number reported that they were registered at a different address. Unfortunately, we did not have the resources to check the registers at these other addresses, so we have to recognize that there will be some uncertainty about the total valid rate of registration.

Table 7.3 provides a first look at the patterns of registration. Since, as Table 7.1 showed, failure to register remains an issue across all generations, we include all generations in this analysis. However, we restrict the analysis to those who told us that they were British or Commonwealth citizens, and who were thus eligible to register.

Table 7.3. Registration among those eligible (British and Commonwealth citizens) Row percentages

Ethnic group	Registered to vote at sample address	Said they were registered at another address	Not registered	N
Indian	80	3	18	556
Pakistani	83	2	15	616
Bangladeshi	78	5	17	252
Black Caribbean	80	6	16	535
Black African	66	7	**28**	400
Mixed white/black	74	4	22	81
All minorities	78	4	19	2476
White British	**91**	2	7	2692

Notes: Excludes those for whom details were not sufficient to identify in the registers. Figures in bold are significantly higher at the 5% level than expectation. Chi^2 = 188.8 (12 df), $p < 0.001$.
Sources: BES 2010, EMBES 2010, weighted

The first column shows the percentages who were definitely registered at the sample address, while the second column shows how many reported that they were registered elsewhere. The third column shows the proportions who were not registered either at the sample address or elsewhere. We can see that for every minority the figure is significantly higher than the white British one, being particularly high for the black Africans. And also recall that we have excluded people who were neither British nor Commonwealth citizens and were therefore ineligible. Our measure of the shortfall is very close to that estimated by the Electoral Commission for 2010,[17] and is also remarkably close to estimates from twenty years ago: an analysis of 1991 data by the Office of Population Censuses and Surveys (now the Office for National Statistics) found that 24 per cent of black people, 15 per cent of South Asians, and 24 per cent of 'other' ethnic groups compared with 7 per cent of white people were not registered.[18] While there are several differences in methodology, which make comparison of the OPCS results and ours difficult, it does seem that despite the valiant efforts of organizations like Operation Black Vote, which runs campaigns to encourage ethnic minority registration, the problem remains undiminished.

How, then, are we to explain the lower levels of registration among the ethnic minorities? We first of all asked our respondents themselves (though we should remember that we were only able to ask those who told us that they were not registered—we did not have the data on validated registration until later). The reason most often given was that they were not eligible (28 per cent), although quite a number of these were almost certainly eligible since they were Commonwealth citizens. Next most common was 'I have recently moved' (24 per cent). Other reasons were 'I'm not interested in elections' (10 per cent), 'I didn't know how to register' (8 per cent), 'I never received the application form' (8 per cent), 'I got left off by mistake' (8 per cent), and 'I just couldn't be bothered' (6 per cent).

The reasons that respondents give may often be rationalizations, but reasons such as lack of interest or lack of know-how readily fit into the kind of cognitive explanations that we described at the beginning of the chapter. But as we also mentioned, there are other potential reasons for turning out to vote, and possibly for registering as well, such as partisanship or a sense of citizen duty. Among the first generation, we also expect to find that barriers might include lack of fluency in the English language, and an orientation towards the origin country and its politics rather than to Britain. Reasons like this were not mentioned by our interviewees, but they might still be important. We could speculate that the reasons respondents give will be the proximate ones that spring to mind most readily, rather than more distant ones which might lie behind the proximate reasons.

We therefore explored a wide range of characteristics, among both the white British and the minority samples, to see what was linked with registration. We first looked at the kinds of characteristics described above, which research on the white British has suggested may be important, namely party identification, a feeling of duty to vote, and knowledge about and interest in the British political process. (We also controlled for various demographic factors such as generation, age, qualifications, marital status, gender, income, and housing tenure.) We explored to what extent these characteristics could explain the registration gap between the majority group and the minorities.

Among the white British we found that registration was linked to an individual's age, housing tenure (people renting their accommodation being the least likely to register), and the sense of a duty to vote. (The Electoral Commission's own research confirms these findings.) Interestingly, strength of party identification was not an important predictor of registration, although as we shall see it is an important predictor of turnout. The same predictors were also important for the ethnic minorities (see Table 7.A2 in the appendix). When we pooled the minority and majority samples, we found that these predictors accounted for a large proportion of the minority registration deficit.[19] This is a very different picture from the one we described in the previous chapter on Labour Party allegiance. In the case of party allegiance, predictors such as age, housing tenure, or attitudes towards political issues made very little headway in explaining minority support for Labour. Huge ethnic differences remained in the analogous statistical analyses. But in the case of registration, standard demographic and attitudinal predictors go a long way to explain the ethnic differences. Interestingly, we found little sign of the group processes that were so important in explaining party allegiance. To be sure, some differences remain, especially in the first generation, although these too were explicable in fairly conventional ways.

Thus, as expected, we found that fluency in the English language was a significant predictor of the adult migrants' likelihood of registering, while years since arrival was of borderline significance.

A consistent theme running through all these findings is that of marginality. It is striking that every single one of the relevant predictors revealed by our statistical analysis, apart from duty to vote, involves some degree of social or economic marginality. Thus, young people and recent arrivals in Britain are marginal in British society. People who are not fluent in the English language are clearly marginal (and one suspects marginalized). People dependent on private-sector rented accommodation are marginal when compared with home owners, or even with local authority tenants, who tend to have long-term security of tenure. These categories are all marginal in the sense that they will have lower and more precarious access to resources, lower security, and probably lower respect and recognition in British society too. Moreover, ethnic minorities have markedly higher rates of marginality than do the white British. While we often tend to think of people of Indian heritage as being a more successful group, they too have quite high rates of marginality.

We can only speculate on the precise mechanisms which lead from marginality to lack of registration. Some mechanisms may be very straightforward: for example, people in multi-occupied accommodation may not receive letters from the electoral registration officer addressed to 'the present occupier'. Practical obstacles of this kind are not always recognized by the authorities who design systems and procedures, as they think of people like themselves who live stable predictable lives. Other mechanisms may be of a more psychological kind: if you feel marginal, you may also feel that there is no point in making the effort to register (see Table 7.A3).

Turnout

We next turn to turnout. Overall, the figures in Table 7.1 suggested that, among registered electors, minority turnout rates were not all that different from white British rates. But this could of course hide substantial differences between minorities. Many previous commentators have suggested that South Asians have higher turnout rates than black groups, although these assertions have usually been based on self-report data. Maybe South Asian groups are more likely to succumb to social desirability bias. To explore these issues, we exclude those respondents who were not actually registered, and then compare the self-reported and the validated turnout rates for the different ethnic groups.

Table 7.4. Self-reported and validated turnout
Percentages

Ethic background	Validated turnout	N	Self-reported turnout	N	% of self-reported voters who actually had not voted	N
Indian	75	452	82	540	13	369
Pakistani	78	509	79	613	15	400
Bangladeshi	78	199	81	252	13	170
Black Caribbean	77	435	**74**	549	11	322
Black African	72	286	73	429	13	206
Mixed black/white	**69**	63	**57**	78	10	31
All minorities	76	1971	78	2496	**14**	1509
White British	78	2419	82	2703	**8**	2007

Notes: Base for self-reported turnout includes 'don't knows' but excludes refusals and those who said they were not registered. Measure of validated turnout includes those issued with postal/proxy votes but excludes those not registered at the sample address. Figures significantly different from expectation at the 5% level are emboldened. Chi^2 (validated turnout) = 10.6 (6 df), p > 0.05; Chi^2 (self-reported turnout) = 65.4 (6 df), p < 0.001; Chi^2 (over-claiming) = 34.5 (6 df), p < 0.001;
Sources: BES 2010 and EMBES 2010, weighted

Table 7.4 shows fairly clearly that, once people were registered, turnout rates were pretty similar among minorities and the majority. There is nothing like the shortfall that we found with registration. In particular, if we look at the measure of validated vote, the overall figures are very close indeed, and there is little variation between minority groups. Only the group of mixed black and white heritage had a significantly lower rate of turnout than the majority group. This similarity in majority and minority validated turnout rates (among registered electors) is in line with the previous research (on the 2001 election) carried out by David Cutts and his colleagues.[20] Their research used the marked-up registers, just as ours does, but they were restricted to studying South Asian communities (since they used name-recognition software to identify Hindu, Sikh, and Muslim minorities). Like us, they found no significant difference in the turnout rates of South Asian and non-South Asian registered electors. They also found some evidence consistent with the idea that ethnic communities are able to mobilize electors, with South Asian turnout being higher in areas of higher ethnic concentration. We shall look at this issue shortly.

A second particularly important finding is the absence of any major shortfall for the black Caribbean group. Most previous research has concluded that black electors have lower rates of turnout, but this is not really evident here. If we look at the figures for validated turnout, the black Caribbean turnout is a non-significant single point lower than the white British one. True, the column for self-reported turnout does show a larger (and significant) difference, but this is not to be relied on. Most previous research has in fact used self-report measures, and most past research also (as far as we can determine) fails to exclude people who are not registered. Given the large shortfall in registration that we showed in the previous section, it is certainly true that *eligible* black citizens are less likely to go to the polling booths than are the white British. But the same applies to South Asians too, as Table 7.3 showed. The validated data on registration and turnout clearly indicate that black Caribbean and South Asian rates are effectively the same.[21]

Finally, it is worth noting that the final column of Table 7.4 suggests that overclaiming was more common among minorities than among the white British. This strengthens our argument that we should be particularly cautious when using self-report measures to draw conclusions about ethnic minority turnout rates. The safest approach, in our judgement, is to use the validated measures, despite their limitations. These provide the most conservative estimates, and even so suggest that the majority/minority difference in turnout of registered electors is small. The big story remains the one about differences in registration rates.

We also carried out some further statistical analysis of the data in order to see whether group processes played any role in ethnic minority turnout. We found that very similar psychological factors—strength of party identification, duty, political interest, and political knowledge—were associated with turnout among ethnic minorities just as among the majority group, although these psychological predictors tended to have stronger associations with turnout among members of the majority group. In particular, the measures of political interest and political knowledge were highly significant among the white British, but not significant at all among minorities (see Table 7.A4). This certainly suggests that somewhat different processes are at work, and that theories and empirical findings based on research on the majority group cannot always be extrapolated to minorities. We also found a strong association with canvassing: people who told us that they had been canvassed by one of the political parties showed a significantly higher likelihood of going to the polling booth, suggesting that mobilization can be effective both among the majority and minority communities.

Turning specifically to the role of bonding social capital and group processes more generally (which we can only study in detail among minorities, not among the white British), our evidence suggests that they play an important *indirect* role in turnout. That is to say, bonding social capital is related to one's strength of partisanship, and strength of partisanship in turn is related to turnout. As a result, validated turnout was actually higher when bonding social capital was stronger. Thus, turnout was only 72 per cent among people with the lowest scores on our measure of bonding social capital (the lowest 20 per cent), rising to 83 per cent of those with the highest bonding scores (the top 14 per cent). However, bonding seems to have no effect on turnout once we take account of strength of partisanship (see Table 7.A2). So this association between bonding and turnout is really just an echo or reflection of the relationship between bonding and partisanship that we explored in Chapter 6.

Marginalization or mobilization?

The first big story of the chapter—by no means a new story—is that the main shortfall is with respect to registration. Ethnic minority rates of registration, even in the second generation, are ten points lower than the white British rate. In contrast (and unlike the situation in many other countries), citizenship and hence eligibility is high, and indeed is almost universal in the second generation. And among those who are registered, the ethnic minority turnout rate is not especially different from the majority turnout rate.

The second big story is a rather newer one. This is that, in striking contrast to the results of the previous chapter on party allegiance, registration is largely to be explained by the individual's circumstances and not by group processes. Thus, we are able to explain a large part of the registration gap by individual characteristics, notably by citizens' age, how long they have lived in Britain, and whether they rent in the private housing market; whereas in Chapter 6 individual characteristics explained hardly any of the minority/majority gap in allegiance to the Labour Party. Consistently with this, bonding social capital has no significant relationship with registration, whereas it had a strong and important relationship with partisanship. We see an echo of this role of social processes when we look at turnout among people who are registered, but it is conspicuous by its absence in explaining registration.

How are we to make sense of this contrast between the kinds of processes involved in registration, turnout, and partisanship? And what might the policy implications be?

First of all, it is not perhaps especially surprising that group norms and sentiments have not developed around registration in the same way that they have around partisanship. Filling in the registration form is essentially a private act, and is not the kind of thing to discuss with one's friends or colleagues. Registration is not a topical issue that gets covered in the mainstream media. It is not, we would suggest, the kind of thing on which group norms would spontaneously emerge in the course of social interaction.

Secondly, our statistical analysis of predictors of registration suggested that many of them reflect aspects of marginality. Registration is particularly low among people in private rented accommodation. It is also low among young people, among people who are not fluent in the English language, or who have only recently arrived in Britain. It would be easy to conclude that marginalized individuals are not interested in registration, and that it is in a sense their own fault. But we take a diametrically opposed view. We find that individual attitudes (apart from duty to vote, where minorities score as highly as the majority) are not important predictors of registration (whereas they are quite important in explaining turnout). Moreover, individual attitudes are precisely the kind of things that group norms and values can influence. So in our judgement it would be quite wrong to 'blame the victim'. Instead, we would suggest that registration procedures have been (perhaps unconsciously) designed for people who live stable, established lives (the classic middle-aged, well-educated home-owner), not for people who have to lead more transient lives in multi-occupied accommodation in more deprived areas. There are many such people among the white British, of course, but the key point is that marginality of this sort is much more common among minorities. Practical efforts to reach these groups would appear to us to be a priority, in order to ensure that the marginalized are not excluded from the political process.

Operation Black Vote and the Electoral Commission play important roles in trying to counter these problems with their campaigns to encourage ethnic minority registration. But it is perhaps more surprising that the Labour Party, which is becoming increasingly reliant on minority voters, does not make more effort to overcome the shortfall in registration. Mobilization clearly can be effective in getting out the vote. Perhaps equal effort should be directed to registration.

Appendix: Supplementary tables

Table 7.A1. Logistic regressions of citizenship: first-generation ethnic minorities Coefficients

	Model 1 without controls	Model 2 + controls
Ethnic group		
Indian	−0.74	−1.57
Pakistani (ref)	0	0
Bangladeshi	0.19	0.10
Black Caribbean	1.03	−0.24
Black African	−0.62	−0.90
Demographics		
Gender		0.52
Marital status		0.32
Age (ln)		0.97
Education		−0.02
Income		0.06
Owner (ref)		0
LA/HA tenant		−0.43
Other		−1.26
Middle class (ref)		0
Working class		−0.40
Unwaged or missing		−0.21
Acculturation		
Years in Britain		0.09

Eligibility, Registration and Turnout

Fluency in English		**0.30**
Speaks other language		0.41
Family in origin		0.25
Reasons for migration		
Political		**0.94**
Family reunion		−0.10
Study		**−0.73**
Other		0
Percentage non-white		**1.01**
IMD		−0.004
Constant	0.98	**−5.84**
Nagelkerke R²		0.53
N	*1250*	*1143*

Notes: Within each of the individual regressions, coefficients that are significantly different from zero at the 5% level are emboldened.

Source: EMBES 2010, unweighted

Table 7.A2. Logistic regressions of registration: ethnic minorities and white British (among those eligible)
Coefficients

	All minorities	White British	Combined without controls	Combined with controls
Ethnic group				
White British	–	–	0	0
Indian	−0.21	–	**−0.88**	−0.35
Pakistani	0	–	**−0.79**	−0.19
Bangladeshi	0.10	–	**−0.93**	−0.08
Black Caribbean	−0.24	–	**−0.75**	−0.31
Black African	−0.43	–	**−1.50**	**−0.59**
Mixed white/black	−0.12	–	**−0.97**	−0.22
Demographics				
Gender	0.19	0.14		**0.19**
Marital status	0.12	0.14		0.16
Age (ln)	**1.48**	**0.65**		**1.16**
Education	0.05	0.01		0.04
Middle class (ref)	0	0		0
Working class	−0.08	0.05		−0.03
Unwaged or missing	−0.05	−0.19		−0.09
Income	−0.001	0.01		0.004
Owner (ref)	0	0		0
LA/HA tenant	**−0.46**	**−0.59**		**−0.52**
Other tenure	**−0.60**	**−1.38**		**−0.88**
1st generation	**−0.71**	0.41		**−0.54**
1.5 generation	−0.04	0.29		0.03
2 + generation (ref)	0	0		0
Political engagement				
Party ID strength	0.11	0.01		0.07
Duty to vote	**0.17**	**0.21**		**0.18**
Political interest	0.07	−0.01		0.03
Political knowledge	0.05	0.05		0.04
Efficacy	−0.01	−0.04		−0.02
Newspaper reader	−0.06	0.07		−0.01

(*Continued*)

The Political Integration of Ethnic Minorities in Britain

Table 7.A2. Continued

	All minorities	White British	Combined without controls	Combined with controls
Social capital				
Church member	−0.03	**0.27**		0.03
Associational involvement	−0.04	0.03		0.10
Constant	−4.41	−1.02	2.45	−3.11
Nagelkerke R2	0.13	0.13	0.06	0.16
N	2351	2631	5132	4981

Notes: The dependent variable includes respondents who said they were registered elsewhere. In the pooled analysis, white British 1.0 and 1.5 generations have been pooled with the 2 + generation, and hence the generation terms refer only to minorities. Within each of the individual regressions, coefficients that are significantly different from zero at the 5% level are emboldened.
Sources: BES 2010 and EMBES 2010, unweighted

Table 7.A3. Logistic regressions of registration Coefficients

	1st generation minorities	All generations
Ethnic group		
Indian	**−1.43**	−0.30
Pakistani (ref)	0	0
Bangladeshi	0.13	0.08
Black Caribbean	−0.58	**−0.56**
Black African	**−0.56**	**−0.66**
Mixed white/black	–	−0.58
Demographics		
Gender	0.05	0.15
Marital status	0.19	−0.02
Age (ln)	**1.70**	**1.63**
Education	0.02	0.07
Income	−0.02	0.015
Owner (ref)		0
Council tenant	−0.22	**−0.46**
Other	−0.58	**−0.93**
Working class	0.27	−0.06
Class missing etc	0.13	0.04
1st generation		**−0.81**
1.5 generation		0.04
2+ generation (ref)		0
Political engagement		
Duty to vote	**0.34**	**0.18**
Party ID strength	0.13	**0.24**
Group relations		
Bonding social capital	−0.06	−0.03
Ethnic identification	0.03	0.01
Fraternal relative deprivation	**−0.08**	−0.02
Acculturation		
Years in Britain	0.02	–
Fluency in English	**0.33**	–
Speaks other language	0.29	–
Family in origin	0.17	–

Reasons for migration		
Political	−0.38	–
Family reunion	0.41	–
study	−0.22	–
general	0	–
Percentage non-white	0.24	0.13
IMD	−0.004	0.001
Constant	**−7.49**	**−5.26**
Nagelkerke R2	0.30	0.19
N	*1044*	*2287*

Notes: Within each of the individual regressions, parameter estimates that are significantly different from zero are emboldened.
Sources: BES 2010 and EMBES 2010, British and Commonwealth citizens only

Table 7.A4. Logistic regressions of validated turnout: ethnic minorities and white British (registered electors only)
Coefficients

	All minorities	White British	Combined without controls	Combined with controls
Ethnic group				
White British			0	0
Indian	−0.18		−0.14	0.10
Pakistani (ref)	0		−0.10	0.21
Bangladeshi	−0.16		0.06	**0.76**
Black Caribbean	0.37		−0.08	**0.45**
Black African	0.01		**−0.31**	0.26
Mixed black/white	−0.42		**−0.63**	0.07
Demographics				
Gender	0.02	0.02		−0.01
Marital status	−0.03	0.19		0.12
Age (ln)	**0.61**	0.21		**0.40**
Education	−0.10	0.08		0.00
Middle class (ref)	0	0		0
Working class	0.15	0.04		0.04
Other or missing	0.07	−0.37		−0.11
Income	0.015	0.01		0.004
Owner (ref)	0	0		0
Council tenant	**−0.51**	−0.21		**−0.47**
Other	−0.15	−0.35		−0.30
1st generation	**−0.50**	−0.08		**−0.39**
1.5 generation	**−0.66**	−0.16		**−0.66**
2+ generation (ref)	0	0		0
Political engagement				
Party ID strength	**0.34**	**0.42**		**0.38**
Newspaper readership	−0.13	−0.16		**−0.21**
Duty to vote	**0.23**	**0.47**		**0.39**
Political interest	0.09	**0.24**		**0.16**
Political knowledge	0.08	**0.26**		**0.15**
Efficacy	−0.01	0.00		−0.00
Social capital				
Church member	**0.29**	**0.23**		**0.24**
	−0.20	0.01		−0.07

(Continued)

Table 7.A4. Continued

	All minorities	White British	Combined without controls	Combined with controls
Associational involvement				
Canvassed by party	0.24	0.34		0.32
Constant	−2.60	−4.02	1.25	−3.44
Nagelkerke R2	0.10	0.28	0.01	0.17
N	1866	2366	4363	4232

Notes: Dependent variable includes those issued with postal and proxy votes. Within each of the individual regressions, coefficients that are significantly different from zero at the 5% level are emboldened. Note that in the pooled analysis, white British 1.0 and 1.5 generations have been combined with the 2+ generation, and hence the generation terms refer only to minorities.
Sources: BES 2010 and EMBES 2010, unweighted

Table 7.A5. Logistic regressions of turnout among registered electors: all and first-generation ethnic minorities
Coefficients

	All minorities	Bivariate correlations	1st generation minorities	Bivariate correlations
Ethnic group				
Indian	0.14		−0.18	
Pakistani (ref)	0		0	
Bangladeshi	**0.48**		−0.15	
Black Caribbean	0.18		0.12	
Black African	0.12		−0.02	
Mixed black/white	−0.17		–	
Demographics				
Gender	0.02		−0.13	
Marital status	−0.01		**0.44**	
Age (ln)	**0.71**	**0.10**	**0.49**	**0.14**
Education	−0.08	**−0.06**	−0.03	**−0.12**
Income	0.03	0.01	−0.05	**−0.10**
Owner (ref)	0		0	
Council tenant	**−0.59**		**−0.53**	
Other	−0.12		0.29	
Middle class (ref)	0		0	
Working class	0.13		−0.05	
Unwaged or missing	0.06		0.42	
1st generation	**−0.52**		–	
1.5 generation	**−0.64**		–	
2+ generation (ref)	0		–	
Political engagement				
Party ID strength	**0.35**	**0.17**	**0.38**	**0.21**
Canvassed by party	**0.28**	**0.08**	−0.09	0.01
Duty to vote	**0.25**	**0.13**	**0.26**	**0.09**
Political interest	0.09	**0.09**	**0.33**	**0.09**
Group relations				
Church member	**0.28**	**0.06**	0.09	0.04
Informal bonding	0.03	**0.05**	−0.01	0.06
Associational bonding	−0.03	0.02	0.04	0.03
Associational bridging	0.04	0.00	−0.12	−0.04

Ethnic identification	0.01	0.01	−0.01	−0.02
Relative deprivation	0.02	0.01	0.02	0.00
Acculturation				
Years in Britain			0.01	**0.13**
Fluency in English			−0.17	**−0.09**
Speaks other language at home			−0.09	0.04
Family in origin			0.58	−0.01
Interest in origin politics			**−0.22**	**−0.10**
Uses ethnic media			0.42	0.07
Reasons for migration				
Political			0.79	0.07
Family reunion			−0.28	−0.03
study			**−0.61**	**−0.10**
general			0	
Percentage non-white	**−0.27**	0.04	−0.03	
IMD	**−0.24**	0.07	**−0.24**	
Constant	**−2.57**		**−1.99**	
Nagelkerke R2	0.11		0.19	
N	*1861*		*821*	

Notes: Within each of the individual regressions, parameter estimates that are significantly different from zero at the 5% level are emboldened.

Source: EMBES 2010

Notes

1. On the USA, Hajnal and Lee (2011, Table 5.1) shows Latino and Asian-American turnout. González-Ferrer (2011, Table 4.2) shows participation in a range of European cities. See also Bird et al. (2011) for comparative European data. On Britain see Studlar (1986), Saggar (1998), Anwar (2001) and Purdam et al. (2002).
2. See the MIPEX website of comparative data on access to citizenship in a range of developed countries.
3. There may, however, be some selective incentives since, for example, the information about whether or not one is on the electoral register is used by credit rating agencies.
4. See Barry (1970).
5. Compare Leighley and Vedlitz's (1999) group consciousness model though their research in the USA found no significant effect of closeness to one's group on participation or turnout.
6. See Cutts et al. (2007) and Fieldhouse and Cutts (2008a). Dancygier (2010) also shows that the proportion of co-ethnics in the neighbourhood predicts South Asian immigrant turnout, more so in local than in general elections, but finds little effect for Caribbean immigrants (pp. 97–8).
7. See, for example, Leighley and Vedlitz (1999).
8. Cho (1999) shows that among first-generation Asian-Americans and Latinos the standard SES variables do not predict turnout in the way that they do for the majority group. English-language proficiency and being foreign-born are very important predictors. She explains this in terms of the different socialization experiences of those living in large, minority-language-speaking communities.

The crucial argument is that education (and age) are important predictors only insofar as they lead to socialization into dominant norms and provide political information (explanations we can test).

9. Wong et al. (2005) investigate predictors of registration and turnout (and other forms of political engagement) among Asian-Americans, focusing on role of group resources. Their findings are patchy, but basically they find that ethnic group identity has no predictive power, while church attendance predicts turnout. Other forms of group resource are mainly relevant for the other forms of political engagement. Percentage of life spent in the USA is a significant predictor of registration as is education outside the USA (negative effect). Age, education, political interest, and partisanship are generally significant predictors. White et al. (2008) find very few significant predictors of turnout in their Canadian data. The most important is log years in the host country (which supports their 'exposure' hypothesis). Type of origin country (advanced versus other), SES and education are non-significant. They also investigate years lived in origin country, but this too was non-significant.
10. Swaddle and Heath (1989) provide a detailed study of the discrepancy between official and self-reported turnout rates. Abramson and Claggett (1984) provide evidence on over-claiming by ethnic minorities in the USA.
11. For details of how the validation was carried out see Howat et al. (2011).
12. For a helpful overview of past research see Purdam et al. (2002).
13. See Bloemraad (2006), p. 670.
14. There is quite a large literature on factors influencing acquisition of citizenship. One interesting finding is that immigrants from societies where reverse migration is more difficult tend to naturalize at higher rates (see, for example, Bueker 2005). This may well explain the higher take-up of citizenship among Indian refugees from East Africa, which we noted above. However, it seems implausible that return migration is easier for migrants coming from India than for people coming from Pakistan, or that it is easier for people coming from Africa than from the Caribbean.
15. See MIPEX (2012).
16. However, we should note that the Eurostat figures refer to numbers of grants made, not to the proportion of eligibles who have naturalized. The high numbers may be simply because of the high recent rates of immigration to Britain.
17. The Electoral Commission found that 77 per cent of people from BME communities were registered compared with 86 per cent of white people (white people also including members of the 'white other' census categories). See Electoral Commission (2011).
18. See Smith (1993).
19. In Table 7.A2, most of the ethnic parameter estimates are non-significant, and so it could be said that we have statistically explained the ethnic minority shortfall in registration. However, every single estimate is negative, and, if we pool the minorities, we do obtain a highly significant ethnic minority deficit.
20. See Cutts et al. (2007).
21. It is important to recognize some limitations of these data, however. As we mentioned above, we were not able to validate the registration and turnout of people who told us that they were registered at another address. We have also included

cases where people were issued with postal or proxy votes as ones where a vote was actually cast (which will not always have been true.) These limitations may introduce some biases, but they are likely to be quantitatively fairly minor, and are unlikely to affect the main thrust of our argument. For example, if we exclude the postal and proxy votes, the figures for validated turnout become 76 per cent for black Caribbeans, 72 per cent for Indians, and 75 per cent for Pakistanis. Alternatively if we add to the validated turnout people who said they voted elsewhere (including all those who said they were registered elsewhere to the base), the figures become 69 per cent for black Caribbeans, 65 per cent for Indians, and 75 per cent for Pakistanis. So our results look fairly robust.

8

Voting, Abstention, and Defection

In general, we expect people's vote choice to follow fairly closely from their party identifications, which we described in Chapter 6. However, there are a number of reasons why, when a voter gets to the polling booth, she might put a cross against a different party from her usual one. For example supporters of a particular party might be disillusioned if their party has failed to live up to expectations. In the context of the 2010 general election, the outgoing Labour government had clearly presided over a period of financial turmoil, a major recession, and rising unemployment. We know that there was a big swing away from Labour in 2010, which left the party with a sharply reduced number of seats and brought the Conservative/Liberal Democrat coalition into office. As John Curtice and his colleagues have observed:

> [Labour's] performance ... was by historical standards little short of dire. Labour's share of the total vote, 29.7%, was its second lowest share since 1918; only the party's performance in the calamitous defeat in 1983 was worse. The 6.5 point drop [between the 2005 and 2010 general elections] in its share of the vote almost matches the worst ever reverse between two elections suffered by an incumbent Labour government, that is the 6.7 point drop suffered by the party following the collapse of Ramsay MacDonald's government in 1931. (Curtice et al. 2010, pp. 385–6)

Disillusioned Labour supporters therefore must either have stayed at home on polling day or switched to another party. A particular interest for us is whether minority voters were as liable as other voters to become disillusioned with their party and to defect or stay at home. As we argued in Chapter 6, minorities typically belong to stronger communities than do the white British, and we might well expect community norms and sentiments to sustain Labour turnout even in bad times. And, as members of cohesive communities, minorities might be more susceptible to mobilization by their party's activists.

A second question is whether minorities, when deciding whether to vote or defect, were perhaps moved by somewhat different considerations than the white British. While Chapter 5 showed considerable similarities between minorities' and the majority's views of the most important issues facing the country, there were also clear differences in political agendas that might be relevant. Quite possibly minorities were less swayed by general considerations about the state of the economy, but more influenced by how much (or little) Labour had done for them and their ethnic group. Labour's commitment to helping minorities, and fears about the lack of interest (or even perhaps hostility) from the Conservatives might have led minorities to vote Labour despite the adverse economic circumstances.

Given the predominance of Labour supporters among ethnic minorities, we focus in this chapter primarily on what Labour supporters did on polling day. (The much smaller numbers of ethnic minority Conservative or Liberal Democrat supporters in our sample also makes it more difficult to undertake robust analysis of their behaviour at the general election.) The key questions we address are: Did ethnic minority Labour supporters show greater loyalty to the Labour party than white British Labour supporters, or did they desert Labour at much the same rate? And in deciding whether to remain loyal to, or desert, Labour, were minorities influenced by the same sorts of considerations that influenced the white British, or were there distinct drivers of minority voting?

Overview

Before focusing on Labour supporters, we begin with the overall distribution of the vote in 2010 among all those who turned out to vote. Table 8.1 shows the expected clear parallels between partisanship and vote. Thus, minorities, especially blacks, were much more likely to vote for Labour, just as Table 6.1 showed that they were much more likely to identify with Labour, while the South Asian groups generally had slightly lower levels of Labour voting than did the black groups, but much higher levels than the white British. In these respects, vote distribution closely follows partisanship.

However, it is noteworthy that, among both minorities and the majority group alike, Labour had a larger lead (or smaller deficit) with respect to party identification than it did when it came to vote. Among the white British there was only a slight Conservative lead over Labour of 4 points in partisanship (with the Conservatives on 40 per cent compared with Labour's 36 per cent), whereas when it came to actual voting there was a Conservative lead of 11 points (40 per cent versus 29 per cent). Among ethnic minorities there was a Labour lead of 64 points over the Conservatives in partisanship, but a lead of only 52 points in terms of vote. A natural interpretation of this is that both minority and majority individuals who thought of themselves as Labour

The Political Integration of Ethnic Minorities in Britain

Table 8.1. Patterns of voting in 2010
Row percentages

Ethnic background	Labour	Conservative	Liberal Democrat	Other	N	Labour lead over Conservatives in partisanship	Labour lead over Conservatives in vote
White British	29	40	24	7	2095	−4	−11
Indian	**61**	24	13	2	409	+45	+37
Pakistani	**60**	13	25	2	449	+54	+47
Bangladeshi	**72**	18	9	1	185	+68	+54
Black Caribbean	**78**	9	12	2	371	+76	+69
Black African	**88**	6	6	1	298	+84	+82
Mixed white/black	**68**	16	16	0	39	+60	+52
All minorities	**68**	16	14	2	1751	+64	+52

Notes: Base excludes non-voters (and non-partisans when calculating Labour lead over Conservatives in partisanship). Figures in bold are significantly higher at the 5% level from expectation. Chi^2 = 787.9 (18 df), p < 0.001.
Sources: BES 2010, EMBES 2010, weighted

Table 8.2. Labour voting and partisanship by ethnic group, 1997 and 2010
Cell percentages—partisanship before slash/vote after slash

Ethnic background	1997	N	2010	N	Partisanship change 1997–2010	Vote change 1997–2010
White British	43/47	2721	36/29	1998	−7	−18
Indian	72/78	228	66/61	409	−6	−17
Pakistani	72/81	85	65/60	449	−7	−21
Bangladeshi	52/73	39	78/72	185	+26	−1
Black Caribbean	72/90	66	84/78	371	+12	−12
Black African	77/90	44	88/88	298	+11	−2
Mixed white/black	–		71/68	39		–
All minorities	68/82		75/68	1768	+7	−13
Official result (seats)	43 (418)		29 (258)			−14

Notes: Non-voters/non-partisans (as appropriate) are excluded.
Sources: BES 1997, EMBES 1997; BES 2010, EMBES 2010, weighted

supporters were disappointed in 2010 by Labour's failures in government, and either stayed at home or switched to another party.

A similar story emerges if we look at changes in vote shares over time. We can compare the pattern in 2010 with our equivalent survey after the 1997 general election, thus neatly capturing the beginning and end of the New Labour era. As Table 8.2 shows, there was quite a contrast between the two elections. In 1997, Labour vote outstripped Labour partisanship, whereas it was the other way round in 2010, and Labour partisanship outstripped vote. As a result, there was a drop in Labour's share of the vote among all minorities, while there was less change in partisanship, and indeed an increase in Labour partisanship among the two black groups. (One should be cautious about the large increase in Labour partisanship among the Bangladeshi group because of the very small sample size in 1997.) We also see that the fall in the Labour vote was larger among the white British (Labour voting falling by 18 points) than among minorities overall (down 14 points), though it was largest of all among voters of Pakistani background (down 21 points), almost certainly because of their opposition to Labour's adventures in Iraq and Afghanistan.

Overall, then, Labour clearly under-performed in 2010 in comparison with 1997, and did so both among minorities and the majority. But there are also suggestions in the table that some minorities, notably the two main black groups, might have been less likely to abandon Labour than were Indians, Pakistanis, or the white British. We look at this in more detail in the next section.

Were minorities more loyal to Labour?

We next consider the extent to which majority and minority voters deviated from their Labour partisanship when they went (or failed to go) to the polling booth. In particular, do we see any greater or lesser tendency on the part of ethnic minorities in general or specific minorities in particular to remain loyal to Labour? In Table 8.3, we select Labour partisans only (that is, we select those people who told us in 2010 that they thought of themselves as Labour), and show whether they abstained, voted Labour, or defected to a different party at the 2010 general election.[1] Because of the problems with self-reports of

Table 8.3. Voting patterns in 2010 among Labour partisans
Row percentages

	Abstained (did not vote or register)	Voted Labour	Defected to another party	N
White British	31	57	12	803
Middle class	24	60	16	333
Working class	31	58	11	357
North/Scotland/Wales	32	58	10	522
South & Midlands	30	57	13	281
Ethnic minorities				
Indian	36	59	3	294
Pakistani	43	50	5	331
Bangladeshi	42	56	7	143
Black Caribbean	43	55	2	356
Black African	54	45	2	314
Mixed white/black	63	33	1	48
All minorities	43	53	4	1499

Notes: Ineligibles excluded. Figures in bold are significantly different at the 5% level from expectation. Chi^2 (ethnic differences) = 127.5 (12 df), p < 0.001.
Sources: BES 2010, EMBES 2010, weighted

turnout that we discussed in the previous chapter, we use our validated data here: we include as Labour voters or defectors to another party only those people who, according to the marked-up registers, actually voted. Similarly, the abstention category includes those who either did not vote or were not registered according to the marked-up registers.[2] We need to take non-registration into account, since it is an important way in which Labour partisanship might fail to translate into actual votes.

As with the changes over time, we see significant differences between the majority and minorities in rates of abstention and defection from Labour. Although the percentage voting in line with their Labour identity is lower among minorities (53 per cent versus the white British 57 per cent), there is a clear pattern for white British Labour partisans to be more likely to switch to a different party than the ethnic minority Labour partisans, who were more likely to fail to vote or fail to register.[3] Abstention, of course, while damaging to a party's electoral chances, is not nearly as damaging as defection, which gives a vote to a rival party.

Another angle on this is to look at vote switching between 2005 and 2010. Here the picture is even clearer. While we do not wholly trust recall data, we do find overall that a higher proportion of 2005 Labour-voting minorities (58 per cent) turned out again for Labour in 2010, compared with an equivalent figure of 50 per cent for the majority group, with the majority group being much more likely to switch to another party (26 per cent) than were minorities (only 11 per cent). We also see a clear difference between minorities, with the two main black groups having higher loyalty to Labour than the two main Muslim groups (see Table 8.A3 in the Appendix).

So while all groups deserted Labour to some extent between 2005 and 2010, rates of desertion were lowest among the black groups and highest among the white British. This is satisfyingly in line with the constituency analysis that has been conducted by John Curtice and his colleagues. Their analysis indicated that the average fall in Labour's share of the vote was much less (only 0.7 point on average) in seats with a large minority population than the average constituency fall (6.5 points) in Britain as a whole.

Explaining patterns of abstention and defection

The standard account given by political scientists of why voters might depart from their usual partisan identities when they enter the polling booth gives pride of place to the incumbent government's record or performance over the previous parliament.[4] And of course the 2005–10 Parliament had seen the disastrous recession of 2008, for which many voters must have held Labour responsible. It would hardly be surprising if voters, including those who thought of themselves as Labour partisans, had punished the party at the polls as a result. As Harold Clarke and his colleagues have argued:

> The [2010] contest occurred in the wake of one of the biggest shocks to the British economy since the Great Depression of the 1930s. A financial crisis, a deep recession and rising unemployment captured the attention of a worried electorate and prompted demands for government action...Knowing 'what' they were concerned about, voters focused heavily on the 'who' of electoral choice. Given Labour's lengthy tenure in office, widespread unhappiness with Prime Minister Gordon Brown, and the prevailing economic distress, voters clearly were open to—indeed, searching for—alternatives in 2010. (Clarke et al. 2011, p. 252)

Our findings in Chapter 4, where we showed that minorities shared these concerns about the economy, provides a straightforward explanation for why Labour voting was lower than Labour partisanship among minorities just as it was among the majority. However, it is less clear whether these concerns over the state of the economy can explain why minorities were less likely than the majority to defect from Labour to other parties. It is in theory possible that minorities were less affected by the recession than were other British citizens, or that they were less likely to blame the Labour government for these difficulties. This is something we need to check, although on the surface it seems pretty implausible: evidence on the labour market indicates that minorities are likely to be even harder hit in a recession than is the majority.[5] It might also be the case that there were other aspects of the government's record, perhaps immigration, on which minorities had rather different views from the majority (as we saw in Chapter 4), and therefore evaluated Labour more favourably. An alternative line of explanation would be to focus on the kind of group processes that we discussed in Chapters 6 and 7. In other words, minorities might not be so swayed by Labour performance, and might be more anchored in their partisanship as a result of community norms and sentiments. First of all, however, we need to check how much leverage is provided by the standard accounts prioritizing disappointment with Labour's record and leadership.

So how did Labour partisans from the minority and the majority feel that they had fared under Labour? We have a number of questions, asked both of minorities and the majority group, asking for their evaluations of how well the Labour government had handled a range of central responsibilities. Both surveys asked respondents how well Labour had handled crime, immigration, the NHS, the risk of terrorism, and the economy generally. We also asked how they thought the war in Afghanistan had been going, how they thought their own personal finances and the national economy had fared, and what they thought about the party leaders. We asked:

How well do you think the last government handled each of the following issues? Crime in Britain, immigration, the National Health Service, the risk of terrorism in Britain, the economy in general.

What is your impression of how the war in Afghanistan is going right now: very well, fairly well, fairly badly, or very badly?

Now a few questions about economic conditions. How does the financial situation of your household now compare with what it was 12 months ago?

How do you think the general economic situation in this country has changed over the last 12 months?

Now let's think about party leaders for a moment. Using a scale that runs from 0 to 10, where 0 means strongly dislike and 10 means strongly like, how do you feel about Gordon Brown; David Cameron; Nick Clegg?

We focus primarily on Labour partisans in order to compare like with like, since these evaluations, particularly ones which explicitly mention Labour, tend to be highly coloured by one's partisanship. We also show the results for Conservative partisans, Liberal Democrat partisans and non-partisans to illustrate just how highly-coloured evaluations can be.[6] Table 8.4 shows the net figures as these highlight the differences. That is, we subtract the percentage of positive evaluations from the percentage of negative ones (ignoring people who either did not know or gave a middling response). We can thus see immediately on which topics the balance of opinion was most unfavourable to Labour.

Table 8.4. Net evaluations of Labour record and party leaders
Net differences

	White British Conservative partisans	White British non-partisans	White British Liberal Democrats	White British Labour partisans	Ethnic minority Labour partisans	All ethnic minorities
Evaluations of government record						
Immigration	−85	−63	−50	−36	**+10**	−1
Afghanistan war	−53	−60	−59	−49	−51	−53
The economy	−68	−32	−26	+31	**+24**	+7
Crime	−25	−4	+21	+29	+31	+20
Risk of terrorism	+15	+18	+37	+53	**+46**	+34
The NHS	+3	+19	+21	+59	+53	+43
Evaluations of economic situation						
Household financial situation	−41	−40	−31	−31	−37	−36
General situation	−54	−57	−47	−43	−55	−54
Liking for party leaders						
David Cameron	+86	+1	+9	−36	−14	−4
Nick Clegg	−25	−5	+73	−23	−12	−1
Gordon Brown	−70	−35	−24	+44	+50	+28

Notes: Figures in bold indicate where the evaluations of ethnic minority Labour partisans are significantly different at the 5% level from evaluations of white British Labour partisans.
Sources: BES 2010 and EMBES 2010, weighted

Table 8.4 shows some interesting patterns. First of all, it is clear that Labour partisans were much more positive about Labour's record and leader than were Conservative or Liberal Democrat partisans or the non-partisans. This is unsurprising: a standard aspect of the psychological theory of selective perception is that partisans are more likely to view their party's record in a favourable light, and it is also likely that some people who were particularly negative about the government's record might have changed their partisanship anyway. (Without a panel study we cannot of course adjudicate between the contributions of these two processes.) Partisanship bias is largest in evaluations of party leaders, and smallest for judgements about one's household or the national economy generally.

We also see that, even among Labour partisans, there were pretty negative evaluations of Labour's handling of immigration and of the war in Afghanistan, as well as fairly negative perceptions of how the economy had fared. However, Labour partisans were fairly charitable in their assessments of how Labour had handled the economy, and very positive about Gordon Brown's leadership. (Partisans of other parties were much more likely than Labour partisans to blame Gordon Brown for Britain's economic problems.)

In contrast to the differences between Labour, Conservative, and Liberal Democrat partisans, minority/majority differences among Labour partisans are pretty small: on most items apart from immigration, Labour-supporting minority respondents had very similar views to their white British peers. As the table shows, on most items the differences were modest, although minorities were slightly more gloomy than the white British Labour partisans about their household and the national economic situation.[7] The only item on which there was any substantial difference was Labour's handling of immigration, where minorities were much more favourably disposed towards the Labour record.[8] This is of course entirely consistent with our findings in Chapter 4, where we showed that minorities were generally less inclined to restrict immigration than were the white British. Maybe this helps to account for their loyalty to Labour.

In addition to the general evaluations of the government's record that were included in both EMBES and the BES, we also asked in EMBES (but not in the BES) how minorities felt their ethnic and religious groups had fared over the last few years. We asked:

Thinking about the past few years, have things generally got better or worse for ethnic minority groups in Britain, or have things stayed much the same?

And thinking about the situation of [respondent's ethnic group] people, have things generally got better or worse, or have they stayed much the same?

And thinking about the situation of [respondent's religion] people, have things generally got better or worse, or have they stayed much the same?

Table 8.5. Net perceptions of how ethnic and religious groups had fared over the last few years: Labour partisans
Net differences

	All	Indian	Pakistani	Bangladeshi	Black Caribbean	Black African	Mixed black/white
Better-worse for minorities	+14	+16	**−13**	+12	+22	+30	+21
...for own ethnic group	+16	+26	**−13**	+21	+18	+28	–
...for own religious group	−5	+14	**−36**	**−8**	+2	+5	+22

Notes: Figures in bold indicate the evaluation was significantly different from expectation. Chi^2 (for ethnic minorities) = 59.5 (10 df), p < 0.001, Chi^2 (for own ethnic group) = 94.3 (8 df), p < 0.001; Chi^2 (for own religious group) = 126.4 (10 df), p < 0.001.
Source: EMBES 2010, weighted data

In Table 8.5, we show the net perceptions of whether the situation has got better or worse. We subtract the percentage who thought things had got worse from the percentage who thought things had got better. Positive signs in the table therefore indicate that respondents were on balance pleased with progress, and negative signs indicate that they were on balance disappointed with progress.

The results are not what we might have expected, given the generally unfavourable economic circumstances of Britain over the last few years, and the negative perceptions in Table 8.4 about how one's household and the country had fared economically. Instead, there is a remarkable story with all groups, except those of Pakistani background, being on balance rather positive about progress. The discrepancy between these rather positive findings and the negative economic perceptions may well be because, when answering these broader questions, minorities have taken into account a wider range of changes that have made their lives easier, and not simply material or economic conditions. For example, there is some evidence that prejudice against minorities has been declining, especially among young white people.[9] So the positive perceptions of progress may well have very little to do with government action but with changes in the broader social context. If this interpretation is correct, we would expect these perceptions to have little influence on patterns of abstention or defection.

People of Pakistani background, on the other hand, are much more negative, especially so on whether things have gone well for their religious group, with an astonishing net figure of −36. While the Bangladeshi group is also on balance negative about how things have gone for their religious group, they are not nearly as negative, suggesting that this is partly but not solely a Muslim issue. Almost certainly, these negative perceptions reflect the growing Islamophobia in British society since 9/11 that Clive Field has documented.[10] The greater concern among people of Pakistani than of Bangladeshi background may possibly reflect the fact that Pakistan itself is in the forefront of the

Voting, Abstention, and Defection

so-called War on Terror (which in some ways is destabilizing Pakistan itself, with Western incursions into Pakistani airspace and territory for military interventions).

To check whether any of these considerations can explain ethnic minority loyalty to Labour, we undertook some statistical analysis of the data. We restricted our analysis to Labour partisans, and tested whether these different perceptions of Labour's record, of the party leaders, and of their own personal and national economic fortunes could explain patterns of abstention and defection. We also took into account strength of partisanship and other attitudes and experiences (duty to vote, political interest, political knowledge, and whether they were canvassed) that were important in predicting registration and turnout in Chapter 7. We expect these to be important in explaining abstention.[11]

We also need to take into account tactical voting. In our statistical analysis, we exclude self-reported tactical voters, since we assume that different processes (such as distance from contention) will drive this rather than government performance per se.[12] In fact, only a small proportion of ethnic minorities voted tactically—less than 5 per cent compared with 8 per cent among the white British. We suspect that this may be because minorities are relatively likely to reside in safe Labour seats, or in constituencies where the Labour Party was very much in contention.

In Table 8.6, we show how much difference each measure is estimated to make to the probability of a Labour partisan either abstaining or defecting to one of the other parties. For example, in column 1 the figure of +15 for 'private renter' indicates that white British Labour partisans who rented privately were 15 percentage points *more* likely to abstain than were home owners (other things being equal). Conversely, in column 1 the figure of −16 for 'duty to vote' indicates that people who strongly agreed with the duty to vote were 16 points *less* likely to abstain than were people who disagreed with the duty to vote (other things being equal). The figures thus tell us how large a difference each measure makes, and they also tell us whether the difference is positive or negative.[13]

We only show estimates in Table 8.6 where the measure made a significant difference for at least one of the four contrasts (that is, for white British abstention and defection or ethnic minority abstention and defection).[14] The first striking result is that none of the retrospective evaluations of Labour's handling of the economy, the war in Afghanistan, or assessments of personal or national finances made any significant difference to defection or abstention. This is in part because any differences they might have made were swamped by evaluations of the party leaders. In other words, people who thought that Labour had handled the economy well were also highly likely to think well of Gordon Brown, and it was this positive evaluation of Brown

Table 8.6. Explaining departures from Labour support (Labour partisans only) Average marginal effects

	White British		Ethnic minorities	
	Did not vote	Switched to another party	Did not vote	Switched to another party
Labour handled crime badly	+3	+6	+1	**+4**
Liking for Gordon Brown	**−14**	**−18**	**−10**	**−6**
Liking for David Cameron	**+10**	+2	**+6**	+2
Liking for Nick Clegg	−7	**+13**	0	**+5**
Strength of Labour partisanship	**−12**	**−9**	**−12**	**−7**
Duty to vote	**−16**	−2	**−9**	−1
Political interest	**−12**	−2	**−10**	**+4**
Political knowledge	−6	**+9**	**−9**	**+5**
Not canvassed	+6	0	**+10**	+2
Canvassed by party other than Labour	**+10**	**+12**	+5	**+6**
Canvassed by Labour (reference)	0	0	0	0
Renter in social housing	+5	−4	**+6**	−2
Private renter	**+15**	−4	**+17**	−2
Home-owner (reference)	0	0	0	0
(pseudo) R²	0.28		0.18	
N	759		1502	

Notes: Emboldened figures indicate that the underlying coefficient is significant at the 5% level. Non-voting includes non-registration.
Sources: BES, EMBES 2010; Labour partisans only and tactical voters excluded

that ended up doing most of the work in the statistical analysis. If we remove evaluations of the leaders from the statistical analysis, we do in fact find that evaluations of Labour's handling of the economy made a fairly large difference to abstention and defection. The crucial point is that the two measures tend to go together, and we should not really attempt to make fine distinctions between them. In short, the analysis supports the idea that negative evaluations by Labour partisans of their party's performance and leader made a substantial difference to their likelihood of abstaining or defecting.

A second striking result is the similarity in the patterns for white British and for ethnic minorities. To be sure, the magnitudes are sometimes rather smaller among minorities, but the general pattern is identical. In particular, we see that strength of one's Labour partisanship and liking for Gordon Brown are strongly associated with loyalty to Labour; abstention is linked to lack of political interest or knowledge and with weaker feelings of duty to vote; defection to another party is (relatively weakly) linked to a liking for Nick Clegg (but not David Cameron) and to negative evaluations of Labour's handling of crime. Overall, any differences in the predictors of majority and minority abstention or defection are ones of detail, and given the very small numbers of minorities who defected to another party (limiting our statistical power), we should be careful not to draw strong conclusions. This is hardly earth-shattering stuff, but it is consistent with the story from Tables 8.1 and 8.2 (and with our previous research on the calculus of vote choice).[15]

More interesting, perhaps, are the predictors that failed to predict: while ethnic minorities were in general very similar to the majority in their evaluations of Labour's record, we saw in Table 8.4 that they were much more supportive of Labour's record on immigration. However, our statistical analysis suggests that this was not an important predictor of (absence of) defection from Labour partisanship, and it seems unlikely that it could explain minorities' greater loyalty to Labour.[16] So, while we have a plausible story to tell about the similarities between minorities and majority in their sources of desertion from Labour, we have not really made any progress in explaining why defection to another party was so much rarer among minorities. As expected, we also found that evaluations of how well one's ethnic or religious group had fared also played no role.

More surprisingly, we also found no significant effect of bonding social capital on the likelihood of defection, although our measure of the extent of group consensus on Labour values (which we developed in Chapter 6) was significantly related to defection: that is, people who belonged to ethno-religious groups which more strongly endorsed Labour values were less likely to defect (for details see Table 8.A5). So here we find an echo of the group processes that we described in Chapter 6.

Another avenue of enquiry is to look at the role of mobilization by the parties. In other words, rather than focusing on the characteristics of the voters, perhaps we need to shift our focus to look at the behaviour of the parties, and in particular at their efforts to win the votes of ethnic minorities. We saw in Chapter 7 that being canvassed by a political party had a strong relationship with turnout (as many other studies have also shown), and mobilization by political parties has often been suggested as a major means of getting out the minority vote.

We asked a question in our survey about whether people had been canvassed, and if so by which party. We also asked if they had been contacted by a co-ethnic, in order to tap the idea of ethnic mobilization. Table 8.7 shows an important story.

The key finding here is that minorities were much less likely to be canvassed than were the white British electors.[17] Moreover, if they were canvassed, Labour canvassing outweighed Conservative or Liberal Democrat canvassing by 3:2, in a way that is not apparent among other electors. It seems that the Conservatives and Liberal Democrats simply did not pursue ethnic minority voters as hard as Labour did, and that even Labour did not try especially hard—possibly because many minorities live in safe Labour seats. There is a great deal of evidence that parties target their efforts at marginal seats, where

Table 8.7. Canvassing (all respondents)
Column percentages

	White British	Ethnic minorities
Not contacted by any party	46	71
Contacted by Labour	38	21
Contacted by Conservatives	41	14
Contacted by Liberal Democrats	34	12
Contacted by Greens	6	1
Contacted by UKIP	9	1
Contacted by Respect	0	1
Contacted by co-ethnic canvasser from Labour party	–	8
N	2643	2779

Notes: Percentages do not sum to 100 since respondents could be canvassed by more than one party. Chi^2 (contrasting not contacted, contacted by Labour and contacted by other party) = 351.2 (4 df), p < 0.001.
Sources: BES 2010, EMBES 2010, weighted

their efforts are most likely to make a difference to the election result.[18] And, indeed, we also found that minorities living in marginal seats were more likely to have been canvassed. This may not be the whole story, but all the same it is likely that all parties are (perhaps unintentionally) ignoring ethnic minority electors because so many of them reside in safe Labour seats.[19]

We saw in Table 8.6 that Labour partisans who were not canvassed by any of the parties were significantly less likely to turn out and vote. Hence, lack of canvassing is clearly a potential explanation for high rates of minority non-voting. Even more strikingly, Table 8.6 also shows that Labour partisans who were canvassed by a party other than Labour were also more likely to defect to another party. Both phenomena hold true for minorities and majority alike.[20] In other words, the high rates of abstention by ethnic minorities, and the very low rates of defection to other parties, may in part reflect the lack of effort that the parties put into winning over minority voters.

We also checked whether being canvassed by a co-ethnic was more effective. There were some hints that this was indeed the case, but the numbers were rather small and results did not reach statistical significance.[21] There has also been a great deal of discussion as to whether ethnic minority candidates are more appealing to ethnic minority voters. From an analysis of constituency results, John Curtice and his colleagues suggested that 'Whereas selecting an ethnic minority candidate may be somewhat advantageous for Labour in an area with a relatively large ethnic minority population, it seems that the opposite may be the case where a white population predominates' (Curtice et al. 2010, p. 394). There is also quite a large literature from other countries suggesting that minority candidates might have greater appeal to minority voters. However, our more detailed investigation failed to find robust evidence that this applies in Britain.[22] This could be because, in the British context, there is a trade-off between policy representation and symbolic representation. A co-ethnic MP in the 'wrong' party might be able to do much less to advance minority interests in Parliament than a white MP in the 'right' party. In other political systems, where individual representatives have much more freedom of manoeuvre than British MPs have, the ethnicity of the candidate may matter more to voters.

A cautionary tale

Evidence of how Labour partisans might react when their votes are sought in earnest by another party comes from the experience of the Respect Party, which made substantial inroads into Labour's ethnic minority heartlands in 2005, although it was much less successful in 2010.

The Respect Party was founded in 2004, running on a radical left-wing agenda and strongly opposed to Britain's involvement in the Iraq and Afghanistan wars. Interestingly, it did not campaign on issues such as redress for racial discrimination: probably because of its Marxist leanings, it preferred a traditional socialist focus on class rather than racial issues. It contested twenty-four seats, primarily those with large numbers of Muslim voters, in 2005. Following internal dissension and splits, it only contested eleven seats in 2010. One of its most notable figures is the former Labour MP George Galloway (who was expelled from the Labour Party in 2003 for his strident opposition to the Iraq war). Galloway won the Bethnal Green and Bow constituency in 2005, and unsuccessfully contested the Poplar and Limehouse constituency at the 2010 general election. However, in 2012 he successfully contested the by-election in Bradford West, overturning a safe Labour majority with a 37 per cent swing.

Too few of our respondents were resident in the small number of seats contested by Respect for us to use the survey data to analyse the party's impact on defection from Labour. However, we can look at constituency results. While this has its own drawbacks (notably the risk of the so-called ecological fallacy: inferences that hold true when areas are compared may not apply to comparisons between individuals), it has the merit of being based on the hard facts of the actual results. It is also very interesting in its own right.

For example, in East Ham (a constituency with a large Muslim electorate) the Respect candidate won 20.5 per cent of the vote in 2005, and the Labour share fell by 19.2 points. But there was no Respect candidate contesting the seat in 2010, and the Labour share bounced back, increasing by 16.8 points—very different from Labour's average loss in 2010 of 7.4 points. Similarly in West Ham, Respect won 19.5 per cent of the vote in 2005, with the Labour share falling by 18.7 points. But when, in 2010, there was no Respect candidate contesting the seat, Labour's share recovered by 10.9 points. However, dramatic inroads into Labour's share of the vote were not confined to the 2005 election. In 2010, the Respect candidate won 25.1 per cent of the vote in Birmingham Hall Green (another constituency with a large Muslim electorate), and Labour saw its share of the vote fall by 9.4 points.

This should remind us forcibly, as indeed should Respect's success in the Bradford West by-election of 2012, that loyalty to Labour is by no means unquestioning among Muslims, who, as we saw in Chapter 4, continued to be exercised about the war in Afghanistan in 2010. Respect's success indicates that, if active attempts are made to win over Muslim voters, then substantial inroads can be made. This also helps to put some of our other results into perspective. For example, we found earlier that attitudes towards the war in Afghanistan seemed to make no difference to whether a Labour partisan defected to another party or not. One possible explanation for this might be that the war no longer had the potential to undermine Labour support among Muslims, but this does not fit with our survey evidence about the issues which exercised Muslim voters in 2010. A better interpretation is surely that the other main parties, unlike Respect, failed to canvas actively on the war. We also suspect that if a rival party canvassed actively for minority votes on the issue of redress of discrimination, Labour support among black voters could also be eroded.

The constituency results are also consistent with our concept of 'collective party identification' that we developed in Chapter 6. There can be short-run departures from a community's collective identity in the light of particular circumstances, such as the intervention of Respect candidates in 2005, but there will also be a homing tendency to revert to the collective identity if the special circumstances disappear—as we saw in the constituencies where Respect stood in 2005 but not in 2010.

Minority loyalty or party inertia?

Ethnic minority support for Labour at the polls declined between 1997 and 2010 much as it did among other groups of British voters, and largely for similar reasons, to do with failures of the economy and leadership. The minority vote for Labour also lagged behind minority Labour partisanship, much as it did among other Labour partisans. Ethnic minority support for Labour is not unconditional, therefore—it is not a bloc vote that can be taken for granted.

On the other hand, the form that ethnic minority disappointment with Labour took was somewhat different from that of the majority: minorities were less likely to defect to a different party, and instead were more likely to stay at home or even to fail to register. A major part of the explanation for the absence of defection to other parties, we suspect, was simply that other parties made little effort to win over minority voters in safe Labour seats. All the main parties, including Labour, concentrated their campaigning on marginal seats, and this meant that, possibly inadvertently, they allowed Labour to continue its dominance among minority voters. Even Labour did not campaign as much in its safe seats as it did elsewhere, and this will have contributed to minorities staying at home.

So while we found some traces of greater minority loyalty to Labour, echoing the role of group norms and sentiments that we described in Chapter 6, we feel that party inertia played a crucial role in explaining minorities' low rates of defection from Labour to other parties. The success of the Respect Party in eating into Labour's share of the vote in 2005, and to a lesser extent in 2010, in constituencies where there were largeish numbers of Muslim voters, should warn Labour against complacency. If other parties seriously wished to win over minority voters, active campaigning on issues that minorities care about would be a good way to start.

Appendix: supplementary tables

Table 8.A1. Partisanship and vote in 2010 (all minorities)
Row percentages

	Abstained (did not vote or register)	Voted Labour	Voted Conservative	Voted Liberal Democrat	Voted for other party	N
Non-partisan	72	15	6	5	1	459
Labour partisan	43	53	1	2	0	1499
Conservative partisan	36	2	59	3	0	221
Liberal Democrat partisan	47	4	1	49	0	226
Other partisans	47	9	0	9	34	37

Source: EMBES 2010, weighted data

Table 8.A2. Multinomial logistic regression of departures from Labour identity
Parameter estimates (reference: voted Labour)

	Abstained (did not vote or did not register)	Defected to another party
Ethnic group		
White British (ref)	0	0
Mixed white/black	0.79	0.59
Indian	−0.19	−0.47
Pakistani	0.08	−0.17
Bangladeshi	−0.44	−0.53
Black Caribbean	−0.05	−0.97
Black African	−0.04	−1.22
Demographics		
Age (ln)	−1.13	0.35
Gender	−0.25	−0.39
Marital status	−0.16	0.04
Education	−0.02	0.13

Continued

Table 8.A2. *Continued*

	Abstained (did not vote or did not register)	Defected to another party
Income	−0.02	0.06
Middle class (ref)	0	0
Working class	0.00	−0.10
Unwaged or missing	0.01	−0.25
Owner (ref)	0	0
LA tenant	**0.50**	**−0.85**
Other tenure	**0.90**	0.00
1st generation	0.26	**−0.47**
1.5 generation	0.08	**−0.42**
2nd generation (ref)	0	0
(Pseudo) R^2	0.09	
N	2257	

Notes: Includes tactical voters; validated measures of voting and non-voting. White British are coded as second+ generation. Parameter estimates significant at the 0.05 level are emboldened.

Sources: BES 2010, EMBES 2010, Labour identifiers only, unweighted

Table 8.A3. Vote and vote change among 2005 Labour voters
Row percentages

	Did not vote	Voted Labour again in 2010	Switched to another party in 2010	N
White British	25	50	26	844
Indian	27	60	13	255
Pakistani	34	51	15	269
Bangladeshi	36	48	17	113
Black Caribbean	28	63	9	277
Black African	35	62	3	191
Mixed white/black	40	53	7	26
All minorities	31	58	11	1131

Sources: BES 2010, EMBES 2010, weighted data

Table 8.A4. Distributions of different ethnic groups' opinions on key performance measures: Labour partisans only
Percentages

	White British	All minorities	Indian	Pakistani	Bangladeshi	Caribbean	African
Labour handled crime fairly or very badly	23	21	**27**	18	13	22	15
…immigration badly	57	31	**39**	27	32	**43**	16
…NHS badly	12	14	**19**	15	16	13	7
…risk of terrorism badly	14	15	**16**	19	18	16	8
…economy generally badly	23	24	24	28	22	**29**	17
Afghanistan war going badly	72	65	66	**72**	66	66	58
H'hold financial situation worse	44	49	44	46	**58**	**53**	51
Economic situation worse	67	67	70	62	70	70	63
Like Gordon Brown	65	68	69	61	**77**	56	**79**
Like David Cameron	21	30	34	34	**46**	**14**	28
Like Nick Clegg	25	28	30	32	29	**11**	**34**
Tactical Voter	8	5	6	5	5	4	4

Notes: Figures in bold indicate that the percentage for the particular ethnic group is significantly different, at the 5% level, from the average expectation for all ethnic minorities.

Sources: BES, EMBES 2010, weighted data

Table 8.A5. Expanded model for explaining deviations from Labour support among ethnic minority Labour identifiers: multinomial logistic regression
Parameter estimates

	Abstained	Switched to another party
Evaluations		
Labour handled crime fairly or very badly	0.08	0.09
...immigration badly	−0.05	0.17
...NHS badly	0.07	0.26
...risk of terrorism badly	0.07	0.13
...economy generally badly	−0.02	−0.23
Think Afghanistan war is going badly	0.01	−0.19
H'hold financial situation worse	0.04	0.28
General economic situation worse	0.15	0.21
Things got better/worse for own ethnic group	−0.08	−0.02
Liking for Gordon Brown	**−0.12**	**−0.24**
Liking for David Cameron	0.09	0.09
Liking for Nick Clegg	0.03	**0.20**
Political engagement		
Strength of partisanship	**−0.45**	**−0.75**
Duty to vote	**−0.63**	**−0.37**
Political interest	**−0.20**	0.25
Political knowledge	−0.06	0.29
Canvassing		
Not canvassed	**0.66**	0.57
Canvassed by other party than Labour	0.21	**1.38**
Canvassed by Labour (reference)	0	0
Group relations		
Ethnic identification	0.07	−0.09
Bonding social capital	−0.04	−0.06
Fraternal relative deprivation	−0.03	−0.15
Labour values	0.01	**−0.05**
(pseudo) R^2	0.21	
N	1271	

Notes: Parameter estimates significant at the 5% level are emboldened. The models also include controls for age, gender, marital status, ethnic group, tenure, generation, class (NS), education (NS), income (NS), IMD (NS), and percentage non-white (NS).
Source: EMBES 2010 unweighted, Labour partisans only, tactical voters excluded

Notes

1. Table 8.A1 in the appendix shows the vote distributions for non-partisans and partisans of other parties. It shows that there were some modest movements in the opposite direction—from non-partisans and other partisans towards Labour—but much smaller in magnitude than the movements away from Labour.
2. Including non-registration as well as non-voting in the category of abstention is perhaps stretching the term from its normal usage. However, we were unable to think of a simple term that encapsulated both non-voting and non-registration, and in any event for some Labour supporters failure to register might have been driven by disillusionment with the party's performance. In practice, if we exclude from the base those who were not registered we obtain the same story with low

percentages of minorities defecting to other parties (5 per cent overall). The self-report data also show the same pattern (6 per cent defecting to other parties).
3. Without controls, all minorities except Indians showed a significantly higher rate of abstention than the white British, and all minorities except the mixed group showed a lower rate of defection. However, after controls for potential confounding variables, only the two black groups showed significantly lower rates of defection (see Table 8.A2).
4. See, for example, Clarke et al. (2004, 2009).
5. See Li and Heath (2008), although the disproportionate effect of recession on minorities was more evident in the early 1980s and early 1990s recessions than it has been since 2008.
6. Non-partisans should not be equated with the US concept of 'independents', since non-partisans in Britain are typically people with lower levels of political interest or knowledge.
7. Differences between the various minority groups were fairly modest too. See Table 8.A4 in the appendix to the chapter.
8. On the items about how Labour had handled the various responsibilities, a significantly higher proportion of minorities answered 'don't know', but apart from this there was little difference in the pattern of responses, except for Labour's handling of immigration.
9. See Ford (2008).
10. See Field (2007, 2011).
11. We also controlled for all the standard demographic measures, specifically for the natural logarithm of age, gender, marital status, income, class, highest educational level, housing tenure, and, for ethnic minorities, generation. We then removed from the final models variables that were consistently non-significant, retaining only those that were significant for at least one contrast. On this criterion, age, income, class, and highest educational level were removed from the models.
12. See, for example, Heath and Evans (1994), Fisher (2004). However, we should note that there appeared to be some confusion among our respondents, quite a few of whom gave their preferred party as the same as the one they had previously reported voting for. We do not count these respondents as tactical voters, therefore, and retain them in the sample.
13. The models fitted are multinomial logistic regressions with robust standard errors. For continuous or ordered variables the average marginal effects compare the 10th and the 90th percentiles.
14. There were, however, some differences with the demographic variables. For the ethnic minorities, but not for the white British, age, being male, and being single significantly increased abstention. There were also some significant differences between minorities.
15. There are several differences of detail from our findings in Sanders et al. (forthcoming), but this is not surprising given that the analysis in this chapter is looking at deviations from a Labour identity rather than vote choice in general.
16. To be sure, Labour's record on immigration, as we saw in Chapter 6, was modestly associated with Labour partisanship, so it would be wrong to say that immigration

is unconnected with Labour support. However, the key point for the present chapter is that it fails, among those who identified with Labour in 2010, to explain whether or not they voted Labour rather than defecting to another party.
17. We also checked results for the ethnic minorities within the BES survey. Within the main BES the minority/majority difference was not as large: 56 per cent of minorities rather than the 71 per cent in EMBES reported that they had not been contacted by any of the parties, but this was still significantly higher than the figure for the white British.
18. See for example Karp et al. (2008), Johnston and Pattie (2012), and Sobolewska et al. (2012).
19. Sobolewska et al. (2012) shows that the mean majority in the elector's constituency in 2005 was only 19 votes for the white British electors and 7,457 votes for an ethnic minority elector.
20. Johnston and Pattie (2012) have also shown, using a different dataset, a powerful effect of being canvassed by a particular party on voting for that party.
21. In a bivariate analysis we found that defection from a Labour identity to a vote for one of the other parties was significantly more likely if canvassed by a co-ethnic canvasser from a different party, but this result was no longer significant after the standard controls.
22. See, for example, Barreto (2007) on the USA, Bergh and Bjorklund (2011) on Norway, and Teney et al. (2010) on Belgium. For our analysis see Fisher et al. (in preparation).

9

Varieties of Political Engagement: Activists and Dissidents

While participation in general elections is an important aspect of the democratic process, the repertoire of political action in Britain is considerably wider than simply voting. Citizens may write to their MP, local councillor, or local newspaper to complain or ask for action (or engage in their contemporary electronic equivalents). They can form or join pressure groups or campaigning organizations that will attempt to directly influence government. They can take to the streets in protest. All of these can be seen as varieties of 'voice',[1] where citizens actively attempt to influence the political process rather than passively following whatever political elites decide to put before them. And these different forms of voice, including peaceful protest, can be seen as potential ways in which minorities might be integrated into the political process. In particular, they give opportunities for groups who feel that their concerns are being sidelined by political elites to bring pressure to bear. While elites, even in democracies, are never too pleased to be challenged, they nevertheless recognize that the expression of dissident voices through non-electoral activities is a legitimate aspect of the practice of democracy. Indeed, the classic study of the civic culture by Gabriel Almond and Sydney Verba saw a balance of active involvement and passive acceptance (which they termed participant and subject cultures) as the mark of the most successful democracies.[2]

So a key question for us is whether minorities participate in these alternative methods for bringing pressure to bear on political elites in the same way that other British citizens do. Our expectation is that new migrants, given their somewhat marginal position in British society, might find access to these alternative forms of participation more difficult. But we also expect to find that this is another area where there is gradual convergence across generations, recent arrivals in Britain being the least likely to be familiar with British ways of influencing the political process but the second generation adapting to the British model. Certainly, research in other European countries has suggested that migrants, particularly those from less-developed countries, have lower levels of participation than native populations (although this European research has not been able to investigate participation among the second generation).[3]

There are many possible ways of categorizing the various forms of non-electoral political participation or voice. Researchers have tended to counterpose more orthodox or conventional forms of political participation, such as voting, joining a political party, and contacting politicians, with what they see as unorthodox or unconventional involvement, such as protests, demonstrations, marches, and even terrorist violence. Some scholars have distinguished elite-supporting from elite-challenging forms of participation, while others have distinguished between citizen-oriented and cause-oriented actions. Another useful distinction might be between individual and collective action—between those activities that are done with others, and those activities that one does on one's own.[4]

In our survey, we asked about a number of forms of participation (although lack of questionnaire space meant that we could not cover the full range that we would have liked to). We asked whether the individual had been active in a voluntary organization, had volunteered to get involved in politics or community affairs, was a member of a political or citizens group, had signed a petition, had participated in a boycott of a particular product, had given money to a political cause, or had participated in a protest, like a rally or a demonstration.

While people who had participated in one form of participation were also relatively likely to participate in others, cluster analysis suggested that these forms of participation fall into two somewhat distinct camps. In the first camp we have the organizational forms of participation (being active in a voluntary organization, volunteering, and belonging to a political or citizens group), and in the second camp we have the more ad hoc or informal activities such as signing a petition, participating in a boycott, or going on a protest.[5] (Tables 9.A1 and 9.A2 show the associations between the different forms.) As a shorthand, we shall term these respectively 'organizational' and 'informal' forms of collective participation. Broadly speaking, we can think of the more organizational forms of participation as being on balance elite-supporting, while the informal ones tend to be somewhat elite-challenging.

A number of different general theories have been suggested in political science, sociology, and social psychology for understanding why people might engage in various forms of collective political action of the sort described above. A classic approach emphasized the role of a shared sense of grievance or injustice—a perception that the government was making unfair or morally objectionable decisions, or failing to address legitimate sources of concern—in stimulating voice or protest. This seems logical, since most protests or petitions are overtly about some public issue. The protests about the Labour government's decisions to go to war in Iraq and Afghanistan, and more recently about the current Conservative/Liberal Democrat coalition government's austerity measures, are obvious examples.

Another sort of grievance which might be relevant is the sense of fraternal relative deprivation which we introduced in Chapter 6. This has often been found by social psychologists to be important in stimulating collective action.[6] Thus, when people feel that the group to which they belong suffers from unfair treatment compared with, say, the treatment the majority receive, then this may provide an incentive to get together and protest. The Civil Rights movement in the USA would be a classic example of this, while closer to home the Troubles in Northern Ireland ultimately stemmed from long-standing grievances about the exclusion of Catholics, and the inequalities of opportunity that they faced. Given the powerful role that a sense of fraternal relative deprivation played in explaining partisanship in Chapter 6, we clearly need to take it seriously in this chapter too.

Implicit in the concept of fraternal relative deprivation is the notion of group identity: you can hardly have a feeling of fraternal deprivation unless you also conceive of some people as being brothers or sisters in adversity. Many theorists have suggested that a sense of group identity is an important factor in collective action, while specialists in minority participation have emphasized the role of ethnic or race consciousness as a driving force behind political participation.[7] Some writers have suggested that ethnic identities will only be important if they have become 'politicized' in the way that they were in the US civil rights movement. This may well be true, although to be honest the argument looks a bit circular.

A very different approach focuses on the role of individual and group resources. The main idea behind this shift in focus is that it is not all that easy to turn a shared grievance into an organized protest or political action. The experience of economic hardship or other forms of disadvantage on their own are unlikely to lead to political participation. Effective organization needs resourceful individuals who can take the lead. These will often be more educated individuals, who also tend to have greater self-confidence that they can make a difference (a greater sense of political 'efficacy', in political science terminology). By and large, the same kinds of individual attributes and resources associated with electoral participation also seem to be involved with non-electoral forms of action.[8]

Collective action will also be helped by group resources such as might be provided by ethnic communities. Collective action essentially presupposes doing something with other people, rather than acting in a purely individualistic way. Social ties may be important as ways of mobilizing friends, or passing information, or reinforcing the sense of grievance. In the context of ethnic minorities, bonding social capital might well be important for mobilizing group members—Marvin Olsen has termed this the 'ethnic community' hypothesis.[9] Meindert Fennema and Jean Tillie have demonstrated the importance in the Netherlands of what they term 'civic community' for ethnic minority participation.[10] In the USA, black churches have also been found to be particularly important in stimulating African-American political action, and there is some evidence that mosques can play a similar role.[11]

A final theme is that of the nature of the alternatives available to the citizen. In particular, protest might be a 'weapon of the weak'. Thus, Michael Lipsky has argued that 'protest is correctly conceived as a strategy utilized by relatively powerless groups in order to increase their bargaining ability' (1968, p. 1157). If conventional channels of electoral participation fail to secure redress of one's grievances, perhaps because one's views are unpopular or because one's agenda is excluded from mainstream party politics, and one does not have the clout through conventional lobbying or pressure group politics, taking to the streets may be the only alternative left. The powerful don't usually need to go out and protest or join pressure groups, as they can usually work from within the system to secure their objectives.

How might these theories apply to the different forms of participation? And to which groups? Well, we might expect more disadvantaged groups, such as blacks and Bangladeshis perhaps, to turn towards protest, if the theory of protest as the weapon of the weak is correct. The theory of fraternal relative deprivation would also suggest that there might be high levels of protest and other informal types of participation among blacks, while grievance theories might predict higher levels of protest and mobilization on the part of Muslims, in view of their concerns over Iraq and Afghanistan. Given their greater collective resources (for example, through bonding social capital), we might also expect to see higher involvement of the South Asian groups in organizational forms of political action.

It is not entirely clear, therefore, whether levels of non-electoral participation among minorities will be higher, lower, or similar to majority levels. While the marginal situation of minorities in British society might depress participation (in a similar way to its effect on minority rates of registration), grievances such as those over the wars in Iraq or Afghanistan or over discrimination and unequal opportunities might give powerful reasons for collective action, while collective resources might well facilitate some forms of collective organization.

Documenting the differences

So let us turn straightaway to our evidence on minority and majority patterns of participation. We asked our respondents:

Now a few questions about how active you are in politics and community affairs.
  Over the past few years, have you volunteered to get involved in politics or community affairs?
  Over the past few years, how active have you been in a voluntary organisation, like a local community association, a charity, or a sports club?
  In the last 12 months, have you participated in a protest, like a rally or a demonstration, to show your concern about a public issue or problem?
  .... signed a petition, to show your concern about a public issue or problem?
  .... participated in a boycott of a particular product or service?
  .... given money to a political cause or advocacy organisation (other than a political party)

The first two questions, but not the others, were also asked in the main BES.

Table 9.1 shows the distribution by ethnic group in the more organizational forms of participation, while Table 9.2 shows participation in the more informal types. (Note that giving money to a cause tended to be slightly more strongly associated with the organizational forms of participation, and so is included in Table 9.1.)

As we can see, some forms of organizational participation are much more common than others. The most common is being active in a voluntary organization, but this is very broadly defined, and as soon as politics is specified, percentages fall off very sharply. It is only a tiny minority who

Table 9.1. Participation in voluntary organizations
Cell percentages who over the last few years had...

Ethnic background	Been active in a voluntary organization	Volunteered to get involved in politics or community affairs	Given money to a political cause	Been active in a political or citizens group	N
White British	46	12	–	–	2759
Indian	46	14	7	3	586
Pakistani	36	16	6	3	667
Bangladeshi	39	16	6	1	270
Black Caribbean	46	15	7	3	597
Black African	52	23	7	4	524
Mixed black/white	45	14	9	2	81
All minorities	44	16	7	3	2779

Notes: Question for donating money to a political cause refers to 'last twelve months'. Coding for being active in a voluntary organization includes very, somewhat, and a little active. Figures in bold are significantly higher than expectation at the 5% level. Chi^2 (active) = 52.8 (6 df), p < 0.001; (volunteered) = 35.8 (6 df), p < 0.001.
Sources: EMBES 2010, BES 2010, weighted data

Varieties of Political Engagement: Activists and Dissidents

Table 9.2. Participation in protest, petition, or boycott
Cell percentages who in last twelve months had...

Ethnic background	Signed a petition	Participated in a protest or demonstration	Participated in a boycott	N
White British	27	5	–	868
All minorities (MCDS)	17	3	–	518
Indian	22	7	6	586
Pakistani	20	7	11	667
Bangladeshi	18	9	8	270
Black Caribbean	20	6	5	597
Black African	16	4	3	524
Mixed black/white	31	5	10	93
All minorities (EMBES)	20	6	7	2707

Notes: Figures in bold are significantly different at the 5% level from expectation in the EMBES survey. Chi^2 for petitioning in the MCD survey = 17.1 (1 df) $p < 0.001$; for protest = 4.3 (1 df), $p < 0.05$.
Sources: EMBES 2010 for ethnic minorities; MCDS 2009 for the white British

actually engage in higher-cost political activities, such as giving money to a political cause. As all previous writers have shown, non-electoral forms of civic participation are much rarer than electoral forms, and this applies to the white British as much as to ethnic minorities.

Majority/minority differences with respect to these forms of organizational participation prove to be surprisingly small, indeed non-existent. Unfortunately, the full range of participation questions was not asked in the main BES. The only two areas where we can make a direct comparison is on activity in a voluntary organization (not necessarily a political one) and volunteering to get involved in political or community affairs. For neither of these forms of organizational involvement is there a significant majority/minority difference.[12] The picture is slightly different, though, when we look at the more informal types of participation.

Table 9.2 shows the more informal forms of participation. As expected, signing a petition is the most common activity, but it is of course a very low-cost activity. Higher-cost activities (in terms of time if not money), such as going on a protest or demonstration, are very much rarer. Again, this is a standard finding from research on non-electoral forms of participation.

Questions on signing a petition or going on a protest were not asked in the main BES, but we do have very similar questions from another nationally representative survey which also had an ethnic minority booster sample, the MCDS.[13] The wording was slightly different, and so we show the MCDS estimates for both white British and for ethnic minorities, as well as the ethnic minority figures from EMBES.[14]

The MCDS indicates that the white British were more likely to sign a petition (27 versus 17 per cent for minorities), and to go on a protest (5 versus 3 per cent). The MCDS also showed quite a big difference in majority/minority rates of engaging in the more individualistic activity of writing to the local council—23 per cent of white British had done so, compared with only 12 per cent of minorities. So our judgement is that overall participation rates, while showing a broadly similar profile, probably are somewhat lower among ethnic minorities.

However, we find relatively little difference between the different minorities. There is a modest tendency in the EMBES data for black Africans to be more involved in voluntary organizations, and to be less engaged in protests or the other less formal types of action. But generally differences are small and not significant. There are hints that people of Bangladeshi background are slightly more inclined to engage in protests, but this does not apply to other notionally weak groups like the black Caribbeans. Nor is there much evidence that groups with stronger bonding capital, such as the Pakistanis, are more inclined towards organizational forms of participation. These results for non-electoral participation thus parallel our findings in Chapter 7 on electoral participation: remember that we found small differences between minorities in electoral participation, but a clear shortfall among all minorities in registration rates compared with the white British.

Chapter 7 also showed that registration rates were significantly lower among the first-generation migrants, and as we noted, European research has also found that non-electoral forms of participation are lower among migrants. It is therefore of considerable interest to chart the patterns of generational change, which we do in Table 9.3.

With the exception of giving money to a cause, we find fairly large and significant generational differences in all types of participation, with the first generation in every case having significantly lower rates of participation.[15] Conversely, minority participation rates in the second generation are as high

Table 9.3. Generational differences in political participation
Cell percentages

	Minorities			White British	
	1st generation	1.5 generation	2nd + generation	All ages	Aged 18–45
Active in voluntary organization	39	50	50	46	45
Volunteered	14	21	16	12	11
Given money to a cause	6	7	8	–	–
Signed petition	14	22	28	27	26
Joined protest	4	6	10	5	4
Joined boycott	2	9	12	–	–

Notes: Figures in bold are significantly lower than expectation in the EMBES sample. Chi^2 (active) = 32.1 (2 df) $p < 0.001$; (volunteered) = 9.5 (2 df) $p < 0.01$; (donated) = 3.5 (2 df), NS; (petition) = 78.8 (2 df) $p < 0.001$; (protest) = 26.8 (2 df) $p < 0.001$; (boycott) = 95.1 (2 df) $p < 0.001$.

Sources: BES 2010 for white British active and volunteered, EMBES 2010 for ethnic minority figures, MCDS for white British petitioning and protest

Varieties of Political Engagement: Activists and Dissidents

or higher than those among their white British peers. This strongly suggests that these non-electoral forms of participation are learned in Britain; in other words they may be more westernized forms of political participation.

Who participates?

Next, we turn to consider the possible drivers of the different forms of participation. How successful are the various theories that we sketched out in the introduction? What roles do grievances and resources (both individual and collective) play in fostering these different forms of participation? And how different are the drivers of non-electoral participation from those of registration and turnout? For this exercise we necessarily have to restrict ourselves to the ethnic minorities, since the relevant questions (about both predictors and outcomes) were not available in the main BES.

We included measures of all the main concepts raised by the theorists, namely grievances and fraternal relative deprivation, individual resources (both socio-economic and more psychological ones), and collective resources (including both ethnic identification and bonding social capital). As usual, we also include standard controls for variables such as age, gender, and generation. We run the same model for a selection of outcomes, namely being active in a voluntary organization, volunteering, signing a petition, going on a protest or demonstration, and participating in a boycott.

What we expect to find is that all the different sorts of non-electoral participation are associated with greater individual resources, with non-participants having fewer resources, although possibly the more informal forms of involvement may not be quite as strongly linked to individual resources, on the theory that protest is a weapon of the weak. We also expect that organizational forms of participation will be more strongly associated with collective resources, while informal types of involvement might be more strongly associated with grievances and fraternal relative deprivation.

In Table 9.4, we show how much difference each predictor is estimated to make to the probability of engaging in each form of activity. For example, in column 1 the figure of +5 for 'discrimination' indicates that minorities who reported that they had experienced discrimination on the grounds of race or religion were 5 percentage points *more* likely to be active than were people who did not report discrimination (other things being equal). Conversely, in column 1 the figure of −3 for 'female' indicates that women were 3 points *less* likely to be active than were men (other things being equal), although in this case the difference was not statistically significant. The figures thus tell us how large a difference each predictor makes to the probability of engaging in each activity, and they also tell us whether the difference is positive or negative. In

Table 9.4. Predictors of non-electoral participation
Average marginal effects

	Active in voluntary organization	Volunteered	Signed petition	Joined protest	Joined boycott
Individual psychological resources					
Political efficacy	**+13**	**+8**	+3	+3	+1
Political interest	**+15**	**+15**	**+14**	**+4**	**+5**
Political knowledge	+1	+2	**+6**	0	**+4**
Socio-economic resources					
Education	**+12**	**+6**	**+9**	+2	**+3**
Middle class	+2	+2	+5	+1	**+4**
Working class	−4	−2	−1	−1	+1
Other class or missing (ref)	0	0	0	0	0
Home owner	**+7**	**+4**	+1	0	−2
Tenant in social housing	+4	+2	+1	0	−1
Other tenures (ref)	0	0	0	0	0
Grievances					
Fraternal relative deprivation	**+5**	**+4**	**+4**	+2	**+4**
Discrimination	**+5**	**+4**	**+6**	+2	**+3**
No party represents me	**+4**	**+3**	+1	+2	+2
Affirmative action	−1	+2	**+6**	+1	**+3**
Asylum	+3	**+4**	**+7**	+1	**+5**
Afghanistan	−3	−1	**+5**	+2	**+4**
Ethnic identification	+2	−1	**−6**	−1	−2
Social capital					
Informal bonding	**−8**	−2	−1	−1	0
Associational bonding	**+24**	**+12**	**+9**	**+6**	**+3**
Church member	**+6**	+2	0	−2	−1
Demographics					
Age	**−6**	+2	+1	**−3**	−2
Female	−3	−1	−1	−1	+2
1st generation (ref)	0	0	0	0	0
1.5 generation	+4	+2	**+5**	+2	**+6**
2nd plus generations	**+5**	0	**+7**	**+3**	**+6**
(pseudo) R^2	0.15	0.14	0.14	0.13	0.19
N	2,548	2,546	2,547	2,548	2,548

Notes: Emboldened figures indicate that the underlying coefficient is significant at the 5% level. The models also include controls for ethnic group.
Source: EMBES 2010, unweighted

interpreting these figures, we need to bear in mind how common or rare each activity was (as shown in Tables 9.1 and 9.2). In other words, we would expect our measures to make more difference in the case of the more common forms of engagement, such as being active in a voluntary organization or signing a petition, than with rarer forms of engagement, such as going on a protest or participating in a boycott. And this is basically what we see.

There are some variations from one outcome to another, but we should not put too much weight on small variations, given the small numbers engaging in some of the forms of participation. Given that we are testing for lots of predictors for lots of outcomes, we are bound to obtain quite a lot of statistically significant estimates just by chance alone. We need to look for general patterns, of which there are some pretty clear ones, rather than focusing on particular estimates, a number of which are bound to be 'false positives'.

First, we find some consistent patterns across all forms of participation. It is striking that education, political interest, and a sense of political efficacy are pretty consistently important, while our other measures of resources, such as social class and housing tenure, have much patchier effects. (We also tested whether income had a significant relationship with the different forms of participation, but its role was negligible, except for making a donation—where more affluent individuals were unsurprisingly more likely to make a donation.) This suggests that the underlying mechanism is not really about economic resources but about psychological ones.[16] Nor is there any sign of protest being a weapon of the weak. Individuals with weaker economic or psychological resources, for example less-educated or working-class individuals, show no sign of being more disposed to engage in protests or boycotts.

The second consistent, and substantively important, pattern is for grievances, broadly construed, to be positively associated with participation. While our estimates are not always statistically significant, there is a clear pattern for our measures of fraternal relative deprivation, of individual experiences of discrimination, and progressive views on affirmative action, asylum, and the war in Afghanistan to have positive signs across the board, and they seem to be most important for signing a petition or joining a boycott. To be sure, grievances do not make as much difference as psychological resources to the probability of being active in a voluntary organization, volunteering, or signing a petition; but it is probably fair to say that psychological resources are relatively more important for the organizational forms of participation, whereas grievances are relatively more important for informal forms. Interestingly, answers to our question whether *'any of the parties in Britain represents your views reasonably well'* (reviewed in Chapter 5) also show a consistent pattern: feelings that views were not represented were consistently associated with an increased probability of non-electoral participation.

Associational bonding capital also makes a difference across the board, in almost exactly the same way that psychological resources and grievances do. We should, however, be rather sceptical of its large role in predicting volunteering or being active in a voluntary organization: our measure of associational bonding capital is whether the respondent belonged to an ethnic or cultural association, and it is highly likely that it will be precisely these associations in which our respondents were being active. So the strong association is almost circular or tautological. However, there is nothing tautological in belonging to an ethnic or cultural association and going on a protest or participating in a boycott. They are conceptually quite distinct. One plausible interpretation, although not the only one, is that ethnic associations are vehicles for mobilizing members to engage in other forms of participation.

Interestingly, however, churches do not seem to play as significant a role in this respect as they do in the USA.

It is also quite striking that neither ethnic identification nor informal bonding lead to increased participation. If anything, the reverse is true.[17] One possibility is that informal bonding and ethnic identification both lead one away from involvement in mainstream British politics and towards a focus on more ethnic concerns. However, we should not make too much of this, since most of their effects shown in Table 9.4 are very modest in size.

Finally, we observe that there are consistent patterns of generational differences across all the outcomes, somewhat more so for the informal forms of participation. This confirms our findings in Table 9.3, and demonstrates that they are robust findings that cannot be explained away by age, education, or even by political interest and knowledge of British politics.

Comparing electoral and non-electoral participation

How similar are these drivers of non-electoral participation to the drivers of registration and turnout that we explored in Chapter 7? Do different sorts of people engage in non-electoral forms of participation, especially perhaps the informal or elite-challenging kinds, from those who engage in more organizational or conventional forms of participation, and from those who register and turn out to vote?

If we run the same analyses on registration and turnout that we have just applied to non-electoral forms of participation, some striking differences and only a couple of similarities emerge. First, the only attributes that are by and large *positively* associated with all the main types of electoral and non-electoral participation are:

- Interest in British politics
- Home ownership

And the only attribute that is *negatively* associated with all the main types of political participation is:

- Membership of the first generation

Attributes that generally have *reversed* associations, positive with non-electoral but negative with electoral participation, and which thus work in opposite directions, are:

- Feelings of fraternal relative deprivation
- Feelings that no party represents me

While attributes that have a positive association *only with non-electoral participation* are:

- Grievances related to issues of asylum, war, and equal opportunities
- Experiences of racial or religious discrimination
- Membership of a cultural association

Further analysis shows that the following attributes have a positive association *only with electoral participation* (registration and turnout) but not the non-electoral forms:

- Duty to vote
- Strength of partisanship
- Age

We must remind readers of our usual caveats about the dangers of inferring causation from these statistical analyses, and about the probability that the effects of some predictors will have been masked by other predictors included in the analysis. Nevertheless, the clear upshot of these comparisons between electoral and non-electoral forms of participation is that a distinct subset of ethnic minorities is taking advantage of the various non-electoral opportunities for voice. Whereas electoral participation is widespread and reflects strength of partisanship and norms of civic duty, non-electoral forms are much less widespread, but give opportunities to people who feel that their grievances are not being addressed by the mainstream parties. Non-electoral forms, whether through voluntary organizations, marches, or other forms of protest, give alternative avenues for the British equivalents of the dissidents who protest in non-democratic countries. They enable them to voice their concern over issues that are largely excluded from the mainstream political agenda.

Voluntary organizations, marches, and protests are thus important alternative forms of political integration. It is the second generation in particular that takes advantage of these alternative forms of elite-challenging activism, and we suspect that they are very similar to other British citizens in these respects. We found no real systematic differences between the various ethnic minorities in these patterns, and we suspect that (if we exclude the less-participatory first generation) there would be no systematic differences from the white British either.

Integrative dissidence

So where does this leave us? Substantively, it looks pretty clear that, just as with electoral participation, minorities' forms of non-electoral participation are not all that dissimilar from those of other British citizens. If the BES had included more of our measures, we could be even clearer, but all the same we have no grounds for supposing that second-generation minorities in general, or any minorities in particular, are distinctively less integrated or differently integrated than the white British. To be sure, participation is indeed lower among the adult migrants, just as it was in the case of electoral registration. Lower participation among the first generation has often been reported before in other countries, and can readily be explained in much the same way that we explained first-generation shortfalls in registration and turnout. But the key point is that the one point five and second generations have participation profiles that are almost certainly very similar to those of their white British peers, and which have most probably been learned in Britain.

These rather British forms of activism and dissident behaviour are important as they give alternative vehicles for individuals and groups who feel neglected by mainstream political bodies. It is particularly noteworthy that individuals who feel fraternal relative deprivation or who feel that none of the mainstream parties adequately represents them are inclined towards protest and dissent. While the authorities are typically more likely to praise dissidents in other countries but to repress home-grown dissidents (for example through the police tactic of 'kettling' protestors on demonstrations), peaceful protest remains an important mechanism for the excluded to bring pressure to bear on the authorities. In this respect, we regard it is an important aspect of political integration, and one where, once again, second-generation minorities resemble their fellow British citizens, and are going with the grain of British political practices.

Appendix: Supplementary tables

Table 9.A1. Associations between different forms of non-electoral participation (ethnic minorities only)
Log odds ratios

	Volunteered	Active in citizens group	Given money to cause	Signed a petition	Joined protest	Joined boycott
Active in voluntary organization	3.5	1.5	1.2	1.3	1.8	1.0
Volunteered		2.2	1.4	1.5	1.8	1.2
Active in citizens group			1.6	1.5	1.4	1.3
Given money				1.6	1.7	1.3
Signed petition					2.5	2.5
Joined protest						2.0

Notes: Log odds ratios significant at the 5% level are emboldened.
Source: EMBES 2010

Table 9.A2. Cluster analysis of the different forms of non-electoral participation
Cluster analysis: final cluster centres

	Cluster 1 (Non-participants)	Cluster 2 (Volunteers)	Cluster 3 (Petitioners)	Cluster 4 (Activists)
Active in voluntary organization	0.29	1.00	0.00	0.96
Volunteered	0.01	0.78	0.05	0.44
Given money	0.03	0.08	0.07	0.44
Active in citizens group	0.01	0.07	0.02	0.14
Signed petition	0.00	0.48	1.00	0.94
Joined protest	0.01	0.10	0.14	0.49
Joined boycott	0.02	0.02	0.22	0.68
N	1987	463	166	154

Notes: The figures give the proportion of the members of each cluster who reported that they engage in each type of activity. They should be thought of as cell proportions, not as column or row proportions.
Source: EMBES 2010

Notes

1. We use the term voice following A. O. Hirschman's classic distinction between exit, voice, and loyalty. See Hirschman (1970).
2. See Almond and Verba (1963).
3. See, for example, Aleksynska (2011). Aleksynska's data source is the European Social Survey. It is implicit in the article that the native-born include members both of the majority group and of minority groups. Similar results using the same source are reported by de Rooij (2012).
4. Some of the key treatments of these issues are to be found in Milbrath (1965), Verba et al. (1978), Barnes and Kaase (1979); Inglehart (1990), and Norris (2004).
5. The cluster analysis in table 9.A2 shows four types of individual: those with generally low levels of participation (cluster 1), those with generally high levels of participation in all the different modes (cluster 4), those who tend to specialize in organizational activity (cluster 2), and those who tend to specialize in more informal forms of activity (cluster 3); although clusters 2 and 3 are not especially clearly demarcated.
6. See van Zomeren at al. (2008) for a review and synthesis.
7. Classic statements of this approach are by Miller et al. (1981), Shingles (1981), and Bobo and Gilliam (1990). Empirical studies that have used US data to test these approaches include Leighley and Vedlitz (1999), who propose five models: (1) SES, (2) psychological resources (interest and efficacy), (3) social connectedness, (4) group identity/consciousness, and (5) group conflict/threat. They find support for SES, psychological resources, and social connectedness theories. Wong et al. (2005) investigated the role of group resources on a composite measure of political engagement (contacting government officials, donating money to a campaign, signing a petition, taking part in a protest or demonstration, serving on a board, working on a political campaign) among Asian-Americans. They examined effects of group identity, group consciousness, and organizational membership. Results are patchy,

but essentially they find that group identity is not a significant predictor of engagement, but sense of linked fate, US identity, church attendance, and Asian-American organizational membership are significant predictors. Santoro et al. (2012), studying Mexican-Americans, find evidence for a curvilinear relationship between bridging ties and protest activities.
8. The classic statement is that of Verba et al. (1993), who use their resource model of time, money, and civic skills to explain the minority/majority gaps in political participation (a very broad measure, including voting, contacting officials, etc). Their main predictors are educational level, high school government, English spoken at home (not significant [NS]), vocabulary, family income, free time (NS), working (NS), retired, job level (NS), job skills, organizational affiliation, organizational skills, church attendance (NS), church skills, and citizenship.
9. See Olsen (1970) for a pioneering discussion of black political engagement. For a more general account see McVeigh and Smith (1999).
10. See Fennema and Tillie (1999) and Tillie (2004). An important element of their approach is an emphasis on the interlinking of different ethnic associations within a particular ethnic group. In ways not dissimilar to our approach in chapter 6, they show that these properties of ethnic groups play an important role over and above individual attributes.
11. There is a huge US literature on the role of churches on political participation. On Black churches see, for example, Calhoun-Brown (1996), Jones-Correa and Leal (2001), and Brown and Brown (2003). On the role of mosques see Jamal (2005).
12. We also checked on minority/majority differences within the BES, and again there was no significant difference for these two forms of organizational participation.
13. The MCDS was directed by Miles Hewstone and funded by the Leverhulme Trust. The fieldwork was carried out by Ipsos MORI, who interviewed a total of 1,666 adults aged sixteen years or more across England between 9 October 2009 and 8 February 2010. A random location quota sample approach was adopted. The sample was designed to comprise two main elements: 1. A core sample designed to deliver a nationally representative sample of the adult (aged sixteen years or more) population living in private households in England, with sufficient total sample size to provide 800 interviews with white British residents. 2. An ethnic minority sample designed to boost interviews with adults (aged sixteen years or more) belonging to eligible ethnic minority groups, living in private households in England, to a minimum of 800.
14. The MCDS question wording was:

Have you personally ever tried to make an impact on improving your community, for example, by writing to the council, joining a local action group, or anything of that sort?

    A. *Written to council or local councillor about community issue*
    B. *Joined or helped a local action group*
    C. *Gone on a protest or demonstration about community affairs*
    D. *Joining other crime prevention groups*
    E. *Signed a petition*
    F. *Other (please specify)*
    G. *Nothing*

15. Martinez (2005) also finds important generational differences in Latino unconventional participation in the USA.
16. We also tested whether socio-economic resources such as income, class, and housing tenure had indirect effects mediated by our measures of psychological resources. However, when we dropped all the potential mediating variables from the model, the effects of socio-economic resources (other than education) remained generally non-significant.
17. The absence of any effect of ethnic identification is also in line with Leighley and Vedlitz's (1999) research in the USA.

10

Satisfaction or Disaffection from British Democracy?

So far our evidence has painted a very positive picture of ethnic minority political integration. Despite some evidence that both ethnic minority issues (notably for the redress of discrimination) and ethnic minority personnel (witness minorities' under-representation in Parliament) are excluded from mainstream British politics, this does not seem to have had the negative consequences for political integration that we feared. What we have found is actually a very positive picture. Migrants came positively oriented towards British democracy, and strongly agree with the democratic principle of the duty to vote. They, and their children, feel that Labour represents their interests reasonably well. They have high levels of political involvement and allegiance to a political party (primarily to Labour) comparable with what is found among other British citizens. Minorities also show comparable levels of turnout as the majority group, and broadly comparable levels of the various non-electoral forms of participation too. To be sure, we also found worryingly low rates of registration, and there were also various other barriers facing the first generation. But this is a much more positive picture than that found in many other countries, and there was little sign that exclusion has led to large-scale withdrawal or lack of engagement, although we did find that the sentiment 'no party represents me' was associated with a turn away from conventional electoral politics towards protest.

One final aspect of political integration which we will explore in this concluding chapter is the extent of minority satisfaction with or disaffection from British democracy, and the extent to which minorities trust major British institutions. Do minorities feel that the British political system is a legitimate one that provides them with adequate means for articulating and redressing their grievances and gives them an adequate stake in British decision-making? Or are there signs that exclusion, either political or socio-economic, has led to discontent and disaffection?

Satisfaction or Disaffection from British Democracy?

We are particularly concerned in this chapter about the second (and later) generation(s). As we have seen throughout this book, there have been some major generational changes—as, for example, in non-electoral participation, where the second generation seems to have learned British modes of protest. It can also be argued that it is the integration of the second generation that provides the sternest test of whether Britain has successfully offered equality of opportunity to its ethnic minorities. As we have emphasized, the first generation came to Britain with generally very positive orientations towards democracy. But have the second generation become disillusioned or embittered by their experiences of life in Britain?

Overall, we might expect the second generation to be more or less as satisfied as other British citizens. Across generations we have usually seen convergence with British norms and practices: in the case of commitment to democratic norms, the first generation was more enthusiastic than the white British, but the second generation has converged with typical British levels. Conversely, in the case of the different forms of participation, the first generation was less likely to vote and less likely to join protests, but the second generation looks very similar to other British citizens in these respects.

On the other hand, there are several respects in which minorities, especially the second generation, might be expected to be less than wholly satisfied with British political institutions. As we saw in Chapter 5, their political concerns to secure redress for discrimination and exclusion are not well integrated into British politics, with the Conservative Party in particular failing to address issues of racial discrimination or inequality anywhere in its 2010 manifesto (or indeed in earlier manifestos). Previous research has suggested that experiences of discrimination may be particularly likely to undermine a sense of British identity, and by implication to foster disaffection.[1] Muslims may also feel more excluded and rejected in the light of growing 'Islamophobia'.[2] As we showed in Chapter 8, people of Pakistani background certainly showed evidence of much greater discontent than other ethno-religious groups with the progress that had been made in recent years.

The second generation may be more aware of these exclusions and inequalities, and hence may be more disenchanted than the first generation. While the first generation came with notably positive orientations towards British democracy, quite possibly because British democracy and freedom compares favourably with political practice in some of the countries of origin, the second generation may be more critical, since they will be making comparisons not with their parents' origin countries but with Britain's own claims of equal opportunities and fairness. The second generation may thus employ a different (basically British) frame of reference when evaluating what life and politics have to offer in Britain. There is some circumstantial evidence from previous work on the labour market that the first generation's frame of reference is more oriented to their contemporaries in their countries of origin, while the second generation's frame of reference is more oriented to their contemporaries in Britain.[3] The same might well apply in politics.

Another possibility which has been raised by politicians and commentators rather than by academic researchers is that some groups, particularly Muslims, who are socially and residentially more separated from British society may be less likely to feel a part of the British political community. This has been a key element of politicians' repudiation of multiculturalism. The politicians' central thesis is that some groups, notably young Muslim men, may feel less committed to British society and British values, in part because multiculturalism has allowed them to lead separate lives apart from the mainstream. Thus, British Prime Minister David Cameron has argued:

> But these young [Muslim] men also find it hard to identify with Britain too, because we have allowed the weakening of our collective identity. Under the doctrine of state multiculturalism, we have encouraged different cultures to live separate lives, apart from each other and apart from the mainstream. We've failed to provide a vision of society to which they feel they want to belong. We've even tolerated these segregated communities behaving in ways that run completely counter to our values... This hands-off tolerance has only served to reinforce the sense that not enough is shared. And this all leaves some young Muslims feeling rootless. And the search for something to belong to and something to believe in can lead them to this extremist ideology. Now for sure, they don't turn into terrorists overnight, but what we see—and what we see in so many European countries—is a process of radicalisation. (Cameron 2011)

While David Cameron's main purpose was to criticize multicultural policies, the thesis that social segregation might have adverse consequences for political integration could hold true whether or not multicultural policies are to blame. It also raises the important question of whether processes of intergenerational change have operated at the same rate and to the same degree among all minorities alike. Have groups which have been slower to integrate socially, such as some of the South Asian ethno-religious minorities, also been slower to converge politically with mainstream British norms and practices?

A directly contradictory thesis holds that contact with the white British actually goes in the opposite direction, and leads minorities to become more aware of the prejudice and discrimination that persists in Britain. People who remain within the ethnic enclave may be insulated from harassment or offensive behaviour. But as the second generation becomes more socially integrated, it may also become more exposed to and aware of discrimination. As a result its members may become more disaffected from British society. As a shorthand, let us term this a paradox of social integration: as minorities become more integrated in their social lives, so they may become more disaffected.[4]

Satisfaction or Disaffection from British Democracy?

Our primary concerns in this chapter, then, are first to document differences between minorities, and across generations, in levels of satisfaction with British democracy and trust in British institutions. We shall then turn to explore possible explanations, focusing on the one hand on social separation and lack of social integration into the mainstream, and on the other on exclusion, and the resulting perceptions of inequality of opportunity and feelings of fraternal relative deprivation.

Documenting the differences

We begin by reporting the differences between the main ethnic groups and the white British with respect to various indicators of satisfaction with and trust in British democracy. A first, summary question that we asked was:

> On the whole, are you satisfied or dissatisfied with the way that democracy works in this country?

We also asked a set of more specific questions on trust in Parliament, politicians, and the police. These questions allow us to corroborate the findings from the satisfaction question and to check the robustness of the findings.[5] We asked:

> Now, thinking about British political institutions like Parliament, please use the 0 to 10 scale to indicate how much trust you have for each of the following, where 0 means no trust and 10 means a great deal of trust.
> the Parliament at Westminster
> British politicians generally
> the Police

These questions were also asked in the main BES, and so we can compare minority and majority responses. Table 10.1 shows the comparisons.

Strikingly, on all but one of these indicators of satisfaction and trust, the overall minority level of confidence in British democracy and institutions is either significantly higher than, or no different from, the white British average. However, there is also considerable variation around the minority average. Most importantly, people of black Caribbean background, together with those of mixed white/black background, are significantly more dissatisfied and distrusting than are white British. Conversely, people of South Asian background and of black African background are significantly more satisfied and more trusting than the white British average.

There is no sign here that the predominantly Muslim groups have low trust or satisfaction. Table 10.2 provides a detailed breakdown of these sentiments by religion, and shows that the groups with the highest dissatisfaction are in

Table 10.1. Satisfaction with democracy and trust in institutions
Cell percentages

Ethnic background	Satisfied with democracy	Trust Parliament	Trust politicians	Trust police	N
Mixed black/white	47	24	14	48	93
Black Caribbean	52	21	20	42	594
White British	59	34	24	68	2760
All minorities	71	43	35	64	2782
Indian	73	45	37	70	582
Black African	77	51	40	62	524
Pakistani	74	44	37	70	667
Bangladeshi	77	54	41	68	270

Notes: Satisfied includes those saying very or fairly satisfied. Trust questions were asked as 0 (no trust)–10 (a great deal of trust) scale; the percentages above are for those reporting greater trust than the midpoint, i.e. scoring more than 6 on the scale (don't know responses included in the base). Figures in bold are significantly different from the white British figure at the 5 per cent level. Chi^2 (satisfaction) = 183.4 (6 df), $p < 0.001$; (trust Parliament) = 184.7 (6 df), $p < 0.001$; (trust politicians) = 138.7 (6 df), $p < 0.001$.
Sources: BES 2010, EMBES 2010; weighted

Table 10.2. Religious differences in satisfaction and trust
Cell percentages

Religious affiliation	Satisfied with democracy	Trust parliament	Trust politicians	Trust police	N
Anglican (white British)	67	41	27	71	817
Anglican (minorities)	71	33	29	49	120
Catholic	67	40	34	58	206
Pentecostal	72	45	39	55	255
Other Christian	60	35	29	55	257
Hindu	74	45	37	75	234
Sikh	73	47	34	67	164
Sunni Muslim	75	46	38	70	935
Other Muslim	75	46	41	66	204
Other religion	68	39	32	65	30
None (minorities)	52	25	22	44	362
None (white British)	53	28	20	65	1459

Notes: Figures in bold are significantly lower at the 5 per cent level than expectation. Chi^2 (satisfaction) = 182.1 (11 df), $p < 0.001$; (parliament) = 162.5 (11 df), $p < 0.001$; (politicians) = 129.8 (11 df), $p < 0.001$; (police) = 166.0 (11 df), $p < 0.001$.
Sources: BES, EMBES, weighted

fact the non-religious, followed, at a considerable distance, by the various Christian groups. Muslims, in fact, are the most satisfied and trusting of all the religious groups.[6]

Some of the differences observed in Tables 10.1 and 10.2 might well be due to age and generational differences. As we saw in Chapter 3, the first-generation adult migrants express higher levels of agreement with the duty to vote than do white British citizens, although they have a somewhat lower interest in British politics and lesser political knowledge. However, across

Satisfaction or Disaffection from British Democracy?

Table 10.3. Generational differences in political trust and satisfaction
Cell percentages

	Ethnic minorities			White British	
	1st	1.5	2nd +	All ages	Age 18–45
Satisfied with democracy	**77**	**68**	52	59	53
Trust Parliament	**50**	**38**	26	34	32
Trust politicians	**43**	**30**	20	24	23
Trust police	**71**	60	47	68	68
N	1288	443	975	2760	1021

Notes: Figures in bold are significantly higher than expectation at the 5 per cent level (EMBES sample only). Chi^2 (satisfaction) = 158.2 (2 df), $p < 0.001$; (trust Parliament) = 143.8 (2 df), $p < 0.001$; (trust politicians) = 147.3 (2 df), $p < 0.001$; (trust police) = 131.1 (2 df), $p < 0.001$.
Sources: BES 2010, EMBES 2010, weighted

generations Chapter 3 showed clear evidence of convergence towards British norms. The sense of civic duty declined from its initially high level to one closer, but still above, the British norm, while political knowledge and interest increased towards, but not quite reaching, British levels.

Because of the historical patterns of immigration to Britain, there are big differences in the distribution of the different groups across generations. As a first step, then, we must check patterns of generational change. This is done in Table 10.3.

Table 10.3 shows a dramatic decline in satisfaction and trust across generations. Starting from very positive and trusting responses in the first generation—much more trusting than those of the white British in most cases—by the second generation, minorities appear to have converged with their peers.

A striking exception to this general rule, however, is trust in the police, which falls to a level well below that of the white British. In every other major sentiment or behaviour that we have investigated in this study, we find convergence with British levels, not departure from them. Convergence occurs with the duty to vote, political interest and knowledge, allegiance with a political party, turnout, and other forms of participation. In all these cases, the figures for the second generation are closer to the white British patterns than they were in the first generation, and in many cases they are not significantly different from the majority-group level (see Table 10.A1 for a summary of these trends). But in the case of trust in the police, the second-generation figure is 20 points lower than that of the white British eighteen–forty-five year olds.

Before attempting to explain this alarming result, we clearly need to check how robust the finding is. In particular, can it be straightforwardly explained by standard demographic processes? Perhaps young people are generally more distrustful of the police. And does this low level of distrust apply to other ethnic groups, or is it primarily a phenomenon among black youth?

Table 10.4. Satisfaction and trust: second-generation minorities compared with their white British peers
Average marginal effects

Ethnic background	Satisfied with democracy	Trust Parliament	Trust politicians	Trust police
Mixed black/white	−10	−9	−10	**−18**
Black Caribbean	**−11**	**−18**	**−11**	**−29**
White British	0	0	0	0
Indian	+6	−1	+1	**−11**
Black African	**+10**	+3	+2	**−18**
Pakistani	**+11**	+3	+4	−8
Bangladeshi	**+17**	**+14**	+8	−9

Notes: Figures in bold are significantly different from zero at the 5 per cent level. Differences are average marginal effects estimated in models that also control for age, gender, marital status, highest qualification, class, housing tenure, income and generation.
Sources: BES 2010, EMBES 2010, weighted

We have therefore estimated how different members of the second generation are from their white British peers, taking account of their demographic profile (that is, taking account of their age, gender, marital status, education, social class, and housing tenure). Table 10.4 then shows the minority/majority differences. Thus the figure of −10 in the top left-hand cell of the table shows that people of mixed white/black heritage were 10 percentage points less likely than the white British (set to zero) to feel satisfied with democracy. (This can be compared with the corresponding gap of 12 percentage points in Table 10.1, indicating that the demographic control variables have accounted for a small part of the original gap.)

Table 10.4 shows two important patterns. First, we see that major ethnic differences remain in the second generation, with the South Asian and black African groups showing higher levels of satisfaction with democracy and broadly similar levels of trust in Parliament and politicians as their white British peers. Conversely, the black Caribbean and black/white mixed groups show significantly less satisfaction and trust. Secondly, we see that every single one of our second-generation minority groups, including the Indians, who generally have come closest to the white British norms, express significantly lower levels of trust in the police. Both of these are remarkable findings, with potentially important implications for government.

Explaining ethnic and generational differences

So how are we to explain these patterns? One obvious candidate for explaining black disaffection must be the discrimination and accompanying feelings of fraternal relative deprivation that we have discussed in earlier chapters.

Thus, in Chapter 5 we saw that feelings of fraternal relative deprivation were associated with the sentiment that 'no party represents me', while in Chapter 6 this sentiment of being unrepresented was strongly associated with lack of allegiance to any political party. And in Chapter 9 we saw that experiences of discrimination and of fraternal relative deprivation were associated with the various forms of dissident (elite-challenging) behaviour, while grievances and a feeling that 'no party represents me' were also important. So here we have a clutch of sentiments predicting disengagement from conventional party politics that might well be associated with dissatisfaction and distrust of political institutions more generally.

In previous chapters we have also explored the role of a variety of indicators of social capital and social ties. Given the prominence accorded by politicians to the dangers of social segregation, and the rival academic theory of the economic and political benefits of cohesive ethnic communities, we clearly need to explore these too. The evidence from previous chapters broadly supports the idea that social ties with co-ethnics tend to increase political integration rather than diminish it. Thus, in Chapter 5, informal bonding capital reduced the likelihood of feeling that 'no party represents me', while in Chapter 6 associational bonding capital was associated with positive forms of political engagement (specifically, reducing the likelihood of not identifying with any political party). In Chapter 7, we saw that church membership was associated with higher rates of turnout, while in Chapter 9 we saw that associational social capital was associated with all the different forms of non-electoral engagement. Overall, then, bonding social capital seems to have beneficial effects on political integration, rather than the corrosive effects that many commentators have suggested, although the evidence does not all point in the same direction: for example, in Chapter 9 associational social capital was associated both with elite-challenging protest and with notionally elite-supporting volunteering.

We must, as ever, be very careful about inferring causal processes from these statistical associations. But it is not difficult to invoke potential mechanisms that might lead fraternal relative deprivation on the one hand or membership in ethnic organizations on the other to inhibit or foster political integration.

Before carrying out the detailed statistical analysis, however, it will be instructive to see how some of these potential explanatory mechanisms vary across generations. The key point is that, if an attribute shows no sign of change across generations, or changes in the 'wrong' direction, it has not got much chance of explaining the decline in trust and satisfaction. Table 10.5 shows the generational differences in feelings of exclusion and bonding social capital.

So what we see here is relatively modest change across generations in the various indicators of bonding social capital. In particular, membership of

Table 10.5. Generational differences in feelings of exclusion and in bonding social capital
Cell percentages

	1st generation	1.5 generation	2nd + generation
Feelings of exclusion			
Fraternal relative deprivation	43	50	49
Reports discrimination	26	32	39
No party represents me	22	34	41
Bonding social capital			
Friends primarily co-ethnic	57	49	**42**
Member ethnic organization	31	37	34
Co-ethnic church member	95	91	**83**
N	1308	448	993

Notes: Rows 2, 4 and 5 reproduced from table 2.9. Figures in bold are significantly lower at the 5 per cent level than expectation. Chi^2 (relative deprivation) = 19.4 (2 df), $p < 0.001$; (discrimination) = 74.3 (2 df), $p < 0.001$; (no party represents me) = 93.0 (2 df), $p < 0.001$; (co-ethnic friends) = 70.1 (2 df), $p < 0.01$; (ethnic organization) = 2.3 (2 df), $p > 0.05$; (church member) = 165.9 (2 df), $p < 0.001$.
Sources: BES 2010, EMBES 2010, weighted data

ethnic or cultural associations shows virtually no change, and so can hardly explain the rise in disaffection. The other two measures of bonding social capital (friendship and church membership) show modest *declines* across generations, but this is the 'wrong' direction of change for explaining the divergence in trust of the police: a decline in bonding social capital would be expected to make minorities more similar to their white British peers, not more dissimilar. (In the case of friendship patterns, our measure asks what proportion of one's friends are from the same ethnic background, and hence any decline in bonding implies a growth in bridging, although not necessarily bridging with white British friends.)

Running in the opposite direction, we then see generational *increases* in all our three measures of sentiments of exclusion, the increases in reported discrimination and in the feeling 'no party represents me' being strikingly large. Thus, these look to be plausible candidates for explaining the rise in disaffection.

Our next step, therefore, is to model the data on satisfaction and trust. A major problem is that we do not have measures in the main BES of these measures of exclusion and bonding social capital. We cannot therefore test how far feelings of exclusion and so on explain minority/majority differences. We can, however, explore whether they explain generational and ethnic differences, and this may in turn give us some clues about the explanation of any minority/majority differences.

We therefore carry out the same kind of analysis that we conducted in the previous chapter. We look at how much difference our various predictors make to the probability of being satisfied with democracy, trusting Parliament, and so on. The results are shown in Table 10.6. Our particular interest is in the role of feelings of exclusion and of bonding social capital, but we also include the other measures that were important in the Chapter 9 analysis. In addition, we include the measure of whether people thought that things had got better or worse for ethnic minorities, which we introduced in Chapter 8.

As we can see from Table 10.6, the main predictors of satisfaction and trust do tend to vary from topic to topic. For example, interest in politics and a feeling that one can influence public affairs are important predictors of trust in Parliament and in politicians, but not for the other two outcomes. Women tend to be less trusting and satisfied with democracy than men, but the position is reversed in the case of trust in the police.

However, there is a very clear and consistent story told by Table 10.6 about the role of our various indicators of exclusion. In particular, feelings of fraternal relative deprivation have by far the largest association with trust, people who feel strongly that ethnic minorities are not treated fairly expressing much lower levels of trust and satisfaction than those who believe that minorities are treated fairly. The difference of 20 points or more is the largest that we have seen in any of our analyses in any of the chapters in this book.

The feeling that 'no party represents [my] views reasonably well' also has a strong relationship with disaffection, a finding that mirrors its relationship with protest and dissident behaviour that we saw in Chapter 9. Disapproval of the war in Afghanistan also recurs, just as it did in Chapter 9, as a significant but relatively minor source of disaffection (although the other issues that we explored in previous chapters did not figure). Individual experiences of discrimination on the other hand are unimportant as predictors of trust, but our subjective measure of whether things had got better or worse for minorities in recent years was a consistently important predictor.[7] So, overall, this is a powerful story of feelings of exclusion leading to disaffection.

The other stories told by Table 10.6 pale into insignificance alongside the role of exclusion. Most crucially, we find that ethnic bonding capital is not a major player. It has some rather patchy effects, but few of them are significant. There is certainly no sign that bonding and leading a separate life within an ethnic community is associated with disaffection, or the reverse.

However, we do find some evidence consistent with what we termed the paradox of social integration if we look at the *indirect* effects of social integration rather than the direct ones that Table 10.6 captures. Are people who are more exposed to British social contacts, for example through friends, neighbourhood, work, church, or membership of voluntary organizations, more likely to perceive discrimination and to feel relative deprivation? The short answer is that they are, although the association is not especially strong. Our evidence, then, is consistent with the hypothesis that contact with the majority group will lead people to be more aware of discrimination and inequality of opportunity, and this will in turn feed into the disaffection. Moreover, this

Table 10.6. Predictors of ethnic minority satisfaction and trust in British politics
Average marginal effects

	Satisfied with democracy	Trust Parliament	Trust politicians	Trust police
Feelings of exclusion				
Reports individual discrimination	−3	−1	0	**−7**
Fraternal relative deprivation	**−23**	**−21**	**−18**	**−28**
Feels no party represents me	**−16**	**−17**	**−16**	**−15**
Feels it's got worse for minorities	**−6**	**−7**	**−5**	**−5**
Opposes Afghanistan war	−1	−3	**−5**	−4
Bonding social capital				
Friends primarily co-ethnic	**+9**	0	+3	+1
Member ethnic organization	−3	−1	−2	0
Member ethnic church	+1	+2	−1	**+6**
Individual psychological resources				
Feels one has political influence	**+3**	**+8**	**+7**	0
Interested in politics	+2	**+12**	**+9**	**+5**
Socio-economic resources				
Education	−1	−1	−2	0
Middle Class	+2	**+4**	0	0
Working class	+2	**+5**	**+4**	**+3**
Other class or missing (ref)	0	0	0	0
Home owner	−1	−3	−2	**−7**
Social housing tenant	−3	**−6**	−2	**−10**
Other tenures (ref)	0	0	0	0
Demographics				
Age	**+7**	**+4**	**+5**	**+3**
Female	**−5**	**−4**	−1	**+5**
1st generation (ref)	0	0	0	0
1.5 generation	−3	**−7**	**−9**	−5
2nd + generations	**−9**	**−12**	**−12**	**−11**
(pseudo) R^2	0.16	0.15	0.13	0.16
N	2633	2631	2632	2633

Notes: Figures in bold are significantly different from zero at the 0.05 level. Differences are average marginal effects estimated in models that also control for ethnic group, ethnic density, and neighbourhood deprivation. In the case of continuous or ordered predictors, AMEs are calculated comparing the 10th and 90th percentiles.
Sources: 2010 BES, EMBES, weighted

finding holds true of the second generation, as well as overall, and is also present in all the main ethnic groups.

However, we must emphasize that the paradox of social integration is only a minor player in our story. The major player is undoubtedly feelings of exclusion, although even these feelings are unable to explain all the gaps either between black Caribbeans and other minorities or between the generations. Feelings of fraternal relative deprivation go some considerable way to explain these gaps, but we must not over claim.

Inequalities of opportunity

Now one has to be very careful when interpreting these associations between subjective measures of fraternal relative deprivation and satisfaction with democracy. We have a big story, but the data do not allow us to make strong and definitive causal assertions of the form that 'minorities' feelings that they are not treated fairly cause them to lose confidence in democracy'. Our evidence is consistent with this claim, and we happen to believe that it is probably true; but survey data cannot prove causality. What we can say unambiguously is that minorities who express feelings of fraternal relative deprivation or who believe that none of the main political parties looks after their interests tend also to have less confidence in British political institutions.

However, as we have observed throughout this book, feelings of relative deprivation have an empirical foundation. They are not just *post hoc* rationalizations dreamed up by people who were already disaffected owing to some other unknown reason. We know from previous work, using entirely different data and replicated by other scholars, that ethnic minorities do suffer ethnic penalties in the labour market. We know from a series of rigorous field experiments that ethnic minority applicants for jobs do not receive the same treatment as white British applicants. We know that minorities are over-represented in the prison population, and it was not all that long ago that Sir William Macpherson was reporting on institutional racism within the police. In all these respects, it would be hard to deny that minorities actually do experience inequality of opportunity, and in this sense suffer a degree of socio-economic exclusion. At the very least, the evidence in support of our claim is considerably stronger than any evidence that has thus far been brought against it.

It is also reasonable to claim that perceptions of political exclusion—the feeling that 'no party represents my views' is not entirely without external support either. We saw in Chapter 4 that minorities do have a variety of distinctive political concerns, especially the shared concern about redress for racial discrimination. And while an important part of our story has been the way in which the Labour Party has historically passed legislation to outlaw discrimination and to promote equality of opportunity, neither of the two main parties made any fresh proposals in their 2010 manifestos, despite the accumulated evidence that the previous legislation had failed to prevent continued inequality of opportunity for minorities. And while there has been progress in the election of minority MPs to Parliament, minorities are still under-represented in the House of Commons. So, once again, minorities' perceptions have an external foundation: they cannot be dismissed as merely subjective epiphenomena.[8]

But while we are surely right to emphasize the real inequalities of opportunity that minorities face, and the likely implications of these inequalities for trust in British political institutions, we also need to emphasize the many ways in which minorities, especially the second generation, are integrated into British political life. Second-generation engagement in the electoral process and participation in the various legitimate channels of non-electoral participation are not especially different in profile or level from those of other British citizens. So there is something of a contrast between the minority/majority similarity in patterns of political engagement (at least in the second generation) and the dissimilarity in trust in the police. There is also a second contrast between the similarity in behaviour but dissimilarity in political trust of people from mixed or black Caribbean backgrounds when compared with other minorities or with the majority group. Even when we control for all the potential predictors included in Table 10.6, we still find that people of black Caribbean background are significantly less satisfied and significantly less trusting than most other groups. But this contrasts with a general absence of significant differences between black Caribbeans and other minorities when it comes to registration, turnout, or other forms of political action.

It is beyond our expertise or remit to provide a detailed explanation of minorities' much greater lack of trust in the police than in Parliament or politicians. Lack of trust in the police can perhaps be explained by a continuation of the kinds of problems described by Sir William Macpherson in his report following the police failures over the Stephen Lawrence enquiry. While there has undoubtedly been some progress over the ensuing years, a parliamentary enquiry into the Macpherson report ten years on recently concluded that major problems remained. The Home Affairs Committee of the House of Commons' conclusions were:

> 15. The police have made tremendous strides in the service they provide to ethnic minority communities and in countering racism amongst its workforce. 67 of Macpherson's 70 recommendations have been implemented fully or in part in the ten years since his report was published... Police leaders have shown a clear commitment to increasing awareness of race as an issue throughout the service.
>
> 16. A number of concerns remain outstanding. Black communities in particular are disproportionately represented in stop and search statistics and on the National DNA Database; in fact, the gap has increased since 1999. Black people are over-represented in the criminal justice system for a number of complex factors; but this does not justify this level of disproportionality. In addition, being subject to higher levels of stop and search and inclusion on the DNA Database perpetuates black people's over-representation in the criminal justice system. We repeat our warning that any gains made by the use of stop and search may be offset by its potentially negative impact on community relations.

17. We are disappointed that the police service will not meet its target to employ 7 per cent of its officers from ethnic minority communities nationally by 2009 and that BME officers continue to experience difficulties in achieving promotion, as well as being more likely to be subject to disciplinary procedures. The police service must now focus its efforts on tackling issues of discrimination within the workforce. (Home Affairs Committee 2009)

So, just as with feelings of relative deprivation and perceptions that no party represents their views, lack of trust in the police may well have a real foundation in the unequal treatment that minorities experience within the police force and criminal justice system.

But how are we to explain the apparent paradox between the relatively high participation rates of the black groups, which are effectively the same as those of other minorities in the second generation, and their markedly greater feelings of disaffection? In a sense, we have here what might be termed a 'paradox of exclusion'. Perceptions of exclusion seem to lead to subjective disaffection on the part of second-generation black citizens but not to the behavioural consequences of exclusion—withdrawal or protest—that we had anticipated at the beginning of the book. How can we reconcile these apparently contradictory findings?

It is perhaps useful to begin by reviewing our empirical evidence on our key measure of perceived socio-economic exclusion, notably the feeling of fraternal relative deprivation. As we showed in Chapter 6, all three black groups (but especially those of Caribbean heritage) were significantly more likely to feel a sense of fraternal relative deprivation than were other minorities (Table 6.4). And this, as we have emphasized before, is consistent with the evidence on ethnic penalties in the labour market.

However, fraternal relative deprivation has very different associations with the different outcomes that we are interested in. Thus, as we have just seen in Table 10.6, it has a powerful but *negative* relationship with trust and satisfaction; it has a modest (but positive) association with protest (Table 9.4); it has no significant association with registration or turnout (Tables 7.A3 and 7.A5); but it then has a strong but *positive* relationship with Labour allegiance (Table 6.7).

One possibility is therefore that Labour allegiance and socio-economic exclusion are pulling in opposite directions when it comes to minorities' actual behaviour. In effect, they may be cancelling each other out. In other words, minorities in general and black groups in particular might well have had much lower rates of participation (as comparable groups appear to in some other countries) if it were not for their incorporation into the Labour Party. Admittedly, this is a counterfactual claim which we cannot directly test, but it is perhaps relevant that in several other Western countries minorities do indeed show much lower rates of participation.

Perhaps, then, what is distinctive about Britain is the role that the Labour Party has played in incorporating minorities, especially black groups. To be sure, we must also recognize the way in which black groups embraced the Labour Party rather than turning to more militant or separatist strategies. Kalbir Shukra gives an insightful account into the divisions within minority groups in the 1960s over the form that their relationship, if any, with the Labour Party should take, and the later struggles within the Labour Party over the formation of black sections have likely also been crucial.[9] As Kalbir Shukra explains:

> For the 1970s' black radicals mobilization had meant moving people on to the streets to protest and campaign but LPBS turned protest into a question of votes... LPBS's electorally oriented politics turned political issues and black anger into a question of black faces in office... the success in electing hundreds of black councillors and four black MPs in 1987 reinforced the view that black representation, rather than real mobilization, could achieve change for black people. (Shukra 1998, p. 73)

The end result has been that for much of the last thirty years the Labour Party has been distinctively associated both with black activists inside the party and with proposals and legislation designed to achieve some redress for discrimination. As we argued in Chapter 6, the legacy of these efforts to advance black interests has been the evolution of community norms and sentiments in favour of the Labour Party, and these community sentiments have been particularly strong among the groups for whom socio-economic exclusion and relative deprivation has been of most pressing concern. In a sense, then, community norms (and community activists) may have channelled black feelings of exclusion and disaffection away from mobilization in the streets and into electoral politics.

But this legacy of pro-Labour community sentiments cannot be taken for granted, as the inroads made by the Respect Party into safe Labour seats demonstrated in 2005, and again in 2012 in Bradford. True, the Respect Party campaigned on issues that had much greater appeal to Muslims than to black groups, but there is no reason to suppose that black support for Labour should be taken for granted any more than Muslim support.

The tension between community sentiments of support for Labour, but unresolved issues over inequality of opportunity, means in our view that Labour should not take black or minority loyalty for granted. While our story is on balance a highly positive one, major challenges remain. For Labour, there is the challenge to preserve its legacy, to recognize the continuing exclusion that minorities experience both in the labour market and in the political sphere, and to continue to be seen as the party that actively looks after minority interests. And for the political class more generally, there is the challenge of dealing with lack of minority representation in Parliament, low levels of electoral registration, inequality of opportunity, and a sense of relative deprivation and disaffection among the excluded. Britain's first-past-the-post electoral system, which incentivizes parties to concentrate on voters in marginal constituencies rather than to look after their core supporters, does not make one hopeful that the parties will rise to this challenge.

We have not in this book attempted to explain the incidence either of 'home grown terrorism' or of the kinds of riots that disfigured many British cities in 2011, since we do not have the right kind of data or research design to tackle these issues. We should not discount them, but terrorism and rioting are actually very rare—and may not be entirely unconnected with exclusion, disaffection, and unequal treatment by the police. Our evidence, however, on Britain's ethnic minority population as a whole indicates that Britain's minorities are just as good democrats as other British citizens. Indeed, we believe that Britain has been fortunate to avoid the minority disengagement found in many other Western countries, and the prolonged Troubles that have blighted Northern Ireland society. We suspect that this good fortune has been in large part thanks to the highly positive orientations towards British society and its democracy which migrants have brought with them, as well as to the efforts of the Labour Party to incorporate minority concerns. But failure to address legitimate grievances over inequalities of opportunity will surely jeopardize this good fortune.

Appendix: Supplementary Table

Table 10.A1. Generational differences in duty, interest, identification, and participation
Cell percentages

	Ethnic minorities			White British	
	1st	1.5	2nd +	All ages	Age 18–45
Agree duty to vote	**92**	88	**81**	76	66
Interested in British politics	**38**	41	**37**	41	34
Non-partisans	19	19	18	22	27
Turnout (among registered electors)	**53**	57	**63**	78	72
Labour vote (among self-reported voters)	**73**	67	**62**	29	28
Active	**39**	50	50	46	45
Volunteered	**14**	21	16	12	11
N	*1288*	*443*	*975*	*2760*	*1203*

Notes: Figures in bold are significantly different at the 5 per cent level than the overall ethnic minority expectation.
Sources: BES, EMBES 2010, weighted

Notes

1. See Maxwell (2006, 2009) and Heath and Roberts (2008), who draw on the Citizenship Survey. Similar results are found in EMBES.
2. See Field (2007, 2011).
3. See Cheung and Heath (2007), pp. 542–3.
4. A somewhat related idea has been put forward by Maxwell (2012), and has been termed an 'integration trade-off'. Maxwell's main point is that social integration may lead to a weakening of ethnic social capital, and hence may reduce the likelihood of ethnic mobilization via self-employment networks (2012, p. 76).
5. We found that, both among the white British in the BES and ethnic minorities in EMBES, the three trust questions and the satisfaction question formed a single dimension.
6. See Maxwell (2010b) for a more detailed examination using the 2007 Citizenship Survey.
7. We also investigated the role of subjective measures of whether things had got better or worse for one's own ethnic or religious group, but these measures were surprisingly not nearly so important.
8. To be sure, this still leaves the interesting question why some individuals are more or less likely to feel a sense of fraternal relative deprivation or to feel that no party represents them. The group differences in, for example, ethnic penalties helps to explain group differences in feelings, but as usual a considerable amount of individual variation is left unexplained.
9. See Shukra (1998), chapter 2.

APPENDIX 1
The Ethnic Minority British Election Survey (EMBES)

EMBES is the first nationally representative probability sample of the ethnic minority electorate in Britain since 1997, when a relatively small 'booster' sample was added to the main British Election Study (BES) post-election survey. The 2010 survey was much larger and was a 'stand-alone' one with a separate sampling frame and fieldwork. The two surveys have been closely coordinated, however, and around half the questions in the EMBES are exact replications of questions in the main post-election wave of the BES. Questions shared with the main BES included all the standard outcome variables, such as registration, turnout, party identification, vote choice, and so on, as well as explanatory variables covering valence issues, perceptions of party positions, and attitudes towards the main contemporary issues. In addition, there were questions in EMBES on ethnic and religious identities, social organization and mobilization, perceptions and experiences of discrimination, and attitudes towards a range of ethnic issues.

The original aim of the survey was to have a probability sample with more or less equal sample sizes (around 500) of the five established groups (as defined in the 2001 Census). The design was to be a clustered, stratified one using the Postcode Address File as the sampling frame, just as in the main BES, with areas of high ethnic minority density being over-sampled and areas with the lowest density (< 2 per cent ethnic minorities) being excluded. We should note however that ethnic minority individuals from these lowest density areas were eligible to be sampled in the main BES. The primary sampling unit (PSU) for the EMBES was the Lower layer Super Output Area (LSOA) in England and Wales (Data Zones in Scotland) whereas for the main BES it was the ward. (Each LSOA contains around 1,500 people. LSOAs are designed to be more homogeneous with respect to population size than are wards.) In EMBES addresses in the selected PSUs were screened for the presence of ethnic minority individuals at the address, the number of addresses issued for screening varying inversely with the ethnic density of the PSU. Over 30,000 addresses were issued for screening in the 620 selected PSUs. To adjust for the over-sampling in higher density PSUs, descriptive statistics are routinely weighted throughout the book.

Respondents to EMBES were paid a conditional incentive of £20. Response rates were between 58 per cent and 66 per cent, depending on the method of treating 'unknowns' in the screening process. This compares very favourably with 1997, when the response rate was 44 per cent. We should also note that in 1997, for cost reasons, areas where the ethnic density was < 10 per cent were excluded from the sampling frame. (For further details of the 1997 survey see Taylor and Thomson 1999, Heath and Saggar 1999.) The achieved sample size in 2010 was 2,787.

The questionnaire was administered face to face by CAPI, including a module which three-quarters of respondents completed themselves on the laptop. There was also a mailback questionnaire. Interviews were conducted in English but translators (aged over twelve) were allowed from within the household, and paper versions of the questionnaire in the main minority languages were provided for use by the household translator in such situations.

Following discussions with TNS-BMRB, our selected fieldwork agency, and agreement with the ESRC, some modifications were made to this initial design. It was agreed, in the interests of maximizing the effective sample size, to aim for larger samples (around 600) of the four larger groups with a smaller target sample of Bangladeshis. We also agreed that if, at the screening stage, a potential respondent from one of the five targeted groups was identified, but on subsequent interview the respondent self-identified as coming from a mixed or some other ethnic minority group, the interview would nonetheless be continued. This decision was taken partly for practical reasons, and partly because self-reported identities, especially for people from mixed backgrounds, are somewhat fluid. We also thought that people of mixed background are an important and growing group in their own right. Table 1 shows the breakdown by ethnic group, using the official census classification, together with the Office for National Statistics' (ONS) mid-year estimates for 2007 (the latest available at the time of writing) of the population aged sixteen and over in England and Wales.

The ONS mid-year estimates shown in Table A1.1 suggest that ethnic minorities, including the Other White category, are now approaching 15 per cent of the population in England and Wales. They will, to be sure, be a somewhat lower proportion of the electorate, since many of the most recent arrivals will not be eligible to vote in a general election (and the proportion of ethnic minorities resident in Scotland is considerably lower than that in England and Wales). However, the great majority of the Indian, Pakistani, Bangladeshi, and Black Caribbean groups, and just under 90 per cent of the Black African group, are eligible to register as either British or Commonwealth citizens. The groups covered in EMBES, therefore, probably made up around 8 per cent of the eligible electorate in 2010. Recently released figures from the 2011 Census confirm that around 8 per cent of the resident population of England and Wales aged 18 and over belonged to the ethnic groups covered in EMBES.

Appendix 1

Table A1.1. The achieved sample sizes in BES, EMBES, and ONS mid-year estimates for 2007 frequencies

Cultural background	EMBES	BES	ONS (%)
White British	0	2761	84.7
Other White	0	44	4.9
Mixed—White/BC	70	7	0.3
Mixed—White/BA	23	8	0.2
Mixed—White/Asian	5	7	0.3
Mixed—White/Other	9	2	0.3
Indian	587	40	2.5
Pakistani	668	12	1.5
Bangladeshi	270	6	0.6
Other Asian	16	10	0.6
Black Caribbean	597	23	1.1
Black African	524	29	1.3
Other Black	6	7	0.2
Other ethnic group	11	27	1.6
Other answers	–	83	–
Refused	1	9	–
All	*2787*	*3075*	100.1

Notes: Unweighted frequencies for BES and EMBES. The figures in the third column are for residents aged sixteen and above. They do not include residents in Scotland.

Sources: 2010 BES post-election wave, EMBES 2010, and ONS mid-year estimates for 2007, table EE2

APPENDIX 2
Coding of the variables

In this appendix, we describe the coding of some of the key socio-demographic variables and the complex variables (derived from more than one item in the questionnaire). Simple variables which are straightforward recodes of individual items are not in general described in this appendix.

Demographic variables

Ethnic group: 1 White British; 2 Other White background; 3 Mixed white/black background; 4 Other Mixed background; 5 Indian background; 6 Pakistani background; 7 Bangladeshi background; 8 Black Caribbean background; 9 Black African background; 10 other ethnic minority background. (Derived from bq101.)

Generation: 1–1.0 generation defined as those born outside UK and who arrived in Britain at age sixteen or older; 2–1.5 generation defined as those born outside UK and who arrived in Britain at ages nought to fifteen; 3–2 + generation defined as those born in UK. (Derived from bq102_1, bq102_2m, and bq102_2r.) Quasi-parents are defined as respondents born abroad who were aged fifty-five or over in 2010 and had been resident in Britain for twenty-five years or more.

Highest educational level: 0 no qualifications, 1 low qualifications (ISCED level 1); 2 lower secondary qualifications such as GCSE or foreign equivalent (ISCED level 2); 3 upper secondary qualifications such as A levels or foreign equivalent or other qualifications below degree level (ISCED levels 3 and 4); 4 degree level qualifications (ISCED level 5). Age of completed education is used to impute a small number of missing values. (Derived from eq63, eq64_2, and bq95_3.)

Housing Tenure: 1 owner; 2 rents from Local Authority, new town development corporation, housing association or housing trust (social housing); 3 other tenures. (Derived from bq93_1 and bq93_3.)

Income: treated as an ordered variable using the bands to which respondents were asked to assign themselves but missing values imputed using the EM algorithm (using age, gender, marital status, class, education, trade union membership, housing tenure, income source, percentage non-white but not ethnic group in order to avoid circularity. (Derived from bq96.)

Appendix 2

Religion: 1 Anglican; 2 Roman Catholic; 3 Pentecostal; 4 Other Christian; 5 Hindu; 6 Sikh; 7 Sunni Muslim; 8 other Muslim; 9 other; 10 none. (Derived from bq106_1, bq106_a, bq106_c, and bq106_m.)

Social Class: derived from respondent's occupation (bq98_1), partner's occupation (bq98_2) and income source (bq97). Seven categories: 1 salariat (professional, managerial or administrative work), 2 clerical, 3 petty bourgeoisie (small business owner), 4 skilled (including foreman), 5 routine work (including sales and service), 6 unwaged (derived from main household source of income), -1 missing data. These are frequently recoded into a three-category schema consisting of middle class (classes 1, 2, and 3), working class (classes 4 and 5), and unwaged/missing (classes 6 and -1). Respondents are assigned to a class based on their own occupational data, unless there is missing data in which case they are assigned on the basis of their partner's occupation (if there is non-missing data on partner's occupation). The retired and those not currently working are assigned on the basis of their last job. If the main household source of income is unemployment benefit or other benefits, this takes precedence over the occupational data.

Explanatory variables

Bonding social capital: sum of five components, namely friends from same ethnic group (scored 2 if all friends and 1 if most friends are from same ethnic group), workmates from same ethnic group (scored similarly), neighbours from same ethnic group (scored similarly), members of place of worship from same ethnic group (scored similarly) and whether taken part in an ethnic or cultural association (scored 2 if taken part). Non-workers and non-members of any religion included in the base, together with don't knows and refusals. (Derived from eq46_1, eq46_2, eq46_3, eq46_4, and eq42.) Re-scored so that range 0–10, mean 2.4, S.D. 2.0.

British practices: Sum of always or sometimes sends Valentine card, sends card to mother/father on Mother's Day/Father's Day, wears a poppy on Remembrance Day. (Derived from eq23_2, eq23_3, and eq23_5.) Range 0–3, mean 1.9. S.D. 1.1.

Discrimination: scored 1 if has experienced discrimination in last five years on grounds of either race or skin colour, language or accent, or religion; otherwise zero. (Derived from eq37, eq39a, eq39b, and eq39c.)

Ethnic identification: sum of black/Asian versus British identity (scored 1 to 5), how much in common with ethnic group (scored 1 to 4), how much in common with British (scored 1 to 4), and how bothered about marrying a white person (scored 1 to 5). Missing values imputed with EM algorithm. All items except eq19 reversed so that high scores represent high ethnic consciousness. (Derived from eq16a, eq17, eq19, and eq33_1.) Re-scored so that range 0–10, mean 4.6, S.D. 1.5. Reliability: Cronbach's alpha = 0.31.

Fraternal relative deprivation: sum of government generally treats *people from my ethnic group* fairly (scored 1 to 5), often a big gap between what *people from my ethnic group* expect out of life and what we actually get (scored 1 to 5 and reversed), non-white people don't have the same opportunities and chances in life as white people, as they are held back by prejudice and discrimination (scored 1 to 5 and reversed), and how much racial prejudice in Britain nowadays (scored 1 to 3 and reversed). Missing values imputed with EM algorithm. (Derived from bq18_a, bq18_2a, eq14_3, and eq24.) Mean 11.6, range 5–18, S.D. 2.4. Reliability: Cronbach's alpha 0.59.

Labour values: Sum of proportions within each ethno-religious group who shared Labour position on spending more on health and social services, protecting rights of the accused, improving opportunities for minorities, unemployment most important issue, sending asylum seekers home, approval of the war in Afghanistan. (Derived from bq40_1 and bq40_2, bq41_1 and bq41_2, bq74_1 and bq74_2, bq12_1, bq72_6, and bq45.) The Labour position was defined as the mean perceived score on items bq40_2, bq41_2 and bq74_2 and as not sending asylum seekers home, approving of the war, and unemployment as most important issue. Respondents were assumed to share this position if their own position on the three scales (bq40_1, bq41_1 and bq74_1 was the same as or more 'progressive' than Labour's, if they disagreed or disagreed strongly with sending asylum seekers home, agreed or agreed strongly that it was right to wage the war, and agreed that unemployment was the most important issue.

Political knowledge: sum of number of correct answers to the four questions asking whether
    Polling stations close at 10.00 p.m. on election day (true), the minimum voting age is sixteen (false), the Chancellor of the Exchequer is responsible for setting interest rates in the UK (false), and any registered voter can obtain a postal vote if they want one—by contacting their local council and asking for a postal vote (true). Range 0–4, mean 2.6, S.D. 1.0.

References

Abramson, Paul R. and William Claggett (1984). Race-related differences in self-reported and validated turnout in 1984. *The Journal of Politics* 46 (3): 719–38.

Alba, Richard D. (1981). The twilight of ethnicity among American Catholics of European ancestry. *Annals of the American Academy of Political and Social Science* 454 (1): 86–97.

Alba, Richard D. (1985). The twilight of ethnicity among Americans of European ancestry: the case of Italians. *Ethnic and Racial Studies* 8 (1): 134–58.

Alba, Richard D. (1990). *Ethnic Identity: The Transformation of White America*. New Haven: Yale University Press.

Alba, Richard D. and Victor Nee (1999). Rethinking assimilation theory for a new era of immigration. Pp. 137–60 in Charles Hirschman, Philip Kasinitz, and Josh DeWind (eds.) *The Handbook of International Migration: the American Experience*. New York: Russell Sage Foundation.

Aleksynska, Mariya (2011). Civic participation of immigrants in Europe: assimilation, origin and destination country effects. *European Journal of Political Economy* 27 (3): 566–85.

All Party Parliamentary Group on Race and Community (2012). *Ethnic Minority Female Unemployment: Black, Pakistani and Bangladeshi Heritage Women*. London: Runnymede Trust.

Almond, Gabriel A. and Sidney Verba (1963). *The Civic Culture: Political Attitudes and Democracy in Five Nations*. Princeton: Princeton University Press.

André, Stéfanie, Jaap Dronkers, and Ariana Need (2009). To vote or not to vote? Electoral participation of immigrants from different countries of origin in 24 European countries of destination. Paper presented at ECSR conference 'Changing societies in the context of the European Union enlargement', 11–12 December 2009, Paris.

Anderson, Benedict (1983). *Imagined Communities: Reflections on the Origin and Spread of Nationalism*. London: Verso.

Anwar, Muhammad (1979). *The Myth of Return: Pakistanis in Britain*. London: Heinemann.

Anwar, Muhammad (2001). The participation of ethnic minorities in British politics. *Journal of Ethnic and Migration Studies* 27 (3): 533–49.

Ballard, Roger (1996). Negotiating race and ethnicity: exploring the implications of the 1991 Census. *Patterns of Prejudice* 30 (3): 3–33.

References

Ballard, Roger (2008). The social and demographic characteristics of Britain's Hindu population. Pp. 25–39 in Diviash Thakrar, Rasamandala Das, and Aziz Sheikh (eds.) *Caring for Hindu Patients*. Oxford: Radcliffe Publications.

Ballard, Roger (ed.) (1994). *Desh Pardesh: the South Asian Presence in Britain*. London: C. Hurst and Co.

Barnes, Samuel H. and Max Kaase (1979). *Political Action: Mass Participation in Five Western Democracies*. Thousand Oaks, CA: Sage.

Barreto, Matt A. (2007). 'Sí Se Puede': Latino candidates and the mobilization of Latino voters. *American Political Science Review* 101 (3): 425–41.

Barry, Brian (1970). *Sociologists, Economists, and Democracy*. Chicago: University of Chicago Press.

Barry, Brian (2001). *Culture and Equality: An Egalitarian Critique of Multiculturalism*, Cambridge: Polity Press.

Bergh, Johannes and Tor Bjorklund (2011). The revival of group voting: explaining the voting preferences of immigrants in Norway. *Political Studies* 59 (2): 308–27.

Berrington, Ann (1996). Marriage patterns and inter-ethnic unions. Pp. 178–212 in David Coleman and John Salt (eds.) *Ethnicity in the 1991 Census, Vol. 1: Demographic Characteristics of the Ethnic Minority Populations*. London: HMSO.

Berthoud, Richard (2000). Ethnic employment penalties in Britain. *Journal of Ethnic and Migration Studies* 26 (3): 389–416.

Bhachu, Parminder (1985). *Twice Migrants: East African Sikh Settlers in Britain*. London: Tavistock.

Bilodeau, Antoine, Ian McAllister, and Mebs Kanji (2010). Adaptation to democracy among immigrants in Australia. *International Political Science Review* 31 (2): 141–66.

Bird, Karen, Thomas Saalfeld, and Andreas M. Wüst (eds.) (2011). *The Political Representation of Immigrants and Minorities: Voters, Parties and Parliaments in Liberal Democracies*. London: Routledge.

Bloemraad, Irene (2006). Becoming a citizen in the United States and Canada; structured mobilization and immigrant political incorporation. *Social Forces* 85 (2): 667–95.

Blossfeld, Hans-Peter and Andreas Timm (eds.) (2003). *Who Marries Whom? Educational Systems as Marriage Markets in Modern Societies*. Dordrecht: Kluwer Academic.

Bobo, Lawrence and Franklin D. Gilliam Jr (1990). Race, socio-political participation, and Black empowerment. *American Political Science Review* 84 (2): 279–393.

Borjas, George J. (1987). Self-selection and the earnings of immigrants. *American Economic Review* 77 (4): 531–53.

Bowler, Shaun and Gary M. Segura (2012). *The Future is Ours: Minority Politics, Political Behaviour, and the Multiracial Era of American Politics*. Los Angeles, CA: Sage.

Brady, Henry E., Sidney Verba, and Kay Lehman Schlozman (1995). Beyond SES: a resource model of political participation. *American Political Science Review* 89 (2): 271–94.

Brown, Colin. (1984). *Black and White Britain: The Third PSI Survey*. London: Heinemann.

Brown, Colin and Pat Gay (1985). *Racial Discrimination 17 Years after the Act*. London: Policy Studies Institute.

References

Brown, R. Khari and Ronald E. Brown (2003). Faith and works: church-based social capital resources and African-American political activism. *Social Forces* 82 (2): 617–41.

Bueker, Catherine S. (2005). Political incorporation among migrants from ten areas of origin: the persistence of source country effects. *International Migration Review* 39 (1): 103–40.

Bulpitt, Jim (1986). Continuity, autonomy and peripheralisation: the anatomy of the centre's race statecraft in England. Pp. 17–44 in Zig Layton-Henry and Paul B. Rich (eds.) *Race, Government and Politics in Britain*. London: Macmillan.

Butler, David and Donald Stokes (1969). *Political Change in Britain: Forces Shaping Electoral Choice*. London: Macmillan.

Butler, David and Donald Stokes (1974). *Political Change in Britain: The Evolution of Electoral Choice*, 2nd ed. London: Macmillan.

Butt, Sarah and John Curtice (2008). Duty in decline? Trends in attitudes to voting. Pp. 1–18 in Alison Park et al. (eds.) *British Social Attitudes: The 26th Report*. London: Sage.

Cabinet Office (2003). Ethnic Minorities and the Labour Market: Final Report. <http://www.cabinetoffice.gov.uk/strategy/work_areas/ethnic_minorities.aspx> (accessed 27 December 2012).

Calhoun-Brown, Allison (1996). African-American churches and political mobilization: the psychological impact of organizational resources. *Journal of Politics* 58 (4): 935–53.

Cameron, David (2011). Speech at the Munich Security conference, 5 February 2011. <http://www.number10.gov.uk/news/pms-speech-at-munich-security-conference> (accessed 8 March 2013).

Cantle, Ted (Chairman) (2001). *Community Cohesion: A Report of the Independent Review Team*. London: Home Office.

Carmichael, Fiona and R. Woods (2000). Ethnic penalties in unemployment and occupational attainment: evidence for Britain, *International Review of Applied Economics* 14 (1): 71–98.

Cheung, Sin-Yi and Anthony F. Heath (2007). Nice work if you can get it: ethnic penalties in Great Britain. Pp. 507–50 in Anthony F. Heath and Sin-Yi Cheung (eds.) *Unequal Chances: Ethnic Minorities in Western Labour Markets*. Proceedings of the British Academy 137. Oxford: Oxford University Press for the British Academy.

Chiswick, Barry (1999). Are immigrants favorably self-selected? *American Economic Review* 89 (2): 181–5.

Cho, Wendy K. Tam (1999). Naturalization, socialization, participation: immigrants and (non-)voting. *Journal of Politics* 61 (4): 1140–55.

Clarke, Harold D., David Sanders, Marianne C. Stewart, and Paul F. Whiteley (2004). *Political Choice in Britain*. Oxford: Oxford University Press.

Clarke, Harold D., David Sanders, Marianne C. Stewart, and Paul F. Whiteley (2009). *Performance Politics and the British Voter*. Cambridge: Cambridge University Press.

Clarke, Harold D., David Sanders, Marianne C. Stewart, and Paul F. Whiteley (2011). Valence politics and electoral choice in Britain, 2010. *Journal of Elections, Public Opinion and Parties* 21 (2): 237–53.

References

Cohen, Robin (1995). Fuzzy frontiers of identity: the British case. *Social Identities* 1 (1): 35–62.

Curtice, John (2012). Bridging the gulf? Britain's democracy after the 2010 election. Pp. 1–20 in Alison Park et al. (eds.) *British Social Attitudes 28*. London: Sage.

Curtice, John, Stephen D. Fisher, and Michael Steed (2005). Appendix 2: the results analysed. Pp. 235–59 in Dennis Kavanagh and David Butler, *The British General Election of 2005*. Basingstoke: Palgrave Macmillan.

Curtice, John, Stephen D. Fisher, and Robert Ford (2010). Appendix 1: An analysis of the results. Pp. 385–426 in Dennis Kavanagh and Philip Cowley, *The British General Election of 2010*. Basingstoke: Palgrave Macmillan.

Cutts, David, Edward Fieldhouse, Kingsley Purdam, David Steel, and Mark Tranmer (2007). Voter turnout in British South Asian communities at the 2001 general election. *British Journal of Politics and International Relations* 9 (3): 396–412.

Daley, Patricia (1996). Black Africans: students who stayed. Pp. 44–65 in Ceri Peach (ed.) *Ethnicity in the 1991 Census*, vol. 2: *The Ethnic Minority Populations of Great Britain*. London: HMSO.

Dancygier, Rafaella (2010). *Immigration and Conflict in Europe*. Cambridge: Cambridge University Press.

Dancygier, Rafaela and Elizabeth N. Saunders (2006). A new electorate? Comparing preferences and partisanship between immigrants and natives. *American Journal of Political Science* 50 (4): 962–81.

Daniel, William W. (1968). *Racial Discrimination in England*. London: Penguin.

Davis, Nancy J. and Robert V. Robinson (2006). The egalitarian face of Islamic orthodoxy: support for Islamic law and economic justice in seven Muslim-majority nations. *American Sociological Review* 71 (2): 167–90.

Dawson, Michael C. (1994). *Behind the Mule: Race and Class in African-American Politics*. Princeton, NJ: Princeton University Press.

De Rooij, Eline A. (2012). Patterns of immigrant political participation: explaining differences in types of political participation between immigrants and the majority population in Western Europe. *European Sociological Review* 28 (4): 455–81.

Diehl, Claudia and Michael Blohm (2001). Apathy, adaptation or ethnic mobilisation? On the political attitudes of an excluded group. *Journal of Ethnic and Migration Studies* 27 (3): 401–20.

DiSipio, Louis (2001). Building America, one person at a time: naturalization and the political behaviour of the naturalized in contemporary American politics. Pp. 67–106 in Gary Gerstle and John Mollenkopf (eds.) *E Pluribus Unum? Contemporary and Historical Perspectives on Immigrant Political Incorporation*. New York: Russell Sage.

Djupe, Paul A. and J. Tobin Grant (2001). Religious institutions and political participation in America. *Journal for the Scientific Study of Religion* 40 (2): 303–14.

Doerschler, Peter (2006). Push-pull factors and immigrant political integration in Germany. *Social Science Quarterly* 87 (5): 1100–16.

Dovidio, John F., Samuel L. Gaertner, and Kerry Kawakami (2003). Intergroup contact: the past, present, and the future. *Group Processes and Intergroup Relations* 6 (1): 5–21.

Downs, Antony (1957). *An Economic Theory of Democracy*. New York: Harper and Row.

References

Dustmann, Christian and Yoram Weiss (2007). Return migration: theory and empirical evidence from the UK. *British Journal of Industrial Relations* 45 (2): 236–56.

Electoral Commission (2005). *Black and Minority Ethnic Survey*. London: Electoral Commission.

Electoral Commission (2011). *Great Britain's Electoral Registers 2011*. London: Electoral Commission.

Equality and Human Rights Commission (2010). *How Fair is Britain? Equality, Human Rights and Good Relations 2010. The First Triennial Review*. London: EHRC. <http://www.equalityhumanrights.com/key-projects/how-fair-is-britain> (accessed 8 March 2013).

Eurostat (2012). Acquisition of citizenship. <http://epp.eurostat.ec.europa.eu/portal/page/portal/product_details/dataset?p_product_code=TPS00024> (accessed 8 August 2012).

Feliciano, Cynthia (2005). Educational selectivity in U.S. immigration: how do immigrants compare to those left behind? *Demography* 42 (1): 131–52.

Fennema, Meindert and Jean Tillie (1999). Political participation and political trust in Amsterdam: civic communities and ethnic networks. *Journal of Ethnic and Migration Studies* 25 (4): 703–26.

Field, Clive D. (2007). Islamophobia in contemporary Britain: the evidence of the opinion polls, 1988–2006. *Islam and Christian-Muslim Relations* 18 (4): 447–77.

Field, Clive D. (2011). Revisiting Islamophobia in contemporary Britain: opinion-poll findings for 2007–10. Pp. 147–61 in Marc Helbling (ed.) *Islamophobia in the West: Measuring and Explaining Individual Attitudes*. London: Routledge.

Fieldhouse, Edward and David Cutts (2008a). Diversity, density and turnout: The effect of neighbourhood ethno-religious composition on voter turnout in Britain. *Political Geography* 27 (5): 530–48.

Fieldhouse, Edward and David Cutts (2008b). Mobilization or marginalization? Neighbourhood effects on Muslim electoral registration in Britain in 2001. *Political Studies* 56 (2): 333–54.

Fiorina, Morris (1981). *Retrospective Voting in American National Elections*. New Haven: Yale University Press.

Fisher, Stephen D. (2004). Definition and measurement of tactical voting: The role of rational choice. *British Journal of Political Science* 34 (1): 152–66.

Fisher, Stephen D., Anthony F. Heath, David Sanders, and Maria Sobolewska (in preparation). Candidate ethnicity and electoral behaviour at the 2010 British General Election.

Fitzgerald, Marian (1987). *Black People and Party Politics in Britain*. London: Runnymede Trust.

Foner, Nancy (1977). The Jamaicans: cultural and social change among migrants in Britain. Pp. 120–50 in James L. Watson (ed.) (1977) *Between Two Cultures: Migrants and Minorities in Britain*. Oxford: Basil Blackwell.

Ford, Robert (2008). Is racial prejudice declining in Britain? *British Journal of Sociology* 59 (4): 609–36.

References

Gardner, Katy and Abdus Shukur (1994). 'I'm Bengali, I'm Asian, and I am living here': the changing identity of British Bengalis. Pp. 142–64 in Roger Ballard (ed.) *Desh Pardesh: The South Asian Presence in Britain*. London: C. Hurst and Co.

Gittell, Ross and Avis Vidal (1998). *Community Organisation: Building Social Capital as a Development Strategy*. Thousand Oaks, CA: Sage.

González-Ferrer, Amparo (2011). The electoral participation of naturalized immigrants in ten European cities. Pp. 63–86 in Laura Morales and Marco Giugni (eds.) *Social Capital, Political Participation and Migration in Europe: Making Multicultural Democracy Work?* Basingstoke: Palgrave Macmillan.

Gordon, Milton (1964). *Assimilation in American Life: The Role of Race, Religion and National Origin*. New York: Oxford University Press.

Guha, Ramachandra (2007). *India After Gandhi: The History of the World's Largest Democracy*. London: Macmillan.

Hajnal, Zoltan L. and Taeku Lee (2011). *Why Americans Don't Join the Party: Race, Immigration, and the Failure (of Political Parties) to Engage the Electorate*. Princeton: Princeton University Press.

Hampshire, James (2012). Race and representation: the BME shortlist debates in Britain. Pp. 33–52 in Terri E. Givens and Rahsaan Maxwell (eds.) *Immigrant Politics: Race and Representation in Western Europe*. Boulder, CO: Lynne Rienner Publishers.

Heath, Anthony F. (1998). The need of data analysis for rational action theory: pros and cons. Pp. 171–87 in Hans-Peter Blossfeld and Gerald Prein (eds.) *Rational Choice Theory and Large-Scale Data Analysis*, Boulder, CO: Westview Press.

Heath, Anthony F., Bob Andersen, John Curtice, and Katarina Thomson (2008). Are Traditional Identities in Decline? Full Research Report ESRC End of Award Report, RES-148-25-0031. Swindon: ESRC.

Heath, Anthony F. and Geoffrey A. Evans (1994). Tactical voting: concepts, measurement and findings. *British Journal of Political Science* 24 (4): 557–61.

Heath, Anthony F., Geoffrey A. Evans, and Jean Martin (1994). The measurement of core beliefs and values: the development of balanced socialist/laissez faire and libertarian/authoritarian scales. *British Journal of Political Science* 24 (1): 115–32.

Heath, Anthony F., Stephen D. Fisher, David Sanders, and Maria Sobolewska (2011). Ethnic heterogeneity in the social bases of voting at the 2010 British General Election. *Journal of Elections, Public Opinion and Parties* 21 (2): 255–77.

Heath, Anthony F., Roger M. Jowell, and John K. Curtice (2001). *The Rise of New Labour: Party Policies and Voter Choices*. Oxford: Oxford University Press.

Heath, Anthony F., Roger Jowell, John Curtice, Geoff Evans, Julia Field, and Sharon Witherspoon (1991). *Understanding Political Change: The British Voter 1964–1987*. Oxford: Pergamon Press.

Heath, Anthony F. and Yaojun Li (2008). Period, life-cycle and generational effects on ethnic minority success in the British labour market. *Kölner Zeitschrift für Soziologie und Sozialpsychologie* 48: 277–306.

Heath, Anthony F. and Jean Martin (2012). Can religious affiliation explain 'ethnic' inequalities in the labour market? *Ethnic and Racial Studies*. Published online. DOI: 10.1080/01419870.2012.657550.

References

Heath, Anthony F. and Dorren McMahon (1997). Education and occupational attainment: the impact of ethnic origins. Pp. 91–113 in Valerie Karn (ed.) *Education, Employment and Housing among Ethnic Minorities in Britain*. London: HMSO.

Heath, Anthony F. and Dorren McMahon (2005). Social mobility of ethnic minorities. Pp. 393–413 in Glenn C. Loury, Tariq Modood, and Steven M. Teles (eds.) *Ethnicity, Social Mobility and Public Policy: Comparing the US and UK*. Cambridge: Cambridge University Press.

Heath, Anthony F., Dorren McMahon, and Jane Roberts (2000). Ethnic differences in the labour market: a comparison of the samples of anonymized records and labour force survey. *Journal of the Royal Statistical Society Series A* 163 (3): 341–61.

Heath, Anthony, Catherine Rothon, and Sundas Ali (2010). Race and public opinion. Pp. 186–208 in Alice Bloch and John Solomos (eds.) *Race and Ethnicity in the 21st Century*. Basingstoke: Palgrave Macmillan.

Heath, Anthony F. and Shamit Saggar (1999). The British General Election Study: Ethnic minority survey 1997. Codebook and data collection instruments. ICPSR 2618. Ann Arbor, Michigan: ICPSR.

Heath, Anthony F., Bridget Taylor, Lindsay Brook, and Alison Park (1999). British national sentiment. *British Journal of Political Science* 29 (1): 155–75.

Heath, Anthony F. and Jane Roberts (2008) *British Identity: Its Sources and Possible Implications for Civic Attitudes and Behaviour*. Research report for Lord Goldsmith's Citizenship Review. <http:/www.justice.gov.uk/docs/british-identity.pdf> (accessed 7 March 2013).

Hewstone, Miles (2009). Living apart, living together? The role of intergroup contact in social integration. *Proceedings of the British Academy* 162: 243–300.

Hirschman, Albert O. (1970). *Exit, Voice and Loyalty: Responses to Decline in Firms, Organizations, and States*. Cambridge, MA: Harvard University Press.

Howat, Nick, Oliver Nordern, Joel Williams, and Emily Pickering (2012). 2010 Ethnic Minority British Election Study: Technical report. London: TNS-BMRB. <http://www.esds.ac.uk/doc/6970\mrdoc\pdf\british_election_study_ethnic_minority_survey_2010_technical_report.pdf> (accessed 8 March 2013).

Inglehart, Ronald (1990). *Culture Shift in Advanced Industrial Society*. Princeton: Princeton University Press.

International IDEA (2012). *Voter Turnout*. <http://www.idea.int/vt> (accessed 8 March 2013).

Jamal, Amaney (2005). The political participation and engagement of Muslim Americans: Mosque involvement and group consciousness. *American Politics Research* 33 (4): 521–44.

Johnston, Ron and Charles Pattie (2012, first published online). Learning electoral geography? Party campaigning, constituency marginality and voting at the 2010 British general election. *Transactions of the Institute of British Geographers* 38 (2): 285–98.

Jones-Correa, Michael A. and David L. Leal (2001). Political participation: does religion matter? *Political Research Quarterly* 54 (4): 751–70.

Jowell, Roger and Patricia Prescott-Clarke (1970). Racial discrimination and white-collar workers in Britain. *Race and Class* 11 (4): 397–417.

References

Karp, Jeffrey A., Susan A. Banducci, and Shaun Bowler (2008). Getting out the vote: party mobilization in a comparative perspective. *British Journal of Political Science* 38 (1): 91–112.

Kinder, Donald R. and Kiewiet, D. Roderick (1981). Sociotropic politics: the American case. *British Journal of Political Science* 11 (2): 129–61.

Koopmans, Ruud and Paul Statham (1999). Challenging the liberal nation-state? Post-nationalism, multiculturalism and the collective claims-making of migrants and ethnic minorities in Britain and Germany. *American Journal of Sociology* 105 (3): 652–96.

Lancee, Bram (2010). The economic returns of immigrants' bonding and bridging social capital. The case of the Netherlands. *International Migration Review* 44 (1): 202–26.

Leighley, Jan E. and Arnold Vedlitz (1999). Race, ethnicity, and political participation: competing models and contrasting explanations. *Journal of Politics* 61 (4): 1092–114.

Lewis, Jeffrey B. and Gary King (1999). No evidence on directional vs. proximity voting. *Political Analysis* 8 (1): 21–33.

Li, Yaojun and Anthony F. Heath (2008). Minority ethnic men in British labour market (1972–2005). *International Journal of Sociology and Social Policy* 28 (5/6): 231–44.

Li, Yaojun and Anthony F. Heath (2010). Struggling onto the ladder, climbing the rungs: employment and class position of minority ethnic groups in Britain. Pp. 83–98 in John Stillwell et al. (eds.) *Spatial and Social Disparities*. London: Springer.

Lipsky, Michael (1968). Protest as a political resource. *American Political Science Review* 62 (4): 1144–58.

Lipsky, Michael (1970). *Protest in City Politics: Rent Strikes, Housing and the Power of the Poor*. Chicago, IL: Rand McNally.

Lopez, David and Yen Espiritu (1990). Panethnicity in the United States: a theoretical framework. *Ethnic and Racial Studies* 13 (2): 198–224.

Macpherson, Sir William (1999). *The Stephen Lawrence Enquiry*. Presented to Parliament by the Secretary of State for the Home Department by command of Her Majesty. Cm 4262_I. London: HMSO.

McVeigh, Rory and Christian Smith (1999). Who protests in America: an analysis of three political alternatives—inaction, institutionalized politics, or protest. *Sociological Forum* 14 (4): 685–702.

Manning, Alan and Sanchari Roy (2010). Culture clash or culture club? National identity in Britain. *The Economic Journal* 120 (542): F72–F100.

Marshall, Monty G. and Keith Jaggers (2011). *Polity IV Country Reports 2010*. <http://www.systemicpeace.org/polity/polity06.htm> (accessed 8 March 2013).

Martinez, Lisa M. (2005). Yes we can: Latino participation in unconventional politics. *Social Forces* 84 (1): 135–55.

Mateos, Pablo, Alex Singleton, and Paul Longley (2009). Uncertainty in the analysis of ethnic classifications: issues of extent and aggregation of ethnic groups. *Journal of Ethnic and Migration Studies* 35 (9): 1437–60.

Maxwell, Rahsaan (2006). Muslims, South Asians, and the British mainstream: a national identity crisis? *West European Politics* 29 (4): 736–56.

References

Maxwell, Rahsaan (2009). Caribbean and South Asian identification with British society: the importance of perceived discrimination. *Ethnic and Racial Studies* 32 (8): 1449–69.

Maxwell, Rahsaan (2010a). Evaluating migrant integration: political attitudes across generations in Europe. *International Migration Review* 44 (1): 25–52.

Maxwell, Rahsaan (2010b). Trust in government among British Muslims: the importance of migration status. *Political Behaviour* 32: 89–109.

Maxwell, Rahsaan (2012). *Ethnic Minority Migrants in Britain and France: Integration Trade-Offs*. Cambridge: Cambridge University Press.

Merton, Robert K. (1995). The Thomas theorem and the Matthew effect. *Social Forces* 74 (2): 379–424.

Merton, Robert K. and Alice S. Rossi (1950). Contributions to the theory of reference group behavior. Pp. 40–105 in Robert K. Merton and Paul F. Lazarsfeld (eds.) *Continuities in Social Research*. New York: The Free Press.

Messina, Anthony M. (1989). *Race and Party Competition in Britain*. Oxford: Clarendon Press.

Milbrath, Lester W. (1965). *Political Participation: How and Why do People get Involved in Politics?* Chicago: Rand McNally.

Miller, Arthur H., Patricia Gurin, Gerald Gurin, and Oksana Malanchuk (1981). Group consciousness and political participation. *American Journal of Political Science* 25 (3): 494–511.

Mitton, Lavinia and Peter Aspinall (2010). Black Africans in England: a diversity of integration experiences. Pp. 179–202 in John Stillwell and Maarten van Ham (eds.) *Ethnicity and Integration: Understanding Population Trends and Processes*, vol. 3. Dordecht: Springer.

MIPEX (2012). Migrant Integration Policy Index. <http://www.mipex.eu (accessed 8 March 2013).

Modood, Tariq (2005). *Multicultural Politics: Racism, Ethnicity and Muslims in Britain*. Edinburgh: Edinburgh University Press.

Modood, Tariq, Richard Berthoud, and others (1997). *Ethnic Minorities in Britain: Diversity and Disadvantage*. London: Policy Studies Institute.

Morales, Laura (2011). Conceptualizing and measuring migrants' political inclusion. Pp. 19–42 in Laura Morales and Marco Giugni (eds.) *Social Capital, Political Participation and Migration in Europe: Making Multicultural Democracy Work?* Basingstoke: Palgrave Macmillan.

Morales, Laura and Katia Pilati (2011). The role of social capital in migrants' engagement in local politics in European cities. Pp. 87–114 in Laura Morales and Marco Giugni (eds.) *Social Capital, Political Participation and Migration in Europe: Making Multicultural Democracy Work*. Basingstoke: Palgrave Macmillan.

Muttarak, Raya (forthcoming). Generation, ethnic and religious diversity in friendship choice: exploring interethnic friendship formation in the UK. *Ethnic and Racial Studies*.

Muttarak, Raya and Heath, Anthony F. (2010). Who intermarries in Britain? Explaining ethnic diversity in intermarriage patterns. *British Journal of Sociology*, 61 (2): 275–305.

References

National Employment Panel (2005). *Enterprising People, Enterprising Places*: Measures to increase ethnic minority employment and business growth. London: National Employment Panel. (June 2005).

Norris, Pippa (2004). Young people and political activism: from the politics of loyalties to the politics of choice?, paper presented at the conference on Civic Engagement in the 21st Century, University of Southern California.

Office for National Statistics (2011). Population estimates by ethnic group 2002–2009. <http://www.ons.gov.uk/ons/taxonomy/index.html?nscl=Population+Estimates+by+Ethnic+Group> (accessed 05 June 2012).

Ogbu, John (1978). *Minority Education and Caste: The American System in Cross-Cultural Perspective*. San Diego, CA: Academic Press.

Olsen, Marvin E. (1970). Social and political participation of Blacks. *American Sociological Review* 35 (4): 682–97.

Patterson, Orlando (2005). Four modes of ethno-somatic stratification: the experience of Blacks in Europe and the Americas. Pp. 67–121 in Glenn C. Loury, Tariq Modood, and Steven M. Teles (eds.) *Ethnicity, Social Mobility and Public Policy: Comparing the US and UK*. Cambridge: Cambridge University Press.

Peach, Ceri (1968). *West Indian Migration to Britain*. London: Oxford University Press.

Peach, Ceri (1996). Black-Caribbeans: class, gender and geography. Pp. 25–43 in Ceri Peach (ed.) *Ethnicity in the 1991 Census, vol. 2: The Ethnic Minority Populations of Great Britain*. London: HMSO.

Petersen, Trond, Ishak Saporta, and Mark-David L. Seidel (2000). Offering a job: meritocracy and social networks. *American Journal of Sociology* 106 (3): 763–817.

Purdam, Kingsley, Edward Fieldhouse, Andrew Russell, and Virinder Kalra (2002). *Voter Engagement among Black and Minority Ethnic Communities*. Research Report July 2002. London: The Electoral Commission.

Putnam, Robert (2000). *Bowling Alone: The Collapse and Revival of American Community*. New York: Simon and Schuster.

Putnam, Robert (2007). *E Pluribus Unum*: diversity and community in the twenty-first century: the 2006 Johan Skytte Prize lecture. *Scandinavian Political Studies* 30 (2): 137–74.

Rabinowitz, George and Stuart Elaine Macdonald (1989). A directional theory of issue voting. *American Political Science Review* 83 (1): 93–121.

Rallings, Colin and Michael Thrasher (2007). *British Electoral Facts 1832–2006*. Farnham, Surrey: Ashgate.

Rice, Tom W. and Jan L. Feldman (1997). Civic culture and democracy from Europe to America, *Journal of Politics* 59 (4): 1143–72.

Runciman, W. Garrison (1966). *Relative Deprivation and Social Justice: A Study of Attitudes to Social Inequality in Twentieth-Century England*. London: Routledge & Kegan Paul.

Saalfeld, Thomas and Kalliope Kyriakopoulou (2011). Presence and behaviour: black and minority MPs in the British House of Commons. Pp. 230–49 in Karen Bird, Thomas Saalfeld, and Andreas M. Wüst (eds.) *The Political Representation of Immigrants and Minorities: Voters, Parties and Parliaments in Liberal Democracies*. London: Routledge.

References

Saggar, Shamit (1998). *The General Election 1997: Ethnic Minorities and Electoral Politics*. London: Commission for Racial Equality.

Saggar, Shamit (2000). *Race and Representation: Electoral Politics and Ethnic Pluralism in Britain*. Manchester: Manchester University Press.

Saggar, Shamit and Heath, Anthony F. (1999). Race: Toward a multicultural electorate? Pp. 102–23 in Geoffrey Evans and Pippa Norris (eds.) *Critical Elections: British Parties and Voters in Long-Term Perspective*. London: Sage.

Sanders, David (2006). Reflections on the 2005 General Election: Some speculations on how the Conservatives can win next time. *Journal of British Politics* 1 (2): 1–25.

Sanders, David, Stephen Fisher, Anthony F. Heath, and Maria Sobolewska (forthcoming). The calculus of ethnic minority voting in Britain. *Political Studies*.

Santoro, Wayne A, María B. Vélez, and Stacy M. Keogh (2012). Mexican American protest, ethnic resiliency and social capital: the mobilization benefits of cross-cutting ties. *Social Forces* 91 (1): 209–31.

Scarman, Lord (1981). The Brixton Disorders, April 10–12 1981: Report of an Inquiry by the Rt. Hon. The Lord Scarman, O.B.E. Cmnd. 8427. London: HMSO.

Shaw, Alison (2000). *Kinship and Continuity: Pakistani Families in Britain*. London: Routledge.

Shingles, Richard D. (1981). Black consciousness and political participation: the missing link. *American Political Science Review* 75 (1): 76–91.

Shukra, Kalbir (1998). *The Changing Pattern of Black Politics in Britain*. London: Pluto Press.

Smith, David J. (1977). *Racial Disadvantage in Britain*. London: Penguin.

Smith, Stephen (1993). *Electoral Registration in 1991*, OPCS Social Survey Division. London: HMSO, London.

Sobolewska, Maria (2005). Ethnic agenda: relevance of political attitudes to party choice. *Journal of Elections, Public Opinion and Parties* 15 (2): 197–214.

Sobolewska, Maria, David Cutts and Edward Fieldhouse (2012). Taking minorities for granted? Ethnic density, party campaigning and targeting minority voters in 2010 British general elections. *Parliamentary Affairs*. doi:10.1093/pa/gss088.

Sobolewska, Maria (2013). Party strategies, political opportunity structure and the descriptive representation of ethnic minorities in Britain. *West European Politics* 66 (2): 329–44.

Statham, Paul (1999). Political mobilisation by minorities in Britain: a negative feedback of 'race relations'? *Journal of Ethnic and Migration Studies* 25 (4): 597–626.

Studlar, Donley T. (1986). Non-white policy preferences, political participation, and the political agenda in Britain. Pp. 159–86 in Zig Layton-Henry and Paul B. Rich (eds.) *Race, Government and Politics in Britain*. London: Macmillan.

Studlar, Donley T. and Zig Layton-Henry (1990). Nonwhite minority access to the political agenda in Britain. *Policy Studies Review* 9 (2): 273–93.

Swaddle, Kevin and Anthony F. Heath (1989). Official and reported turnout in the British General Election of 1987. *British Journal of Political Science* 19 (4): 537–70.

Tajfel, Henri (ed.) (1978). *Differentiation Between Social Groups: Studies in the social psychology of intergroup relations*. London: Academic Press.

References

Taylor, Bridget and Katarina Thomson (1999). Technical appendix. Pp. 272–83 in Geoffrey Evans and Pippa Norris (eds.) *Critical Elections: British Parties and Voters in Long-term Perspective*. London: Sage.

Teney, Celine, Dirk Jacobs, Andrea Rea, and Pascal Delwit (2010). Ethnic voting in Brussels: Voting patterns among ethnic minorities in Brussels (Belgium) during the 2006 local elections. *Acta Politica* 45 (3): 273–97.

Thomas, William I. and Dorothy Swaine Thomas (1928). *The Child in America: Behavior problems and programs*. New York: Knopf.

Tillie, Jean (2004). Social capital of organisations and their members: explaining the political integration of immigrants in Amsterdam. *Journal of Ethnic and Migration Studies* 30 (3): 529–41.

Transparency International (2011). *Corruption Perceptions Index 2011*. <http:///www.Cpi.transparency.org/cpi2011/results> (accessed 8 March 2013).

Uhlaner, Carole J. and F. Chris Garcia (2005). *Foundations of Latino Party Identification*. Irvine, CA: Center for the Study of Democracy Research Monograph Series.

Verba, Sidney, Norman H. Nie, and Jae-on Kim (1978). *Participation and Political Equality*. Cambridge: Cambridge University Press.

Verba, Sidney, Kay L. Schlozman, and Henry E. Brady (1995). *Voice and Equality: Civic Voluntarism in American Politics*. Cambridge, MA: Harvard University Press.

Verba, Sidney, Kay Lehman Schlozman, Henry Brady, and Norman H. Nie (1993). Race, ethnicity and political resources: participation in the United States. *British Journal of Political Science* 23 (4): 453–97.

Warner, W. Lloyd and Leo Srole (1945). *The Social Systems of American Ethnic Groups*. New Haven, CT: Yale University Press.

Watson, James L. (ed.) (1977). *Between Two Cultures: Migrants and Minorities in Britain*. Oxford: Basil Blackwell.

Weakliem, David and Anthony F. Heath (1994). Rational choice and class voting. *Rationality and Society* 6 (2): 243–70.

Weber, M. ([1922] 1978). Ethnic group. Pp. 385–98 in G. Roth and C. Wittich (eds.) *Economy and Society: An Outline of Interpretive Sociology*, vol. 1, Part II. Berkeley, CA: University of California Press.

Werfhorst, Herman G. van de, Erika van Elsas, and Anthony F. Heath (2012). A meta-analysis of second generation immigrant disadvantage in education: comparative findings. Paper presented at the RC28 conference, Hong Kong.

White, Steven, Neil Nevitte, André Blais, Elizabeth Gidengil, and Patrick Fournier (2008). The political resocialization of immigrants: resistance or lifelong learning? *Political Research Quarterly* 61 (2): 268–81.

Wilson, J. Matthew (2012). How are we doing? Group-based economic assessments and African American political behaviour. *Electoral Studies* 31 (3): 550–61.

Wong, Janelle, Pei-Te Lien, and M. Margaret Conway (2005). Group-based resources and political participation among Asian Americans. *American Politics Research* 33 (4): 545–76.

References

Wood, Martin, Jon Hales, Susan Purdon, Tanya Sejersen, and Oliver Hayllar (2009). *A Test for Racial Discrimination in Recruitment Practice in British Cities*. Department for Work and Pensions Research Report 607. London: DWP.

Zomeren, Martijn van, Tom Postmes, and Russell Spears (2008). Toward an integrative social identity model of collective action: a quantitative research synthesis of three socio-psychological perspective. *Psychological Bulletin* 134 (4): 504–35.

Index

Abbott, Diane, MP 89, 90
Abramson, Paul R. 152
abstention 3, 10, 11, 154–173
acculturation 27, 29, 34, 35, 135
Adivasis 22
affirmative action
  attitudes to 69, 71, 73, 75, 96, 114, 183
  policies 69, 130
Afghanistan war, attitudes to 9, 13, 61, 63, 65, 66, 67, 68, 73, 74, 79, 83, 95, 96, 107, 114, 119, 125, 130, 157, 159, 160, 161, 163, 168, 183, 199, 212
African/ black African background 7, 8, 9, 16, 17, 18, 21, 25–26, 29, 31, 32, 33, 35, 38, 44, 45, 67, 68, 79, 80, 106, 112, 120, 138, 139, 140, 180, 193, 196, 208
African-Americans 27, 36, 38, 65, 108, 115, 128, 177
Africanization 22, 23
age
  as predictor 31, 50, 51, 53, 58, 59, 73, 138, 141, 145, 152, 172, 182, 185, 194, 200
  differences 53
agenda *see* political agenda
Akan 26
Alba, Richard 14, 16, 36
Aleksynska, Mariya 57, 187
alienation *see* disaffection
All Party Parliamentary Group on Race and Community 128
allegiance *see* party identification
Almond, Gabriel A. 174, 187
Amin, Idi 22
André, Stéphanie 57
Anderson, Benedict 16
Anglicans 20
anti-discrimination measures *see* redress for racial discrimination
Antigua 20
Anwar, Muhammad 14, 56, 151
apathy *see* disengagement
Arbitration Act 1996 71
arrival, time since 6, 7, 19, 20, 21, 22, 24, 25, 26, 31, 33, 34, 45–46, 50, 51, 58, 61, 117, 129, 137, 138, 142, 174, 208

Asian-Americans 105
Aspinall, Peter 38
assimilation, theories of 6, 14, 27
associations, ethnic or cultural 9, 30, 31, 34, 35, 38, 45, 46, 47, 48, 49, 50, 54, 129, 178, 183, 185, 188, 197, 198, 211
asylum-seekers, attitudes towards 9, 33, 61, 65, 66, 67, 68, 72–3, 75, 95, 114, 119, 130, 183, 185, 212
Austria 19, 36
authoritarian regimes 44, 57
average marginal effects 164, 172, 182, 196
Azad Kashmiris 18, 23

backlash, parties' fear of white 81, 82, 96
Ballard, Roger 37
Bangladesh 25, 42, 44
Bangladeshi/Bangladeshi background 7, 17, 18, 24–25, 29, 31, 38, 42, 43, 44, 45, 48, 49, 52, 53, 61, 63, 67, 70, 106, 111, 113, 119, 128, 156, 162, 177, 180, 208
Barbados 20, 58
Barnes, Samuel H. 187
Barreto, Matt A. 173
Barry, Brian 4, 134, 151
Belgium 19, 36, 173
Bengali language 25
Bergh, Johannes 130, 173
Berrington, Ann 37
Berthoud, Richard 39
Bethnal Green and Bow constituency 167
Bhachu, Parminder 37
Bhownagree, Mancherjee, MP 89
big business interests 93
Bilodeau, Antoine 57
Birādarī 23, 37
Bird, Karen 15, 151
Birmingham Hall Green constituency 168
Bjorklund, Tor 130, 173
Black and Asian interests 92, 94, 95, 106
Black utility heuristic 108, 115
Blair, Tony, MP 66
blasphemy laws 62
Bloemraad, Irene v, 56, 137, 152
Blohm, Michael 38, 43, 56, 57

Index

Blossfeld, Hans-Peter 80
Boateng, Paul, MP 89
Bobo, Lawrence 187
Borders, Citizenship and Immigration Act 2009 88, 133, 139
Borjas, George, J. 37
Bowler, Shaun 64, 79
boycott 11, 175, 178, 179, 181, 182, 183
Bradford West by-election 167, 168, 204
Brady, Henry E. 39
British, white, measurement of 16–18
British citizenship *see* citizenship
British Election Survey (BES) 8, 43, 127, 207
British identity 8, 16, 34, 191
British Nationality Act 1981 87, 97, 132–3
British Nationality (Hong Kong) Act 1997 87
British practices 15, 28, 29, 45, 49, 135, 191, 192, 211
  see also Remembrance Day
Brixton riots 81, 88
Brown, Colin 14, 37
Brown, Gordon, MP 66, 105, 159, 160, 161, 163, 164
Brown, R. Khari 188
Brown, Ronald E. 188
Bueker, Catherine 57, 152
Bulpitt, Jim 14, 81, 82, 97
Butler, David vi, 78, 109, 118, 128
Butt, Sarah 59

Cabinet Office Strategy for Race Equality 85, 103
Calhoun-Brown, Allison 188
Cameron, David, MP 14, 164, 192
Canada 6, 22, 56, 137
candidates (for election as MP) 9, 83, 89, 90, 166
Cantle report 4, 5
canvassing 11, 144, 163, 165, 166, 168, 173
Caribbean/black Caribbean background 7, 10, 12, 16, 17, 18–21, 22, 23, 25, 28, 29, 30, 32, 33, 35, 36, 37, 38, 49, 80, 95, 106, 112, 120, 128, 138, 143, 144, 151, 153, 180, 193, 196, 200, 202, 203, 208
Carmichael, Fiona 39
caste 23
Catholics 2, 20, 22, 26, 176, 194
causation, difficulty of establishing 46, 47, 54, 124, 138, 185, 197, 201
census classification of ethnicity 17, 37
Cheung, Sin-Yi 37, 39, 206
Chinese 7, 17
Chiswick, Barry 37
Cho, Wendy K. 151
Christians 19, 20, 21, 22, 26, 194
church attendance 49, 50, 152, 188
church membership 30, 31, 96, 119, 120, 177, 184, 197, 198, 199

citizenship,
  access to 41, 151, 152
  and eligibility to register 132
  British 4, 6, 8, 10, 20, 21, 22, 23, 24, 25, 26, 46, 50, 52, 132–3, 136–9, 145, 188
  Commonwealth 10, 20, 22, 24, 25, 26, 133
  dual 20, 23, 133, 137
  Indian 23, 137–8
  lack of British 41, 45–46, 129, 132, 135, 136
  legislation 86, 87, 88
  of the United Kingdom and Colonies 19
Citizenship Survey 206
civic culture 57, 174
civic duty *see* duty to vote
civic voluntarism model 47, 58
civil liberties, attitudes to 9, 60, 65–8, 75
  see also crime and rights of accused
Civil Rights movement 176
Claggett, William 152
Clarke, Harold D. v, 14, 56, 57, 58, 60, 78, 159, 172
class
  differences 72–3, 113, 157
  measurement of 211
  middle 31, 32, 33, 34, 72, 93, 112, 157
  trumped by ethnicity 10, 72–4
  working 72–3, 93, 94, 97, 109, 110, 111, 112, 113, 157
Clegg, Nick, MP 164
Cohen, Robin 16, 36
collective action 2, 128, 175–7
collective norms and sentiments 10, 11, 13, 124–5
Commission for Racial Equality 37
Commonwealth Immigrants Act 1962 19, 20, 87
community, ethnic 4, 5, 12, 30, 33, 41, 42, 47, 52, 53, 74, 96, 110, 118, 177, 199
community relations and immigration controls 85
conflict 2, 3, 4, 11, 187
Congo 26, 42, 67
Congolese 31
connectedness, social 187
  see also social ties
consciousness, ethnic/race 28, 128, 151, 176, 187, 211
  see also identification, ethnic
consensus on Labour policies *see* norms of Labour support
Conservative Party 9, 10, 31, 64, 82, 84–97, 104, 106, 107, 108, 112, 113, 116, 117, 154, 155, 160, 161, 165, 191
Constituencies, Parliamentary
  voting patterns 158
  see also marginal seats, safe seats
convergence across generations 7, 9, 12, 13, 51, 53, 54, 73, 174, 191, 195

Index

corruption 51
country of origin 20, 22, 24, 25, 26, 67
'Cricket test' 28
crime and rights of accused
  and party identification 113–4
  Labour's handling of 159, 164
  perceptions of party positions 91–2
  respondents' position on 64–5, 67, 79
cultural integration 27–29
culture clash 29
cultural rights, protection of 61, 70–71, 75
Curtice, John v, 59, 78, 128, 154, 157, 166
Cutts, David 14, 132, 134, 143, 151, 152

Daley, Patricia 26, 38
Dancygier, Rafaela 66, 79, 128, 151
Daniel, William W. 14, 37
Davis, Nancy J. 79
Dawson, Michael C. 38, 108, 109, 115
De Rooij, Eline A. 187
defection 10, 11, 154–173
democracy
  in origin country 49, 57
  legitimacy of 3
  norms and values 6, 44
  satisfaction with 12, 190–206
democratic deficit 12
demonstrations *see* protest
Denning, Lord 37
detention without trial, attitudes to 65–8, 72–3, 75, 95, 96, 107, 129
diaspora, Indian 21, 138
Diehl, Claudia 38, 43, 56, 57
directional theory of vote choice 80
disaffection 4, 5, 7, 8, 11, 13, 135, 190, 198
discrimination, racial
  as explanation of ethnic penalties 32, 109
  concerns about 1, 5, 7, 17, 27, 32, 61, 96, 177
  indirect 1–2, 87
  measurement of 14, 211
  reported experience of 32, 33, 34, 35, 36, 115, 116, 181–3, 185, 192, 196, 197, 198, 199, 200
  see also redress for racial discrimination, relative deprivation
disengagement
  from politics 2, 3, 4, 11, 40, 43, 53, 96, 190, 203
  from politics of origin country 46
DiSipio, Louis 58
Disraeli, Benjamin 74
distrust *see* trust
diversity within ethnic minorities 8
Doerschler, Peter 56
Dominica 20
donations to political causes 11, 175, 178, 180, 183, 187

Dovidio, John F. 38
Downs, Antony 107, 108, 109, 113, 128
Dustmann, Christian 14
duty to vote 9, 41, 48–54, 58, 59, 134–5, 141, 163, 185, 194

East Africa 21, 23
East Ham constituency 167
economy
  Labour's handling of 104, 159, 160, 161, 163, 164
  state of 5, 9, 63, 74, 159, 161
education, priority attached to 63
education
  and ethnic penalties 32
  as predictor 45–6, 49, 50, 57, 58, 59, 72–4, 112, 152, 172, 182–3, 188, 189, 200,
  British 34–5
  measurement of 210
  of migrants 18, 20, 22, 24, 25, 26, 27, 34
  of second generation 34–5
Electoral Commission v, 128, 140, 141, 146, 152
electorate
  composition of 1, 90, 104, 208–9
  year of entry into 117–8, 124, 129–30
eligibility to vote 7, 10, 131, 132, 136, 137–9, 145
engagement, cognitive 135
English
  as predictor 45–6, 47, 50, 142, 145, 151, 188
  fluency in 6, 13, 27, 28, 29, 35,
  help with learning 85
  lack of 28, 33, 41, 44, 135, 142
  language test 85
  main language at home 20, 21, 22, 24, 25, 26, 28, 34
equal protection of interests, principle of 3, 40
Equality Act
  2006 Act 88
  2010 Act 69, 88
  proposals for 84, 86, 97
Equality and Human Rights Commission (EHRC) 79, 84, 88, 102, 103
Equality Commission, proposals for 86, 97
equality of opportunity,
  concern with 12, 13, 61, 70, 96
  in Conservative manifestos 85, 191
  principle of 1, 3, 75, 109
  proposals for 84, 88, 201
  see also inequality of opportunity
Espiritu, Yen 36
ESRC v, 7
ethnic associations *see* associations, ethnic or cultural
ethnic communities *see* community, ethnic

229

Index

ethnic media *see* media
ethnic minority agenda *see* political agenda
Ethnic Minority British Election survey
  (EMBES) 1997 survey 8, 29, 38, 66, 80, 92, 94, 95, 96, 103, 104, 106, 119, 128, 156, 157, 168, 207–9
  2010 survey 7–8, 207–9
ethnic penalties 12, 17, 32, 33, 35, 36, 37, 39, 74, 75, 109, 116, 201, 203, 206
ethnicity
  definition 15–16
  measurement of 17, 210
  trumping class 6, 7, 10, 72, 110, 113
ethno-religious group 8, 18, 75, 116, 119, 120, 121, 122, 123, 124, 130, 131, 191
Europe, attitudes to 80
European Union migrants, exclusion from study 7, 14
Eurostat 139
evaluations
  of party leaders 159–61, 163
  retrospective 116, 117, 130, 159, 160, 163, 164, 165
Evans, Geoffrey A. 172
exclusion
  feelings of 7, 11, 12, 135, 191, 197, 198, 199, 200, 203, 204
  from political agenda 14, 81–104, 105
  political 1, 2, 3, 4, 9, 12, 14, 40, 60, 61, 135, 190, 198, 199, 201
  socio-economic 1, 5, 11, 12, 75, 201, 204
  see also non-representation
experiments, field 1, 14, 201
extremism, outside book's scope 4, 8

false positives 46, 57, 183
family reunion *see* migration, reasons for
family ties in origin country 45–46
Feldman, Jan L. 57
Feliciano, Cynthia 37, 38
Fennema, Meindert 177, 188
Field, Clive D. 162, 172, 206
field experiments *see* experiments, field
Fieldhouse, Edward vi, 7, 132, 151
financial crisis, priority attached to 63
Fiorina, Morris 107, 108, 116, 118, 125, 129
Fisher, Stephen D. 172, 173
Fitzgerald, Marian 82, 103, 104
Foner, Nancy 37
Ford, Robert 172
foreign policy, attitudes to 80
frames of reference 7, 35, 67, 191, 192
France 35
Fraser, Lord 37
fraternal relative deprivation *see* relative deprivation

free market policies, and class cleavage 72
free-rider problem 48
French 26
friendship, co-ethnic 30, 31, 34
  see also social capital, bonding

Galloway, George, MP 167
Garcia, F. Chris 118, 130
Gardner, Katy 38
Gay, Pat 14
gender
  as predictor 45–6, 47, 59, 80, 138, 141, 172, 181, 196
  differences 32, 46, 47
General Election of 1997 156
General Election of 2010 9, 153, 159
generational change/differences 6, 33–35, 39, 41, 51–54, 58, 72–4, 180, 184, 189, 191, 192, 194, 195, 196–8
generations
  definition and measurement of 34, 210
  first 34, 42, 43
  one point five 34
  quasi-parental 34, 35, 39, 52
  second 5, 7, 12, 34
  see also generational change
Germany 19, 36, 40, 43
Ghana 25, 26
Gilliam, Franklin D., Jr. 187
Gittell, Ross 38
González-Ferrer, Amparo 14, 151
Gordon, Milton 27, 38, 66, 88, 105, 159, 160, 161, 163, 164
government spending *see* taxes and spending
Grant, Bernie, MP 89
grievances 5, 11, 175, 176, 177, 181, 183, 185, 197, 205
group solidarity 15, 110, 118, 122, 124, 135, 136
guest-workers 19, 20, 36, 40
Guha, Ramachandra 37
Gujerat 21
Gujerati language 22
Gypsy 17

Hajnal, Zoltan 14, 97, 105, 111, 128, 151
Hampshire, James 104
Heath, Anthony F. 32, 33, 37, 38, 39, 58, 78, 87, 104, 106, 108, 110, 128, 129, 152, 172, 206, 208
Hewstone, Miles v, 38, 188
Hindi 22
Hindus 22, 25, 31, 32, 111, 112, 119, 194
Hirschman, Albert O. 187
housing tenure
  as predictor 73, 113, 163, 164, 182, 184, 200

230

Index

measurement of 210
owners 10, 33, 146, 163, 184
private renters 143, 163
social 73, 111–3, 118, 164, 182, 200
Howat, Nick v, 14, 152

identification, ethnic 29, 38, 45–46, 50, 181, 184, 187, 189, 211
see also consciousness, ethnic/race
identity
  Black/Asian 16, 28, 29
  British 8, 28, 29, 30, 34, 52, 138, 191
  collective 119, 124–5, 168
  dual 29, 38, 52
  ethnic 28, 29, 30, 34, 95, 96, 152, 187
  European 36
  party 94, 105, 121, 128, 129, 130
  social or group 128, 176, 187, 188
ideological dimensions 60, 64, 72, 107, 113, 114, 124
imagined community 16
immigration,
  attitudes to 61, 65, 66, 67, 79, 81
  history of 6, 20–7, 195
  Labour record on 13, 159, 165, 172
  Labour's handling of 159, 160, 161
  legislation 13, 19, 86–8
  policies 82, 83, 84, 85, 86, 87, 97, 107, 108
  priority attached to 63
  rates of 66, 87
Immigration Act 1971 87
income, measurement of 210
India 22, 24, 25, 41, 42, 56, 59
Indian/Indian background 7, 8, 17, 18, 21–23, 29, 31, 32, 33, 37, 38, 43, 49, 65, 67, 69, 95, 111, 112, 113, 114, 115, 137, 138, 140, 142, 143, 152, 156, 162, 178, 179, 194, 196, 209
inequality of opportunity 7, 12, 13, 96, 176, 193, 199, 201–6
see also equality of opportunity
inflation, priority attached to 63
Inglehart, Ronald 187
institutional racism *see* racism
integration *see* cultural integration, political integration, social integration, structural integration
integration trade-off 206
see also paradox of social integration
intermarriage
  attitudes towards 29
  occurrence of 4, 21, 37, 38, 80
International IDEA 56
Ipsos Mori 188
Iraq war 13, 61, 63, 157
Irish 16, 17, 18, 37

Irish Traveller 17
Islamophobia 162, 191
issues, most important 62–64
Italians 16

Jaggers, Keith 58
Jamaica 19, 20, 42, 56, 59
Jamal, Amaney 188
Johnston, Ron 173
Jones-Correa, Michael A. 188
Jowell, Roger 14, 218, 219

Ks, the five 71
Kaase, Max 187
Karp, Jeffrey A. 173
Kenya 22, 24
Khalistan 37, 41
Kinder, Donald R. 128
King, Gary 80
knowledge *see* political knowledge
Koopmans, Ruud 78
Kyriakopoulos, Kalliope 103

Labour Party 6, 9, 10, 11, 13, 64, 66, 82–104, 105–131, 134, 141, 145, 146, 154–73, 176, 190, 201, 203, 204, 205
see also New Labour
Labour Party Black Sections 204
Lammy, David, MP 90
Lancee, Bram 38
language spoken at home 20, 22, 24, 25, 26, 46
Latinos 105, 118, 135
law and order, priority attached to 63
Lawrence, Stephen, murder investigation 65, 79, 81, 202–3
Layton-Henry, Zig 3, 14, 81
Leal, David L. 188
Lee, Taeku 14, 97, 105, 111, 128, 151
left-right ideological dimension 59, 60, 64, 79, 114
legislation on immigration and racial discrimination 87
Leighley, Jan E. 151, 187, 189
Lewis, Jeffrey B. 80
Li, Yaojun vi, 87, 128, 172
Liberal-authoritarian ideological dimension 60, 64, 79
liberal Democrat Party 10, 84, 85, 86, 89, 90, 91, 92, 93, 97, 111, 112, 122, 154, 156, 160, 161, 165, 166, 176
linked fate 108–9, 188
Lipsky, Michael 177
local politics 8, 82, 97, 151
Lopez, David 36

Macdonald, Stuart Elaine 80
Macpherson, Sir William 65, 79, 81, 201, 202

231

Index

Macpherson enquiry 65, 79, 81, 202
Macpherson report – ten years on 202–3
Managing Cultural Diversity Survey (MCDS) 179, 180, 188
manifestos, party 2, 9, 82–103, 191
Manning, Alan 29, 38
marginal seats 165–6, 205
marginalization, socio-economic 10, 142, 145–6
Marshall, Monty G. 58
Martin, Jean 33, 128
Martinez, Lisa M. 189
Mateos, Pablo 37
Matthew effect 103
Mauritius 22, 42, 56, 59
Maxwell, Rahsaan 5, 14, 38, 57, 206
McMahon, Dorren 32, 39, 128
McVeigh, Rory 188
media
　British 42, 135
　ethnic 41, 45, 47 50
　see also readership
Merton, Robert K. 103, 128
Messina, Anthony M. 82, 86, 103
migrants
　involuntary 27, 36, 38
　labour 25
　orientations 40–59, 67, 105, 117, 118, 128, 132, 133, 135, 136, 137, 138, 142, 151, 152, 174, 180, 186, 190, 194, 205
　postcolonial 19, 25, 36, 40
　refugee 26
　twice 32
　voluntary 19, 27, 36
migration
　from Caribbean 20
　from East Africa 21, 23, 37
　from India 21
　from Pakistan 23
　from Sub-Saharan Africa 25
　from Sylhet 38
　net rate 87–8
　reasons for 18, 20, 22, 23, 24, 25, 26, 40, 44–46, 50, 61, 138
Milbrath, Lester W. 187
Miller, Arthur H. 38, 128, 187
MIPEX 151, 152
Mirpur 23, 24
Mirpuri language 24
Mitton, Lavinia 38
mixed heritage/identity 12, 16, 17, 21, 28, 29, 31, 32, 36, 37, 65, 59, 95, 111, 115, 120, 128, 140, 143, 156, 157, 162, 172, 178, 179, 193, 194, 196, 202, 208
mobilization by ethnic community 134, 143, 145–6, 153, 165
Modood, Tariq 37, 78

Morales, Laura 14, 47, 56, 58
MPs, ethnic minority 1, 2, 9, 14, 83, 89, 90, 103
multiculturalism 4, 75, 85, 192
multilevel modelling 121
Muslim Arbitration councils 71
Muslim/non-Muslim differences 72–3, 193–4
Muslims 4, 9, 13, 17, 22, 23, 24, 25, 26, 29, 31, 33, 54, 57, 61, 65, 67, 68, 70–5, 78, 119, 129, 158, 162, 167, 168, 169, 177, 191, 192, 193–4, 204, 211
Muttarak, Raya 36, 37, 38
myth of return 56

Naoroji, Dadabhai, MP 89
nation 16, 18
National Employment Panel 85, 102
National Front 82
Nee, Victor 14
neighbourhood composition 46, 50, 59, 151
neighbours, co-ethnic 30, 31
Netherlands 19, 36
New Labour 66, 86, 88, 92, 104, 111, 118, 130, 156
NHS
　Labour's handling of 159, 160
　pride in 79
　priority attached to 63
Nigeria 25, 26
non-partisans 105, 111, 122, 128, 129
non-registration, reasons for 140–1
non-representation, feeling of 95–96, 183, 184, 190, 197, 199, 201
norms and values
　of Labour support 118, 119, 120, 122, 130, 165, 212
　of voting 48, 51
Norris, Pippa 187

Office for National Statistics (ONS) 37, 140
Ogbu, John 27, 38
Olsen, Marvin E. 177, 188,
'One drop' rule 16, 36
Operation Black Vote 140, 146
opportunities for minorities
　and party identification 114
　perceptions of parties' positions 7, 91–2
　respondents' positions on 9, 68–70, 75
oppositional culture 38
orientations
　learned in origin country 58
　sojourner 40, 41
　towards British politics 5, 6, 8, 12, 53, 191, 205
　towards origin country 4, 5, 8, 12
over-reporting of turnout 135, 144

Pakistan 24, 41, 42, 44
Pakistani/Pakistani background 7, 13, 17, 18, 23–24, 29, 31, 33, 37, 38, 43, 44, 49, 52, 53, 61, 63, 65, 67, 69, 70, 71, 95, 106, 111, 112, 113, 114, 115, 119, 137, 140, 143, 156, 157, 162, 163, 178, 179, 191, 194, 196, 209
panethnicity 16, 35, 36
paradox
  of exclusion 203
  of social integration 192, 199, 200
  of voting 133–4
parallel lives *see* segregation
Parliament, trust in 12, 193, 194, 195, 196, 198, 199, 200, 202
participation, electoral 132–153, 184–5
  see also turnout
participation, non-electoral
  cause-oriented 175
  citizen-oriented 175
  conventional 2, 175
  elite-challenging 175, 197
  elite-supporting 175
  levels of 11, 12, 175, 177, 178–80, 186, 195, 202, 203
  patterns of 187
  predictors of 182–5, 188
partisanship *see* party identification
partisanship bias 160–1
Partition of India 21, 23, 24, 38
partnership, co-ethnic 30, 31
party identification
  collective 119, 124–5, 168
  individual 10, 105–131, 134, 141, 155
  strength of 129–30, 134, 141, 144, 163, 164, 185
Pashtu 24
Patterson, Orlando 36
Pattie, Charles 173
Peach, Ceri v, 37
pensioners' interests 93–4
Pentecostals 20, 21, 26, 31, 119, 120, 194
perceptions
  of minorities' views 95, 201, 203
  of party positions 10, 91–2, 97, 104, 129, 130
  of representation of minority interests 9, 83, 92–4, 104, 106
performance issues *see* valence issues
Petersen, Trond 38
petition 11, 175, 176, 179, 181, 182, 183, 187
Pilati, Katia 47, 56, 58
police, trust in 193, 194, 195, 196, 198, 199, 200, 202, 203
Policy Studies Institute (PSI) 37
political agenda,
  elite consensus 82, 83, 85, 86

ethnic minority 9, 60–75, 78, 109
  mainstream 2, 3, 5, 14, 94, 96
political engagement 2, 4, 5, 6, 7, 8, 10, 11, 12, 13, 14, 40, 41, 42, 44, 47,132, 135, 152, 174–89, 190, 197, 202
  see also party identification, political interest
political integration 2, 4, 5, 6, 12, 14, 27, 28, 30, 31, 42, 185, 186, 190, 192, 197
political interest
  in British politics 41, 42–48, 57, 59, 96, 135, 164, 184, 194
  in politics of origin country 4, 6, 8, 11, 40, 41, 42–48, 57, 59
political knowledge 8, 42, 43, 52, 54, 57, 59, 135, 164, 194, 212
political representation *see* representation
politicians, trust in 6, 193, 194, 195, 196, 199, 200, 202
Polity IV scores 56, 57
Poplar and Limehouse constituency 167
Powell, Enoch , MP 19
practices, British *see* British practices
prejudice, racial 1, 30, 38, 61, 108, 115, 135, 162, 192
Prescott-Clarke, Patricia 14
protecting rights of the accused *see* civil liberties
protest 2, 4, 8, 11, 12, 78, 175, 176, 177, 179–88, 191, 197, 199, 203
proximity theory of vote choice 80
Punjab 21, 23
Punjabi 18, 22, 24
Purdam, Kingsley 14, 151, 152
Putnam, Robert 30, 38

qualifications *see* education

Rabinowitz, George 80
Race Relations Acts 13, 37
Racial and Religious Hatred Act 2006 13
racial terminology 17
racism, institutional 65, 79, 201, 202
Rallings, Colin 89
rational choice theory 107
readership, of daily newspaper 45–46
redistribution, attitudes to 65, 72
redress for racial discrimination
  absence of measures in Conservative manifestos 85, 86, 96–7, 108, 191
  absence of measures in Respect manifesto 167
  concerns with 9–10, 12, 61, 68–70, 80, 82, 83, 84, 85, 86, 87, 88, 90–1, 92, 94, 95, 96, 97, 107, 168, 177, 189, 191, 201, 203, 204
  legislation 87–8
  manifesto proposals 83–9
reference group theory 128

233

Index

refugees *see* migrants, refugee
registration 10, 14, 133, 136–7, 139–141, 145, 146, 158, 181
relative deprivation, fraternal 13, 95, 96, 109, 110, 115–6, 122–3, 128, 135, 176, 177, 181, 183, 184, 186, 193, 196, 197, 199, 200, 201, 203, 206, 211
reliability (of scales) 79
religion
  as predictor 111, 193, 194
  differences 1, 7, 18, 20, 21, 22, 24, 25, 26, 31, 32, 35, 61, 70, 71, 75, 119, 120, 161, 162, 165, 206, 211
  measurement of 211
  see also ethno-religious group
Remembrance Day, wearing poppy on 28, 29, 45–46, 49
representation
  of minority interests 9, 75, 96–7, 105, 204–5
  perceived 91–6, 104
  policy 81–9, 166
  symbolic 83, 89–91, 166–7
  see also non-representation
residence, length of 135
residential concentration 5, 14, 30, 128, 134, 143
  see also segregation
resources
  group 5, 30, 152, 176, 177, 181
  psychological 182, 182, 187, 200
  socio-economic 6, 176, 182, 183, 187, 189, 200
  theory 31, 39, 188
Respect Party 11, 13, 167–8, 169, 204
retrospective voting theory *see* running tally
return migration 4, 7, 14, 36, 40, 41, 56, 138, 152
Rice, Tom W. 57
riots, outside book's scope 205
Robinson, Robert V. 79
Rossi, Alice S. 128
Roy, Sanchari 29, 38
Runciman, W. Garrison vi, 96, 109, 128
running tally explanation of party support 107–8, 116–8
Rushdie, Salman 62, 78

Saalfeld, Thomas 103
safe seats 165–6
Saggar, Shamit v, 8, 78, 80, 103, 104, 106, 112, 128, 151, 208
Saklatvala, Shapurji, MP 89
Sanders, David v, 78, 172
Santoro, Wayne A. 188
satisfaction *see* democracy, satisfaction with
Saunders, Elizabeth N. 66, 79, 128
Scarman report 79, 81, 88

Scottish 18
segregation 4, 5, 6, 11, 14, 192
  see also neighbours, co-ethnic *and* residential concentration
Segura, Gary M. 64, 79
selection
  negative 19, 37
  positive 19, 22, 24, 26, 36, 37, 38, 79
separate lives thesis 4, 5, 8, 11, 16, 41, 42, 44, 47, 50, 54, 74, 192, 199
separate minority party 95, 111
separate religious instruction 71
Sharia law, attitudes to 70–71, 73
Shaw, Alison 37
Shingles, Richard D. 187
Shukra, Kalbir 104, 204, 206
Shukur, Abdus 38
Sikhs 18, 21, 22, 23, 31, 33, 37, 61, 71, 78, 111, 112, 119, 194
Smith, Christian 188
Smith, David J. 37
Smith, Stephen 152
Sobolewska, Maria 14, 80, 90, 104, 129, 173, 217
social capital
  bonding 30, 31, 34, 35, 38, 41, 45, 46, 47, 48, 49, 50, 52, 54, 58, 96, 122–3, 129, 144, 145, 165, 177, 180, 181, 183, 184, 197, 198, 199, 211
  bridging 30, 31, 32, 35, 38, 44, 45, 57, 188, 198
  see also associations, ethnic or cultural
social class *see* class
social desirability bias 50–51, 135, 142–3
social distance 29, 30, 74, 80, 89
  see also intermarriage
social housing *see* housing tenure
social identity theory 128
social integration 8, 29–31, 192–3, 199, 206
  see also paradox of social integration
social ties
  with co-ethnics in Britain 5, 13, 30, 34, 38, 176, 197
  with family in homeland 44–46
socio-economic position
  of minorities 8, 12, 201
  as predictor 112–4, 129, 182, 189, 190, 200
  within minorities 6, 7, 72, 73–4, 75
  see also ethnic penalties, marginalization
sociotropic approach 108, 128
Somali/Somali background 33, 42, 61, 67, 68
Somali language 26
Somalia 26, 42, 67
South Asians 10, 24, 31, 35, 57, 61, 67, 68, 90, 106, 115–6, 119, 120, 124, 134, 140, 142, 143, 144, 151, 155, 177, 192, 193, 196

special provisions at work 71
Sri Lanka 22
Srole, Leo 224
standard of living, priority attached to 63
Statham, Paul 61, 68, 78
Stokes, Donald vi, 78, 109, 118, 128
structural integration 31–33
Studlar, Donley T. 3, 14, 37, 57, 62, 63, 74, 81, 128, 151
Swaddle, Kevin 152
Sylhet 24
Sylheti language 25

tactical voting, *see* voting
Tajfel, Henri 128
Tamil language 22
taxes and spending
  and party identification 113–4
  perceptions of party positions 91–2
  respondents' position on 64–6, 79
  priority attached to 9, 63, 65, 67
Taylor, Bridget 208
Tebbit, Norman, MP 28
Teney, Celine 173
terrorism
  outside book's scope 205
  Labour's handling of risk 159
Thatcher, Margaret, MP 28, 82, 87, 88
Thomas theorem 103
Thomas, Dorothy Swaine 83
Thomas, William I. 83
Thomson, Katarina 208
Thrasher, Michael 89
Tillie, Jean 177, 188
Timm, Andreas 80
TNS-BMRB v, 208
Trade Union
  interests 93–4
  and Labour identification 111–3, 118
traditional dress 71
transnational links *see* social ties
Transparency International index of corruption 59
Trinidad 20
trust
  political 6, 12, 13, 190–206
  social 4, 38
turban, right to wear 37, 62, 78
turnout 3, 10, 14, 42, 56, 132–146, 181
tyranny of the majority 3

Uganda 22
Uhlaner, Carole J. 130
UK 19, 59
Ummah 17
unemployed, interests of 93–4, 97

unemployment
  ethnic minority rate 1, 32, 33, 74, 86, 87–8
  priority attached to 5, 9, 62–3, 73, 74, 78–9, 114, 121, 123
Urdu 24
USA 10, 22, 36, 56, 75

valence
  issues 78
  theory 158–9
validation of turnout 135–6, 143, 158
values
  British 4, 41, 48, 54, 58, 75, 84, 85, 192
  democratic 6, 41, 42, 44
  liberal 74
  progressive 31
  right-wing 31
  see also norms and values
Vaz, Keith, MP 89, 90
Vedlitz, Arnold 189
Verba, Sidney 4, 39, 47, 58, 174, 187, 188
Vidal, Avis 38
'voice' 174, 175, 176, 185, 187
volunteering 133, 175, 178–83, 186, 197
vote switching, *see* defection
voting,
  at 1997 general election 156
  at 2010 general election 10, 155–173
  tactical 163, 172

War on Terror 163
  see also detention without trial, Afghanistan
Warner, W. Lloyd 14
Weakliem, David 128
Weber, Max 15, 37
Weiss, Yoram 14
welfare state
  British 67, 79
  US 79
Welsh 18
Werfhorst, Herman G. van de
West Ham constituency 167
White British *see* British, white
White, Steven 58, 152
Wilson, J. Matthew 128
withdrawal *see* disengagement
women's interests 93–4
Wong, Janelle 152, 187
Wood, Martin 14
Woods, R. 39
working class, *see* class

Yoruba 26

Zimbabwe 26, 67
Zomeren, Martijn van 187

235